Life Sentences

Life Sentences

LITERARY ESSAYS

Joseph Epstein

W · W · Norton & Company · New York · London

"Love" and excerpt from "This Be the Verse" from *Collected Poems* by Philip
Larkin. Copyright © 1988, 1989 by The Estate of Philip Larkin. Reprinted by
permission of Farrar, Straus, & Giroux, Inc. and Faber and Faber Ltd.
"Nero's Deadline," "Very Seldom," and excerpt from "Waiting for the
Barbarians," translated by Edmund Keeley and Phillip Sherrard, from *C.P.
Cavafy: Selected Poems, Revised Edition,* edited by George Savidis. English
translation copyright © 1975 by Edmund Keeley and Phillip Sherrard, revised
edition copyright © 1992 by Princeton University Press.

For information about permission to reproduce selections from this book,
write to Permissions, W. W. Norton & Company, Inc., 500 Fifth Avenue,
New York, NY 10110

The text of this book is composed in Perpetua with the
    display set in Gill Sans.
Composition and manufacturing by the Haddon
    Craftsmen, Inc.
Book design by Jack Meserole.

Library of Congress Cataloging-in-Publication Data

Epstein, Joseph, 1937–
    Life sentences : literary essays / by Joseph Epstein.
        p.   cm.
    ISBN 0-393-04546-3
    1. Epstein, Joseph, 1937–   —Books and reading   2. Literature—History
and criticism.   3. Authors—Biography.   I. Title.
PS3555.P6527L54   1997
809—dc21   976322
                                                                                CIP

W. W. Norton & Company, Inc., 500 Fifth Avenue, New York, N.Y. 10110
                    http://www.wwnorton.com

W. W. Norton & Company Ltd., 10 Coptic Street, London WC1A 1PU

                    1 2 3 4 5 6 7 8 9 0

To Nicholas Charles Epstein,

Welcome to the game, kiddo.

CONTENTS

CONTENTS

INTRODUCTION

I was sorry to find that the word "autodidact" does not appear in the new edition of Fowler's Modern English Usage, because it is a word that, from the moment I first heard it, has troubled me. An autodidact, according to Webster's, is "a self-taught person." But isn't everyone, ultimately, self-taught? I know of late people have become fond of referring to others as their "mentors," and mentor has now become a verb and we even have the activity of "mentoring." As someone who slogged his way through college—which old radicals such as Paul Goodman used to say was a sure sign that one's spirit had been properly broken—sat through endless lectures, and dutifully read all the prescribed books, I have nonetheless never felt that my education was in any but my own hands. Which makes me, I believe, an autodidact, and my guess is that it makes whoever is about to read this book one, too.

The only difference between me and most other people who take great pleasure in reading is that I get my education in public. I have always been fascinated by that phrase—"getting one's education in public"—and didn't quite understand it, either, until it occurred to me that it was devised to cover people precisely like myself. I get my education in public by writing

9

about things that, until I actually do write about them, I don't always really know all that much about. I read up, I think through, I write out, and, the hope is, at the end I am a bit smarter about the subject under study.

The scam, as I see it, is that I am paid for this self-administered education. Nearly every essay in this collection began in the mind of the editor of the magazine who asked for it; the remainder I suggested to these editors, because I found an occasion—the publication of a biography, or the republication or new translation of a classic work—to write about a subject I had long wanted to write about. The reason I wanted to do so is that I recognized a serious gap in my learning that might now be filled; or that I was fascinated enough by my sketchy knowledge of the subject to wish to look further into it; or merely that—to adapt the words I once heard the English humorist Stephen Potter utter when asked why he wrote such peculiar books as *One-Upsmanship, Gamesmanship,* and *Lifesmanship*—I was "out of work, you know."

Like hanging, writing concentrates the mind, with the important advantage that, with the latter, one's corpse isn't carted off afterwards. If one is sufficiently graphomaniacal— as I, after the production of this, my twelfth book appear to be—nothing becomes quite real until one has written about it. Asked his opinion about some matter, E. M. Forster is said to have replied, "How do I know what I think until I have written about it?" Many habitual writers know whereof Forster spoke. Writing, for true writers, means discovery, the acquisition of knowledge, the attainment of revelation.

This is my fourth collection of literary essays; the first appeared in 1985, or twelve years ago. In each of them my method has been the same: to read everything a particular writer has written, to read the most interesting things written about him, and then to attempt to clear my own line of vision to write about the writer and his or her works. In some cases (Edmund Wilson and Aleksandr Solzhenitsyn), vast amounts of reading are entailed; in others (Cavafy, La Rochefoucauld) a good deal less. But the idea is always the same: to be able to say something— I won't say "original" but at least new and interesting about the writer. The more personal attraction is for the writer of these essays himself to gain a surer intellectual purchase on writers whose work he has loved, or disliked, or about which he felt an unsettling dubiety.

What unites this collection of literary essays is the interest of the man who wrote them. The man, as anyone will be able to tell from his book's table of contents, is a sucker for stylish writing. If there is a republic of letters, he has a weakness for its aesthetic aristocrats. But he is on occasion willing to forgo this penchant for moral seriousness, as witness his admiring essays on Theodore Dreiser and Aleksandr Solzhenitsyn. His essays on the poetry of Elizabeth Bishop and Robert Lowell and the fiction of Robert Musil show he still has a taste for the deflation of literary reputation.

He has himself reached an age when he considers all writers—even the great sixteenth-century essayist Montaigne— members of the same club, and the chief literary distinction for him remains that between good and bad writers. His reading ranges widely over time and forms, and he seems to read roughly equal amounts of poetry, fiction, and criticism. His interest in his subjects is in good part biographical. In this connection, he stands with Henry James, who, apropos of Turgenev, wrote to Edmund Gosse: "Yes, I too like what I read better when I know (and like) the author." He is heavily—though he hopes not irritatingly—quotatious. Poor fellow, he continues to read in the old-fashioned hope of getting just a bit smarter about the world. . . . But I had better stop before I go on to supply a review for my own book.

A note on the title: My three earlier books of literary essays— *Plausible Prejudices* (1985), *Partial Payments* (1989), and *Pertinent Players* (1993)—left me in a rigidly rooted rut of absolutely adamantine alliteration. I struggled to find another PP—Portraits in Porcelain? Perusing Peregrinations?—title for this book, and then decided to break the chain with *Life Sentences,* which comes from the title of my essay in this collection on Joseph Conrad. *Life Sentences* is at least a double- and perhaps a triple-entendre, suggesting Conrad's travail with every sentence he wrote on his way to his triumph as an English prose stylist, his dark but dignified vision of men and women's destiny on earth, and his own long confinement to literary creation. A fourth possible meaning is that literature, for those who truly believe in its powers, is also a life sentence, but of a very different order. As such a believer, a true believer in literature, I feel that this particular sentence is one I myself can do, as they say out in the yard, standing on my head.

JE

ACKNOWLEDGMENTS

The essays in this book first appeared in *Commentary, The New Criterion, The Hudson Review,* and *The New Yorker*. The author is grateful to the editors of these journals.

Life Sentences

Reading Montaigne

Michel de Montaigne (1533–1592) put the capital I, the first person, into literature, and while he was at it also invented the essay. When he took up the writing of his *Essays,* in 1572, Montaigne was the first man to write freely about himself, and not for another two centuries, until Jean Jacques Rousseau, would anyone do so with such unabashed candor again. Chiding Tacitus for undue modesty, Montaigne remarked that "not to dare to talk roundly of yourself betrays a defect of thought." This, clearly, was not Montaigne's defect. "I not only dare to talk about myself but to talk of nothing else but myself." That is not quite true; he talks about a great deal else in the *Essays.* Yet there was something to what he said when he added: "I study myself more than any other subject. That is my metaphysics; that is my physics."

Inscribed on the tympanum of the Temple of Apollo at Delphi was the legend, "Know Thyself." This was the project Montaigne set to work on when in 1570, at the age of thirty-seven, he retired from public life to the tower on his estate in Gascony in which he kept his library of a thousand or so books. Montaigne not only believed in the importance of knowing himself but thought there was scarcely anything better, or even else, worth knowing. "I would rather be an expert on me than on Cicero," he writes in his essay "On Experience," and in "On Physiognomy" he writes, "I am wandering off the point when I write about anything else, cheating my subject of me." But the more important point is that he made of the study of himself an epistemology: from knowledge of himself, he believed, all other knowledge flowed.

Had Montaigne not chosen himself for his subject, in time someone else would no doubt have come along to write about himself with the same degree of candor—but not, the great likelihood is, with the same degree of success. What makes Montaigne's invention of the personal essay so extraordinary is that he not only was its first practitioner but may also have been, to date, its best. He set out the program for the personal essay— loose, digressive, elastic, familiar: "free association, artistically controlled," is the way Aldous Huxley described Montaigne's method—and then produced it in a quantity of more than a thousand pages. The impressive, the really quite astonishing thing is that Montaigne never bores on the subject of *me;* far from wishing him to go on to take up other matters, one is always rather pleased when he returns to it, even about such trivial things as his changing taste for radishes.

Montaigne also had the unteachable, the quite unexplainable gift of being absolutely a man of his time who, four centuries later, reads pertinently as a man of ours. As D. P. Walker, the distinguished medievalist, has written:

> In many ways Montaigne was a startlingly original and independent thinker; but this can only be appreciated if one has some knowledge of relevant contemporary and earlier thought, for the most fundamental of Montaigne's new ideas and attitudes have become our own unquestioned assumptions.

Among these are the high valuation he placed on what is individual, private, original, and different. Modern, too—or so one would like to think—is his rejection of all dogmatic systems of thought. (How amusing he would have been on Marx and Freud, the two crushing systematizers of the modern era!) Finally, he strikes the modern note in his self-absorption, which, D. P. Walker avers, was entirely radical for its day. Not until Rousseau's *Confessions* (1781) was there another work of self-portrayal like the *Essays,* and Montaigne's book, though written two centuries earlier, both feels more contemporary and is much wiser.

None of this would have been possible if Montaigne had not been precisely the man he was. "Authors," he wrote,

> communicate themselves to the public by some peculiar mark foreign to themselves; I—the first ever to do so—by my universal being, not as a grammarian, poet or jurisconsult but [as] Michel de Montaigne. If all complain that I talk too much about myself, I complain that they never even think about their own selves.

The American critic Van Wyck Brooks once defined literature as "a great man writing." The definition fits Montaigne exquisitely. But then Montaigne was himself exquisitely well fitted—by birth, by temperament, by talent—for the kind of writing he did.

Born in 1533 at his family's chateau between Bordeaux and Périgord, Michel Eyquem de Montaigne was, on his father's side, the son of a long line of successful merchants who only four generations earlier had purchased their title of nobility and with it the name Montaigne. His mother's was a family of Spanish Jews (named Louppes or Lopez), with connections in Antwerp, who had outwardly accepted Christianity without ever fully dispelling the suspicions of their neighbors. In his excellent biography of Montaigne, the late Donald Frame remarks that most attempts to explain Montaigne's mind and temper by the 25 percent of Jewish blood that ran in his veins have been properly cautious, as is Frame's own:

> Probably attributable to it in some measure are his deep tolerance in an age when that was not in fashion; a rather detached attitude, typical of the Marranos and natural in them, toward the religion he consistently and very conscientiously practiced [Roman Catholicism]; his tireless curiosity, mainly but not solely intellectual; the cosmopolitanism natural to the member of a far-flung family.

In the *Essays,* Montaigne makes only one, insignificant, mention of his mother, while he often refers to Pierre Eyquem de Montaigne, more than once as "the best of all fathers."

Montaigne was indeed fortunate in his father, who though not learned himself had great regard for learning, who had served as mayor of Bordeaux, and who took great care with his eldest son Michel's education (Montaigne had four brothers and three sisters). This education was far from conventional. Montaigne's first tutor was a German who spoke Latin but no French, and so the boy was brought up speaking Latin exclusively until the age of six (his parents and household servants acquired enough Latin to converse with him). When he went off to school he had less luck with Greek and thought himself, as a boy, a lazy and unretentive student. Fortunately, he acquired a love of reading, especially of Latin literature, that would never leave him, even though in later life he regularly demoted the importance of books in his own education.

Little is known about Montaigne's adolescence and early manhood. It is thought that he studied law in Toulouse. In 1557, at twenty-four, he became a *conseiller,* or magistrate, at the *parlement* in Bordeaux. Here he met his dear friend, his soulmate really, Etienne de La Boétie, of whom he wrote that "his was indeed an ample soul, beautiful from every point of view, a soul of the Ancient mold." The loneliness from Boétie's early death is sometimes said to be what caused Montaigne to turn to writing. He married in 1565, and he and his wife subsequently lost all but one of their children, a daughter Léonor.

After the death of his father in 1568, Michel became head of his family and lord over its estates. Complying with a wish of his father's, he translated Raymond Sebond's lengthy *Natural Theology,* which was published in 1569, from Latin into French; his "Apology for Raymond Sebond" would later become the longest of his essays. He resigned from work at the *parlement* at Bordeaux in 1570, retiring to Montaigne, where, in the tower he used as a study, he soon began the experimental writing that would result in the *Essays.* He would later, between 1581 and 1585, serve as mayor of Bordeaux, as his father had done before him, and his mature years were spent with his country riven by civil war over the Reformation. It is almost as if Montaigne had acquired just enough experience out of which to write, yet not so much as to despise the role of somewhat distanced observer that is central to the act of writing.

Montaigne's *Essays* is, as advertised, a great book. It is also in the category of great large books. (In M.A. Screech's lucid new translation, the text of Montaigne's *Essays* runs to 1,269 pages.) I have read in it for years, but have only now for the first time read through it. As in reading other great books of magnitude—*The Decline and Fall of the Roman Empire, War and Peace, Remembrance of Things Past*—one feels a sadness at coming to its conclusion. One has lived in the close company of an extraordinary man, swayed for weeks to the undulations of his mind, and now, at book's end, it is over. The Harvard economic historian Alexander Gerschenkron has told of coming to the end of *War and Peace* with this feeling of sadness so heavy upon him that he paused, sighed, and then turned the novel over and began it again from the beginning.

Montaigne would have appreciated that digression if not

necessarily the point. He is himself the most digressive of writers, always ready to tell a story, often from the chronicles of ancient history which he loved—usually to illustrate a point but sometimes, too, just because he thinks it a good story. In his essays he found the form that best fit the shape of his own mind.

"Essay," it is generally noted, comes from the French verb *essayer:* to try, to attempt. In bringing up this etymology most people wish to underscore the tentativeness of the form. Such modesty does not at all apply to Montaigne, who, while not out for the last word or seeking to be in any way definitive, nonetheless has fairly larger things in mind than the intellectual equivalent of a stroll around the garden.

Nor are the *Essays* merely a variety of disquisitions upon what its author happens to think on such subjects as Vanity, Experience, Sadness, Fear, Liars, and the rest, even though such words appear in the titles of his essays. Montaigne's project was both much more and much less programmatic than this. Better to think of what he wrote not as essays, in the sense we have come to think of the form, but as assays—" 'assays,' " as Professor Screech writes in his introduction to his new translation, "of himself by himself." The critic Erich Auerbach, in his chapter on Montaigne in *Mimesis,* suggests that the word "essay" as Montaigne used it might be rendered "Tests Upon One's Self" or "Self-Try-Outs." On behalf of his own revolutionary endeavor, the quotatious Montaigne cites the pre-Socratic philosopher Thales, of whom he remarks that "when Thales reckons that a knowledge of man is very hard to acquire, he is telling him that knowledge of anything else is impossible." How pleasing it must have been to Montaigne that in his own lifetime the scholar Justus Lipsius called him "the French Thales"!

What Montaigne is after in his essays is a method of discovering the meaning of such truths as he thinks available to man by studying the man he knows better than any other—himself. Sounds, in theory, easy enough. In practice, of course, it isn't. To acquire larger truths about the world by looking into one's heart is only possible if one is able to command an impressive honesty. Many other things are more likely to command *us:* bias, self-deceit, vanity, to name only three from a probably endless list. In the very first of the essays in his book, Montaigne avers that "man is indeed miraculously vain, various, and wandering"—and that, you might say, ain't a hundredth of it.

To italicize the difficulty of his venture, Montaigne writes in his brief essay "On Lying" that upon retiring to his estates, he had hoped to let his mind play upon itself, "calmly thinking of itself." As it turned out, nothing of the kind happened. Instead, his idleness resulted in his being visited by so "many chimeras and fantastic monstrosities" that he began to keep a record of them, "hoping in time to make my mind ashamed of itself." Writing, for him, began as a form of self-administered therapy.

From this failure—a failure that nearly resulted in a nervous breakdown—Montaigne came to discover his form. "Where I seek myself I cannot find myself," he writes; "I discover myself more by accident than by inquiring into my judgment." He began, in his early essays, to consider the thought of the ancient writers, occasionally touching on his own thoughts and experiences. Soon his essays began to feature these thoughts and that experience. His models were Seneca and Plutarch, whom he quotes perhaps more than any other writers. (He claimed the *Essays* were "built entirely of [Seneca and Plutarch's] spoils.") The discrete essays—some 107 of them—are in some ways perhaps better thought of as chapters; they range considerably in length, from a single page to nearly 200 pages. Montaigne called them "this confused medley of mine," and he found other self-denigrating ways of referring to them, not least vividly as *des excréments d'un viel esprit* ("the droppings of an ancient spirit"), "grotesques and monstrous bodies, pieced together of divers members without definite shape, having no order, sequence, or proportion other than accident." In fact, the *Essays* are a running chronicle of the mind of Michel de Montaigne. In his view he never loses the thread of his thought, even if his reader may, and he holds that, though he may seem to contradict himself, "I never contradict the truth."

If ever the maxim about the style being the man applied to a writer, it applied to Montaigne. Erich Auerbach remarks that, after reading a good deal of Montaigne, he thought he "could hear him speak and see his gestures." And Montaigne evidently wrote as he spoke, and spoke as he felt—directly, candidly, straightforwardly:

> The speech I love is a simple, natural speech, the same on paper as in the mouth; a speech succulent and sinewy, brief and compressed, not so much dainty and well-combed as vehement and brusque . . . rather difficult than boring, remote from affectation, irregular, disconnected, and bold; each bit making a body in itself; not pedantic, not monkish, not lawyer-like, but rather soldierly.

Montaigne's was a style at once ironic, playful, metaphoric, slangy, image-laden, self-deprecatory, commonsensical, and never abstract. "His is not an incapacity for abstractions," Donald Frame writes, "but a happy incapacity for expressing it other than concretely." He could ramble, his sentences could be overly elaborate, but always he strove to mesh substance to style, thought to form. He preferred not to be praised for his style, lest style seem to obscure his content. Content was his chief concern, for he felt that the contents of his book and of his mind were "consubstantial." "How I would hate the reputation of being clever at writing but stupid at everything else," he notes. Yet style is the preservative of literature, and Montaigne's is the style of a man you trust. "He was the frankest and honestest of writers," wrote Emerson, who added that he did not know any book "that seems less written."

"I think I am an ordinary sort of man," Montaigne writes, "except in considering myself to be one." The *Essays* demonstrate how extraordinary an ordinary sort of man can be. As the book progresses, ordinariness becomes a kind of virtue, for to be ordinary, by which he means human, is high praise from Montaigne. He has his own little pantheon of heroes—Homer, Alexander the Great, the Theban general Epaminondas, and above all Socrates (revered for his naturalness) occupying prominent places in it. Yet his is chiefly a comic view of life—no matter how high the throne, Montaigne notes, even a king sits upon his arse—if a comic view that, somehow, does not deprive men of their dignity. He laughs at other men by laughing first at himself.

"Everyone recognizes me in my book," Montaigne writes, "and my book in me." Quite as interestingly, everyone recognizes himself in Montaigne. The temptation in reading him is to discover oneself in him—and, of course, to admire him (and oneself) correspondingly. Even Flaubert, who felt little commonality with anyone, felt much in common with Montaigne, whom he claimed to regard as a foster father. Emerson said of the *Essays* that "it seemed to me as if I had myself written the book, in some former life, so sincerely it spoke to my thought and experience." André Gide remarked of Montaigne that "it seems to me that he is myself." Justice Oliver Wendell Holmes, writing to Sir Frederick Pollock, noted: "I told you I believe that late in life I have discovered Montaigne and have read him with enormous delight. The beast knows a lot of things that I fondly hoped had been reserved for me."

Of the two great categories of writers—those who tell us things we do not know and those who formulate those things that have always been in our hearts but which we have had neither the time nor more likely the wit to formulate on our own—Montaigne is foremost among the latter. He claimed for self-knowledge that from it he could understand other men, but it turns out that it works quite well the other way around, so that from our knowledge of him we can learn about ourselves. Along with formulating our own thoughts for us, what makes Montaigne seem so close to us, his readers, is his gift for intimacy. This man who has looked into his own heart has in the course of doing so looked into ours, and reverberations from our own life sound on his nearly every page.

Montaigne speaks to us because he speaks for us. He claims that, for him, "there is no savor without communication." But to whom, in his *Essays,* did Montaigne think he was communicating? When the first two of the ultimately three books of the *Essays* were published in 1580, they were a commercial success if not quite a best-seller. Yet, pleased though he was with this success, Montaigne nonetheless continued to write chiefly for himself. His essays were above all a form of self-discovery. Montaigne says literally up front, in his opening note to the reader, what he is about:

> You have here, Reader, a book whose faith can be trusted, a book which warns you from the start that I have set myself no other end but a private family one. I have not been concerned to serve you nor my reputation: my powers are inadequate for such a design. . . . If my design had been to seek the favor of the world I would have decked myself out better and presented myself in a studied gait. Here I want to be seen in my simple, natural, everyday fashion, without striving or artifice: for it is my own self that I am painting. Here, drawn from life, you will read of my defects and my native form so far as respect for social convention allows: for had I found myself among those peoples who are said still to live under the sweet liberty of Nature's primal laws, I can assure you that I would most willingly have portrayed myself whole, and wholly naked.

After this note, Michel de Montaigne began writing the most personal book in the history of the world.

To write a personal book, it is best to have a personality—

and, to go along with it, the impersonality required by the highest art to set it out properly. "The essays," Virginia Woolf wrote of Montaigne's book, "are an attempt to communicate a soul." Here is a task that requires candor, lucidity, honesty, persistence. For as Virginia Woolf also wrote, apropos not of Montaigne but of all personal essayists of whom he remains the father: "Far beyond the difficulty of communicating oneself, there is the supreme difficulty of being oneself." Discovering who exactly he was is part of the motive behind Montaigne's book. When he said that the study of himself was his metaphysics and his physics, he meant that subjective truth was sufficient for him. "I do not see the whole of anything," he writes. "Nor do those who promise to show it to us."

Intellectual method was of little use to Montaigne. In logic he found crippling, even laughable, limitations—for logic, as he puts it, provides no consolation for gout. Even the senses cannot be counted upon. This notion is at the center of the "Apology for Raymond Sebond," the longest essay in Montaigne's book and the only one with a directly polemical intent. In that essay, Montaigne sets out after rationalism, whose chief internal danger he views as establishing the belief in men that they can achieve universal truth outside religion, through the sheer power of their reasoning. Montaigne mocks the attempt. Jacob Zeitlin, in a brilliant introductory commentary to his 1934–36 translation of the *Essays,* characterizes the "Apology for Raymond Sebond" as an "exercise of the rational process to degrade the principle of reason." It is in the "Apology" that Montaigne writes, "When I play with my cat, how do I know that she is not passing time with me rather than I with her?" This may seem a trivial enough question but is in fact the nub of the matter, asking, in the most particular and concrete terms, how do we know anything? "There is a plague on man: his opinion that he knows something."

Owing to this essay, Montaigne was thought to be hostage

to Pyrrhonism, named after the founder of Greek skepticism. Pyrrhonians doubted the efficacy even of doubt itself. Montaigne writes of them: "If you can picture an endless confession of ignorance, or a power of judgment which never, never inclines to one side or the other, then you can conceive what Pyrrhonism is." Behind the polemic in the "Apology for Raymond Sebond" is Montaigne's concern that men will make the horrendously arrogant mistake of believing that they are in control of their own destinies. "So long as man thinks he has means and powers deriving from himself he will never acknowledge what he owes to his Master." It is in the "Apology" that he writes, "In truth we are but nothing."

Such utterances would lead one to think Montaigne a seriously religious man, even though Sainte-Beuve believed that, in writing an "Apology for Raymond Sebond," he was attempting covertly to attack Christianity. From the *Essays* we have Montaigne's claim that he believes in the orthodoxy of the Roman Catholic Church and that he believes it on the authority of the Scriptures. "The more we refer ourselves to God," he writes, "commit ourselves to Him and reject ourselves, the greater we are worth." He adds: "Socrates' verdict—and mine as well—is that the best judgment you can make about the heavens is not to make any at all." Aristotle, Plato, even the otherwise inevitably sensible Plutarch he finds foolish on the subject of what happens to the soul after death. How should a simpler man, a man like Montaigne (or you and I), know better than they? Outwardly conventional in his religious views and practice, Montaigne appears to have rested in his own version of fideism, or faith based on a deep skepticism about all human knowledge.

Religion as the complicated relations, fueled by faith, between men and God is a subject Montaigne is content to leave alone. Only man's debt to God, which is total, is acknowledged. "But there can be no first principles," he avers, "unless

God has revealed them; all the rest—beginning, middle, and end—is dream and vapors." Quotatious though he is, Montaigne rarely quotes Scripture. Here, as in many another realm, the question he had had engraved on a medal, *Que scay-je?* (What do I know?), which might serve as the motto for the *Essays,* applies most of all. He is instead keen on how to achieve the maximum contentment out of a life down upon which vicissitudes of every sort rain—how to find order and such happiness as is available here on earth.

No small problem, this, not least because of the change-ability that Montaigne finds in himself and, by extension, in human nature. As with his own nature, so with the world at large, everything seems mutable. "For all we know," he remarks of the leading theories of planetary rotation of his day, "in a thousand years' time another opinion will overthrow both." As with knowledge, so with thought:

> Once you start digging down into a piece of writing there is simply no slant or meaning—straight, bitter, sweet, or bent—which the human mind cannot find there.

Not even the truth that the senses convey can be trusted: "The senses deceive the intellect; it deceives them in their turn. (Love someone and she seems more beautiful than she is.)" With theories, opinion, custom, knowledge, even our senses forever changing, Montaigne concludes that he "would rather be guided by results than by reason—for [the two] are always clashing." He reminds his readers of the ideal, much admired by Aristotle and by the Pyrrhonists, of being "astonished by nothing." In the end, Montaigne concludes, only God is. Only God and, one might add, Michel de Montaigne.

This last-named fellow, despite his many protestations about his shortcomings, is far from negligible. For if we cannot trust either knowledge or our senses, and if we can only by our best lights be obedient to but cannot hope to fathom the design of God, what guidance do we then turn to in the hope of living our lives with a modicum of decency, dignity, and contentment? The short answer, for Montaigne, is to understand experience rightly and to quest for understanding human nature, with the additional proviso that "there is no end in our inquiries; our end is in the other world." Yet the short answer is less impressive than the long. The long answer is the *Essays*. In fact, Montaigne claims not to be in the business of supplying answers at all. *"Je n'enseigne pas, je raconte"* ("I do not teach, I tell"), he writes. But, as with most people who claim not to teach, especially writers, he lies.

If Montaigne does teach, he does not preach. Very little self-righteousness pops up in the pages of the *Essays*. He was well aware of the traps implicit in writing about himself: "Condemn yourself and you are always believed; praise yourself and you never are." The author of the *Essays,* unlike so many writers, ancient and modern, never implies that he is the sole repository of virtue, even while freely criticizing his age. His modesty seems suitable, his humility genuine, and if both cannot always be entirely believed, for Montaigne had a delicate ironic touch, neither is ever overdone. ("Don't be so humble," Golda Meir is alleged to have said as Prime Minister of Israel to a member of her cabinet, "you're not that great.") As with any book of this length, there are longueurs in the *Essays,* and Montaigne can sometimes disappoint on a subject he proposes to take up by dissipating it through excessive quotation and digression. But his greatness lies in his temperament.

By temperament I mean that the elements of Montaigne's character, the humors as the medievals would say, were wonderfully well mixed in him. It is the complexity of his character, which he seems not only never to wish to hide but increasingly to divulge, that wins us to him. "I describe myself standing up and lying down, from the front and back, from right and left, and with all my inborn complexities." He could make a joke, he could take a blow, he could live with paradox. To his mind, "Good Luck and Bad Luck are two sovereign powers. There is no wisdom in thinking that the role of Fortune can be played by human wisdom."

Part of the seductiveness of Montaigne's thinking lies in his understanding of both the limitations of, and at the same time the need for, wisdom. Nowhere is this better brought out than in his writing about the body. Montaigne distrusted saints and disliked fanatics because they pretended to despise the body. "Aristippus championed only the body, as though we had no soul," he writes, "Zeno championed only the soul, as though we had no body. Both were flawed." Montaigne, on the contrary, thought the chances for contentment were greatly lessened until the body and soul could be somehow aligned; until such time, the human being was incomplete. He writes openly about his bodily appetites and functions—about food, sex, illness, defecation, death. To separate mind and body, as most systems of thought tend to do, seemed to Montaigne an error of the first magnitude. "May Philosophy's followers, faced with breaking their wife's hymen, be no more erect, muscular, nor succulent than her arguments are!" Part of Montaigne's all-roundedness has to do with his considering everything about life worth considering:

> It is an error to reckon some functions to be less worthy because they are necessities. They will never beat it out of my head that the marriage of Pleasure to Necessity . . . is a most suitable match.

For Montaigne what was finally of interest were the complexities of morality and the conundrum of human nature. Because he sensed that the universities of his day—as in ours—contributed little to either of these matters, he referred to them as "yap shops" and allowed that if he had a son he would prefer he get along with artisans rather than with scholars.

Artificialities came more and more to put Montaigne off; life was too brief to piffle it away on falsities, not least on false learning.

At the beginning of the *Essays* Montaigne is much taken up with the idea of death. One of the early essays carries the title "To Philosophize Is to Learn How to Die"; and later he will write that "dying is without doubt the most noteworthy action in a man's life." But the closer he came to dying himself, the more he was convinced that the great feat was to savor life's pleasures. "It is my conviction that what makes for human happiness is not, as Antithenes said, dying happily but living happily," he writes in "On Repenting." And in "On Experience," the final essay in the book, he observes: "It is an accomplishment, absolute and as it were God-like, to know how to enjoy our being as we ought."

Montaigne's illness—he developed kidney stones in his mid-forties, an illness that killed his father at the age of sixty-seven and would cause his own death at fifty-nine—may have changed his attitudes toward death. He no longer believed, with Seneca, that life was only worthwhile once one could bring oneself to despise it, on the Stoical grounds that nothing is worth having that one fears losing. The "stone," as he sometimes refers to it, gave him anguish and horrendous pain. (Imagine the excruciation of having kidney stones in 1577 and the hideous attempts at cure.) "I am wrestling with the worst of all illnesses," Montaigne writes, "the most unpredictable, the most fatal, and the most uncurable." The stone "unlechered" him, sent him on the road seeking remedies, made him realize afresh the hopelessness of professional knowledge when up against the discordant strength of nature—and, somehow, made him, a man whose full-time task was observing and reporting on himself ("I am loath even to have thoughts that I cannot publish"), even more intelligent.

He reports the pain vividly—talking about "the stubborn

nature of my stones, especially when in my prick," in Screech's unbuttoned translation—without quite complaining about it. "Anyone who is afraid of suffering," he writes, "suffers already of being afraid." Perhaps the stone had the contradictory effect of simultaneously reminding him of the sweetness of life and reconciling him to death. Such, at any rate, he leads one to believe when he writes:

> If I had to live again, I would live as I have done; I neither regret the past nor fear the future. And unless I deceive myself, things within have gone much the same as those without. One of my greatest obligations to my lot is that the course of my physical state has brought each thing in due season. I have known the blade, the blossom, and the fruit; and I now know their withering. Happily so, since naturally so. I can bear more patiently the ills that I have since they come in due season, and since they also make me recall with more gratitude the long-lasting happiness of my former life.

The novelist, dramatist, poet has the advantage over the essayist, autobiographer, philosopher of not having his life called into question—at least not decisively so. And even when it is called into question, the imaginative writer is freed from his ultimate responsibility for that life's not coming close to matching his art in its pretensions. Think only of Tolstoy, who lived with such clownish complications in his domestic life. Think of Baudelaire, a most unpleasant man generally. It is a great blessing that we do not know more about Shakespeare than we now do, but even if it were revealed that he was, say, a cannibal, we should probably not value the plays much less than we now do. But for the "non-imaginative" writer, the writer who writes not out of his imagination but out of his direct experience, the life is held up next to the work, and quite fairly so. As Montaigne himself puts it: "I never read an author, especially one treating of virtue and duty, without curiously inquiring what sort of man he was."

Montaigne himself passes this test not because of his purity, his goodness, his spirituality, but because of his honesty. He describes himself, and through himself men generally, not as they ought to be but as they are—and the picture seems accurate and just and true. Cosmetics are not employed. "I find that the best of the goodness in me," he writes, "has some vicious stain." And toward the end of the *Essays,* when he begins to write in the first-person plural—*je* becoming *nous*—he notes: "Yet within ourselves we are somehow double creatures, with the result that what we believe we do not believe, what we condemn we cannot rid ourselves of."

Montaigne regularly reports his shortcomings—his want of ambition, his laziness, his ineptitude at managing his estates, his wretched memory, his emotional distance from others. "If others were to look attentively into themselves, as I do, they would find themselves, as I do, full of emptiness and tomfoolery." Yet when he says such things you do not feel the touch of con, of someone working you up to like him for admirably admitting to his weaknesses. No, it is his good sense, his psychological penetration, his general bonhomie that wins one to Montaigne. In him religion never descends into piety, conservatism (he thought change in institutions an opening to tyrants) into meanness, skepticism into nihilism. Above all, he understood that "the world is involved in hundreds of questions where both the for and against are false." Montaigne perhaps alone of men famous in history or literature came closest to living the golden mean:

> Greatness of soul [he writes] consists not so much in striving upward and forward as in knowing how to find one's place and to draw the line. Whatever is adequate it regards as ample; it shows its sublime quality by preferring the moderate to the outstanding. Nothing is so beautiful, so right, as acting as a man

should; nor is any learning so arduous as knowing how to live this life naturally and well. And the most uncouth of our afflictions is to despise our being.

A mark of a great, of a world-historical writer is that his work not only translates across national boundaries but across time. Montaigne has met this mark. Each age has found its different lessons in the *Essays,* from the Enlightenment to our own. In our day, perhaps the most important lesson Montaigne has to teach is the need to regard all systems, all general ideas, all "isms" with extreme and comic dubiety. Montaigne was a writer who loved life, and it is in the name of the love of life, which is only another name for the love of reality, that Montaigne's hardy skepticism makes most sense in our own day, when concepts are created almost hourly and when, as Ortega once remarked, to create a concept is to invite reality to leave the room. Part of the splendor of Montaigne, and part of the pleasure of reading him, is that he is always inviting reality back in.

"Between you and me," Montaigne writes, "I have always found two things to be in singular harmony: supercelestial opinions and subterranean morals." What for Montaigne needs to be in harmony are opinions and morals, work and life. What his extraordinary exercise in self-analysis and self-portraiture is in the end about is the disciplining of the moral faculties through rigorous and profound introspection, so that such harmonious order prevails. No artist effectively teaches morality; the best he can hope to do is teach what morality is about. This Montaigne does supremely.

By being a man on whom not much was lost, by studying the complex variousness of human nature through looking first into his own soul, by carefully considering his experience of the world, by not asking the impossible of himself and being suspicious of those who asked it of others, by understanding that man's problem on earth is to attain such wisdom as will help him live a fit and reasonably happy life, Montaigne, for those who read him more than four centuries after he wrote, continues to lessen life's terror and to add to its pleasure. More than this no writer can hope to do, and none has done it better than Michel de Montaigne.

C. P. Cavafy,
A Poet in History

Freaks of literature, like freaks of nature, turn up in odd and unpredictable places. Why, after all, should Buenos Aires produce a Borges, Palmero a Lampedusa, Trieste a Svevo? The only—and perfectly unsatisfactory—answer is, Why not! Nothing in the traditions out of which any of these writers derive could have anticipated their becoming, as all did, writers of world interest. No very good explanation is available, really, just the brute fact of their arrival, writing quite unlike anyone else before them and producing enduring work of universal value. As they come upon the scene out of nowhere, neither do these writers begin or leave anything like a tradition behind them. *Sui generis,* in a class by oneself, is, after all, only another phrase for freakish.

C. P. Cavafy, the Greek poet who lived in the ancient Egyptian city of Alexandria, is another such freak of literature—perhaps the most interesting, idiosyncratic, and unexplainable of them all. Along with Borges, Lampedusa, and Svevo, Cavafy is a poet whose life, whose subject matter, whose point of view is inextricably bound up with his city. "Outside his poems," the Greek poet and critic George Seferis has said, "Cavafy does not exist." But without Alexandria, neither would the poems exist:

"for me," Cavafy wrote, referring to Alexandria in "In the Same Place," one of his late poems, "the whole of you is transformed into feeling."

Even though he wrote his poems in Greek, there is a sense in which Cavafy was more an Alexandrian than a Greek. Proud though he was of his Greek heritage, he did not in fact care to be described as a Greek, much preferring to be thought a Hellene. Alexandria, that city built by Alexander the Great and ruled by the Ptolemies, the site of Cleopatra's grandeur and Mark Antony's destruction, was for centuries the vessel through which so much world history flowed. This, the historical Alexandria, a city always more Mediterranean than Egyptian, was the Alexandria that Cavafy loved. He himself came, through his poetry, to resemble it in being yet another vessel through which history, this time in the form of his extraordinary poetry, flowed.

When Cavafy—whose dates are 1863–1933—lived in Alexandria, it was much less a classical than a preponderantly commercial city. Judeo-Hellenic and Franco-Levantine, it was, in the richly crowded sentence of Patrick Leigh Fermor, "a cosmopolitan, decadent, and marvellous hybrid, old in sin, steeped in history, warrened with intrigue, stuffed with cotton, flashing with cash, strident with cries for baksheesh, restless with conjuring tricks, and, after sunset, murmurous with improper and complicated suggestions." In his day, Cavafy must have made a few improper and complicated suggestions of his own.

Constantine Cavafy was the youngest of nine children born to a family that, by the time he came into the world, had already seen somewhat better and soon would see much worse days. In partnership with his brother, Cavafy's father was one of the leading merchants in the Greek colony in Alexandria; the family firm specialized in cotton and textiles. In this colony, all that counted was wealth, which the Cavafys had in sufficient quantity for the young Constantine to be raised with a French tutor and an English nurse in the house. Constantine's older brothers were sent abroad for their education. Their father, a free spender, died when Cavafy was seven, leaving his wife with very little money and his son with scant memories of him and the mixed blessing of continuing to think himself a rich man's son. Although the family retained something of its old social standing in Alexandria, having been thought upper-class, its position without wealth would henceforth be insecure, living with only the furniture and the memories of former luxuriance. Later Cavafy would tell E. M. Forster that aristocracy in modern Greece was the sheerest pretense, being built exclusively on cash: "To be an aristocrat there is to have made a corner in coffee in the Piraeus in 1849."

Cavafy's mother was now dependent on her sons for survival. At one point, when Cavafy was nine, the family moved to Liverpool, where the family business had a branch. Later the family moved to London, then back to Liverpool, only returning to Alexandria in 1877, when Cavafy was fourteen. In 1882, during the riots of Egyptians against Europeans in Alexandria, the family fled to Constantinople, where it remained for three years. The result was that between the ages of nine and fourteen, Cavafy lived in England, and between nineteen and twenty-two he lived in Turkey. Afterward he returned to Alexandria, where he remained, with infrequent visits to Greece, what might be called a firmly rooted cosmopolitan.

Cavafy, lucky fellow, did not leave many letters behind, nor an extensive diary. He wrote very little prose in his life and easily forbore the literary man's temptation of autobiography. Little is known about some of the most basic facts of his youth: where, for example, he went to school, apart from a year spent in a commercial school for Greek children in Alexandria. I say "lucky fellow," for the paucity of biographical information about Cavafy has spared him the cruelty of biographers poking into his life and career chiefly to find ways of advancing their own.

The hurdle of intrusive biography is the last that any writer has to jump, and any decent-minded reader nowadays has to hope that the writers he admires will find a way to cheat their biographers. In good part, Constantine Cavafy seems to have done so.

The most complete biography of Cavafy in English is a slender (by contemporary standards) volume of 222 pages by the English writer Robert Liddell. It is mainly concerned with putting to rout a good number of falsifications about Cavafy concocted by Greek writers of Freudian or Marxistical bent. An honest writer, Mr. Liddell has composed a book that, in the nature of the case, is full of "seems" and "supposes." Thus: "Cavafy seems never to have had confidants, and unfortunately we do not know whether his emotions were in any way involved in his sexual life." And: "There is no reason to suppose that he was an obsessional homosexual, the slave of his appetites." Mr. Liddell supplies those facts about Cavafy that can be nailed down, and the scarcity of these facts sets one's own imagination to work and turns inquiring minds—as *The National Enquirer* calls them—to the work itself, from which one is left to do one's best to extrapolate the life.

What is known about Cavafy as a young man is that, upon his return to Alexandria, he had, as Mr. Liddell reports, two things to hide from his friends: "homosexuality and acute poverty." He did what he could to alleviate the latter by working briefly as a journalist, then as a broker at the city's Cotton Exchange. (He supplemented his income by dabbling in the market throughout his life.) He began to work in 1889 as an unpaid clerk at the city's Irrigation Office, in the hope of catching on as a salaried employee, which, after showing his usefulness in dealing with documents in foreign languages, he did about three years later. He remained at the Dantesque-sounding location of the Third Circle of the Irrigation Office until his retirement thirty years later. Robert Liddell speculates that his job at the Irrigation Office gave him the kind of freedom he required.

This was the freedom to be Cavafy, which was a leisurely yet full-time job. E. M. Forster, who was in Alexandria during World War I and who was an early admirer and promoter of Cavafy's poetry, described Cavafy as a fixture in the city: "a Greek gentleman in a straw hat, standing absolutely motionless at a slight angle to the universe." Forster was here describing the poet going either from his home to his office or from his office to his home, perhaps stopping to deliver himself of a sentence of extraordinary syntactical complexity and impressive precision. Cavafy's home was an apartment in the old Greek quarter on the Rue Lepsius, where he lived after the death of his mother, with whom he had resided until he was thirty-six; on a lower floor was a brothel, not the sole such institution on the street, which was also known as the rue Clapsius. A hospital and a church were nearby. Cavafy more than once told visitors: "Where could I live better? Below, the brothel caters to the flesh. And there is the church which forgives sin. And there is the hospital where we die."

Cavafy's was the settled bachelor life of the homosexual *homme de lettres.* In Alexandria, people remember him as never being in a hurry. He wore dark suits with vests and thick glasses behind which his large eyes were draped by heavy, hooded lids. He lived in an apartment crowded with old furniture and rugs from his mother's apartment, but, surprisingly for a man steeped in history, not all that many books, and those mostly devoted to ancient Greek history, which he knew exceedingly well. He was an occasional gambler. He is said generally to have paid for his sex; his taste, Robert Liddell reports, ran not to Egyptian or Arab *ingénes* but to young Greek men. From the ages assigned to the men in his more erotic poems, one gathers that his ideal was that of Greek men in their twenties.

As Cavafy grew older and as his vigor diminished, so did

his fear of scandal, and he began writing—and promulgating—poems about the emotions surrounding homosexual love. With age, he grew rather seedy. Owing to the cancer of the larynx that finally killed him, toward the end of his life he walked about with his neck swathed in bandages. He dyed his hair with a solution of his own invention. (Voluptuaries take even less kindly to aging and death than the rest of us, and Cavafy's early poems show him when still at a young age already imagining himself a dessicated old man.) His conversation was measured, affable, and apparently memorable, judging by the number of people who met him who have recalled various of his utterances. All must have sensed that, in this odd duck Cavafy, they were in the presence of a great man. Right they were, too.

Cavafy would supply a fine if anomalous chapter in a book on the history of literary reputation. He was, at least among the cognescenti, a famous poet who in his lifetime never published a book, or at least never offered one for publication. Early in his career he published only a half dozen of the nearly two hundred poems he had already written, many of which he would later repudiate. (The final Cavafy canon, in Edmund Keeley and Philip Sherrard's excellent translation, consists of 175 poems.) Cavafy later brought together a pamphlet of his own devising consisting of only twenty-one poems, which he gave to relatives and a few friends. "Thereafter," writes Professor Keeley, who is Cavafy's best critic, "his method of disseminating his work, along with periodical publication, was through increasingly heavy folders containing broadsheets and offprints, the folders kept up-to-date year after year by Cavafy himself and distributed by his own hand to his select audience of readers, sometimes with revisions inserted by pen." When Cavafy died at seventy, there was no collected edition of his poems, nor had he left instructions for one.

Edith Wharton once claimed that she was fortunate when young not to have been considered promising: all sorts of pressures were removed. Cavafy took this a step further and claimed that he was fortunate to have been neglected. For one thing, a writer in a society where there are no obvious institutions of recognition for artists is automatically released from currying favor; nor need he worry about expressing things that might be impolitic from the standpoint of advancing his career. For another, in such a society a writer may develop at his own pace; he is unlikely to feel, as he might in a different setting, that if he hasn't won this prize by that age, or published that much by this age, he is a dismal failure. A neglected poet, in other words, has time to develop.

Cavafy required such time. The watershed year in his career, all his critics recognize, and as he himself would avow, was 1911, when he was forty-eight years old. (By forty-eight, a poet in America should already have had five books of poems published, an NEA and perhaps a Guggenheim grant behind him, be awaiting a MacArthur, and have tenure locked in. By fifty, if on schedule, he already begins to write much worse.) Not only did Cavafy produce a number of his best poems in the year 1911—including "The God Abandons Antony," "The Glory of the Ptolemies," and "Ithaka"—but, as if by magic, he had found his style: plain, spare, dramatic.

Cavafy found his subject in the Greek world of the Eastern Mediterranean. Many of the best of his poems are set in the two hundred years following the conquests of Alexander the Great. "The great age of Hellas," as C. M. Bowra wrote, "was no subject for his subtle taste." Bowra is surely correct when he adds that Cavafy "was interested not in the great lessons of history but in its smaller episodes, in which he saw more human interest than in the triumphs of heroes." Cavafy had a splendid instinct for capturing the perfect historical detail that demonstrated the continuity of human nature. Often, the deeper Cavafy's poetry takes a reader into history the more the poem makes him think of the present. His famous poem "Waiting for the Barbarians," in which the rulers and citizens of an unnamed ancient city, awaiting at the city walls, are disappointed at the failure of the barbarians to arrive, ends with the lines:

> Why this sudden restlessness, this confusion?
> (How serious people's faces have become.)
> Why are the streets and squares emptying so rapidly,
> everyone going home so lost in thought?
>
> > Because night has fallen and the barbarians have not
> > come.
> > And some who have just returned from the border
> > say
> > There are no barbarians any longer.
>
> > And now, what's going to happen to us without
> > barbarians?
> > They were, those people, a kind of solution.

Today it is difficult to read that poem without thinking of the West *vis-à-vis* the crumbling of Communism. Great poets write poems applicable to events and situations that they themselves could not ever have foreseen. Cavafy's achievement was somehow to write outside time by anchoring his writing as firmly as possible inside time.

Style helped Cavafy immensely in this endeavor. Once he hit his stride as a poet, Cavafy's poems became more and more shorn of ornament. He scarcely ever wrote about nature, and never, *à la* Lawrence Durrell (another of Cavafy's admirers), indulged in Middle Eastern exotica. He wrote in modern Greek, of course, but at least one of Cavafy's critics has suggested that he "thought" his poems in English. (After his early years in England, his Greek was spoken with a slight English accent, and his English, though fluent, was said not to be free of small mistakes—or not always, as an immigrant woman I knew once said, "impeachable.") Reading Cavafy in translation, one doesn't feel—despite Robert Frost's remark about poetry being what is lost in translation—too keen a loss. W. H. Auden has written on this point:

> What, then, is it in Cavafy's poems that survives translation and excites? Something I can only call, most inadequately, a tone of voice, a personal speech. I have read translations of Cavafy made by many different hands, but every one of them was immediately recognizable as a poem by Cavafy; nobody else could possibly have written it.

In their foreword to the *Collected Poems,* Edmund Keeley and Philip Sherrard speak of attending to Cavafy's "formal concerns, for example his subtle use of enjambment and his mode of establishing rhythm and emphasis through repetition." But in their limpid translation, Cavafy's poems read with the clarity and ease of a kind that seems trans-national and outside time. Howard Moss said of Cavafy's historical poems that "the tone [is] contemporary, but the voice timeless." Few of Cavafy's poems are more than two pages long; most are much shorter than that. "Nero's Deadline," if not one of his best, is a characteristic Cavafy poem:

> Nero wasn't worried at all when he heard
> the utterance of the Delphic Oracle:
> "Beware the age of seventy-three."
> Plenty of time to enjoy himself still.
> He's thirty. The deadline
> the god has given him is quite enough
> to cope with future dangers.
>
> Now, a little tired, he'll return to Rome—
> but wonderfully tired from that journey
> devoted entirely to pleasure:
> theatres, garden-parties, stadiums . . .
> evenings in the cities of Achaia . . .
> and, above all, the sensual delight of naked bodies . . .

45

So much for Nero. And in Spain Galba
secretly musters and drills his army—
Galba, the old man in his seventy-third year.

This poem demonstrates Cavafy's stripped-down method, what Joseph Brodsky has called "the economy of maturity": no imagery, no metrical tricks, no rhyme, no surprising or even striking adjectives, nothing ornate; a flat account of an event is given—sometimes told by a participant in the drama of a poem, sometimes (as here) by an offstage narrator—sometimes but not always with an ironic twist added at the end. "Cavafy," wrote George Seferis, "stands at the boundary where poetry strips herself in order to become prose."

But wherein, one might ask, lies the poetry? Often it is in the drama of Cavafy's poems, but not invariably even in that. Strangely, uniquely, I believe, it lies in the absence of metaphors in Cavafy's poems. Cavafy's poems are free from metaphors for the good reason that each of his poems is a metaphor unto itself. In Eliot, in James Joyce, in Yeats, one must, in effect, decode or parse or unpack symbols and myths to extract meaning. The very content of Cavafy's poems requires no such decoding or parsing or unpacking, to learn that this equals that, or that parallels the other.

Through his irony, sometimes through his drama, with the aid of his historical precision and his refusal of undue emphasis or over-dramatization, Cavafy can take a small historical incident, or even a person of tertiary significance, and raise it or him to an impressive general significance. Easier said than done, of course. The details have to be got exactly right, the meaning of the event described perfectly understood.

One of the my favorite among Cavafy's poems is "Alexandrian Kings," which is about a ceremony in which Antony declares Cleopatra's children kings of the known world, which is divided up among them. Kaisarion, the reputed son of Cleopatra and Julius Caesar, is declared the most powerful of them all,

King of Kings. Cavafy describes the child Kaisarion's clothes ("dressed in pink silk, / on his chest a bunch of hyacinths, / his belt a double row of amethysts and sapphires, / his shoes tied with white ribbons / prinked with rose-colored pearls"). He reports that the ceremony was a theatrical success, but makes plain that, in the eyes of the worldly Alexandrians, who enjoyed the event thoroughly on a day when the sky was "a pale blue," it was never more than sheer theater: "they know of course what all this was worth, / what empty words they really were, these kingships."

Plutarch's account of the event, told in his life of Mark Antony, is rather different. In it, the emphasis is on the two gold thrones Antony has set up for himself and Cleopatra. Plutarch describes the clothes of Antony and Cleopatra's children, Alexander and Ptolemy, but not, as does Cavafy, those of Kaisarion. Plutarch tells us that the Alexandrians were offended by the entire performance: "it seemed a theatrical piece of insolence and contempt of his country." In Cavafy, the Alexandrians are less enraged, more cynical. The entire episode is made all the more poignant by the fact, reported later and laconically by Plutarch, that "so, afterwards, when Cleopatra was dead he [Kaisarion] was killed." The attention, in Cavafy's version, is where it ought to be: on the child, who, being history's plaything, is pure victim.

Is this touching up history? Better perhaps to think it poet's history. Cavafy, toward the end of his life, declared himself "a historical poet." He added: "I could never write a novel or a play; but I hear inside me a hundred and twenty-five voices telling me that I could write history." Living in an ancient city, Cavafy had a feel for history, found his inspirations and deepest perceptions in history. The historian's function, in this view, is to show what happened in history; the poet's is to make plain its significance, but in the particular, oddly angled way of poets. In a later poem entitled "Kaisarion," Cavafy recounts how he came to write "Alexandrian Kings." He recounts killing an hour or two on a book of inscriptions about the Ptolemies, where he happened to come upon Kaisarion's name. The poem continues:

> Because we know
> so little about you from history,
> I could fashion you more freely in my mind.
> I made you good-looking and sensitive.
> My art gives your face
> a dreamy, an appealing beauty.
> And so completely did I imagine you
> that late last night,
> as my lamp went out—I let it go out on purpose—
> it seemed you came into my room,
> it seemed you stood there in front of me,
> looking just as you would have
> in conquered Alexandria,
> pale and weary, ideal in your grief,
> still hoping they might take pity on you,
> those scum who whispered: "Too many Caesars."

Not all Cavafy's poems have a classical setting. A handful are set in the Byzantine Empire. A few are of the kind that Marguerite Yourcenar, who translated Cavafy into French, calls his "poems of passionate reflection." (Only one in the *Collected Poems* is uncharacteristically comic: "King Claudius," which considers the Hamlet story from the uncle and step-father's point of view.) Many more are erotic, some among them plainly autobiographically erotic. Connoisseurs of Cavafy almost unanimously rate this latter category least interesting of the various categories of his poems. One is inclined to agree with Mme Yourcenar that these poems tend toward the sentimental.

To be sure, Cavafy is a highly erotic poet, but his is an eroticism recollected in tranquility. None of his poems is in the least pornographic; all of them are post-coital, and generally offer a reminiscence of one or another lover now gone. The ancient world was scarcely bereft of hedonism, and art and the erotic were there almost everywhere intertwined. So were they in Cavafy's own conception of poetry. In such poems as "Very Seldom" and "Understanding" ("In the loose living of my early years / the impulses of my poetry were shaped, / the boundaries of my art were laid down"), he makes unmistakably clear the importance of his homoerotic life to his art. The erotic in Cavafy takes two forms: it is only fleetingly obtainable—and often not even that—and then it evanesces. Art was for him consolation, at moments even compensation, for all that was unobtainable and lost to him in the erotic realm. In a poem with the telling title of "Half an Hour," about a lover whom he would never know, one finds the lines: ". . . But we who serve Art, / sometimes with the mind's intensity, / can create—but of course only for a short time— / pleasure that seems almost physical."

Joseph Brodsky is probably correct when he says that Cavafy's poems, without their "hedonistic bias," would have lapsed into mere anecdotes. Mme Yourcenar, a close student of these matters, felt that Cavafy had gone from the romantic view of homosexuality—"from the idea of an abnormal, morbid experience outside the limits of the usual and the licit"—to the classical view, in which, in her words, "notions of happiness, fulfillment, and the validity of pleasure gain ascendancy." This, too, on the evidence of the poems, seems probably true. Robert Liddell writes that Cavafy's homosexuality "made him what he was" and at the same time warns us that "it can be exaggerated and read into his work where it is not present." Contradictory though it may sound, he is correct on both counts.

Yet the significance of homosexuality in Cavafy's poetry, in my view, cuts deep. I think his homosexuality helped develop his vision of a world in which, first, the gods are fond of playing tricks on mortals: one of his earliest poems refers to men as "toys of fate," and another to "this unfair fate." Second, I think Cavafy's homosexuality intensified his sense that all that is not art is fated to die in this world. Cavafy's is a world that is all past and present and no future. Without religion—and, it is true, Cavafy was born into and died with the rites of the Greek Orthodox Church—without religion, which implies a continuous future, who can escape the grim knowledge that human existence is birth, life and loss, death and oblivion? Homosexuals, having no children, who are the key agency of futurity, get this sad news first. It comes to many of the rest of us rather later. The bone knowledge that everything in life is created to disappear is the beginning of what is known as the tragic sense—and Cavafy had this sense *in excelsis.*

Edmund Keeley makes the point that the tragic sense operates more strongly in Cavafy than does the moral sense. Some commentators have gone further and spoken of Cavafy as amoral. Marguerite Yourcenar speaks of his "absence of moralism," and E. M. Forster even speaks of his "amoral mind." Forster wrote:

> Courage and cowardice are equally interesting to his amoral mind, because he sees in both of them opportunities for sensation. What he envies is the power to snatch sensation, to triumph over the moment even if remorse ensues. Perhaps that physical snatching is courage; it is certainly the seed of exquisite memories and it is possibly the foundation of art. The amours of youth, even when disreputable, are delightful, thinks Cavafy, but the point of them is not that: the point is that they create the future, and may give to an ageing man in a Rue Lepsius perceptions he would never have known.

Cavafy himself seemed to believe that his sensual experiences—however fleeting, however superficial—gave him not only memories on which he could live for long afterwards but put him outside time. One sees this in a poem such as "Very Seldom," written in 1914, when Cavafy was only forty-one but surely anticipating his own old age:

He's an old man. Used up and bent,
crippled by time and indulgence,
he slowly walks along the narrow street.
But when he goes inside his house to hide
the shambles of his old age, his mind turns
to the share in youth that still belongs to him.

His verse is now recited by young men.
His visions come before their lively eyes.
Their healthy sensual minds,
their shapely taut bodies
stir to his perception of the beautiful.

This is, in my view, Cavafy at his most unconvincing. An old man shoring up a few memories of quick jousts against the ruins of old age, indeed of oblivion, is more pathetic than persuasive. In "Their Beginning," a poem recounting the aftermath of an illicit tryst, the two men part, each going off in his own direction, and Cavafy concludes: "But what profit for the life of the artist: / tomorrow, the day after, or years later, he'll give voice / to the strong lines that had their beginning here." After quoting from this poem, W. H. Auden, a strong admirer of Cavafy, laconically remarks: "But what, one cannot help wondering, will be the future of the artist's companion."

This seems not ever to have been a question for Cavafy, to whom the world was not organized into moral compartments. Standard morals, regular virtues, were to him not central; sin, original or unoriginal, was of no interest. In the world of his poems, politics plays as no more than the comedy of state, one man, group, or state squabbling with another man, group, or state for the power to control others. Politics allowed men to behave cruelly to one another but it did not free even those in control from the even crueller twists of fate.

Cavafy tends to admire those who accept fate like King Dimitrios, in the poem by that name, who, when the Macedonians deserted him, slipped off his golden robes, slipped into simple clothes, and "just like an actor who, / the play over, / changes his costume and goes away." In "The God Abandons Antony," the poet invokes Antony to read the writing on the wall, and "Above all, don't fool yourself, don't say / it was a dream, your ears deceived you: / don't degrade yourself with empty hopes like these."

In so many Cavafy poems, disaster lies round the corner, catastrophe waits in the wings. Although action is usually hopeless, inaction is itself a defect. Defeat in life is all but inevitable, and success, when it arrives, cannot for long be sustained. We are, in short, in the hands of the gods, the fates—call them what you will, they are full of dark surprises. The biggest mistake is to think one is in control of one's life for very long. "Fate is a traitor," says the narrator of the poem "Kimon, Son of Learchos," and *perepateia,* or reversal of fortune, is, in Cavafy's world, no more than business as usual. Nothing for it but to be honest about one's emotion, accept one's limitations, and live as best one can without illusions.

This sounds very dark, but, somehow, as it comes through Cavafy's poems, it is not. Marguerite Yourcenar has called Cavafy's "a perspective without illusions, but not desolate even so." He never lets one forget that only fools think the world is arranged for their convenience. His poems fortify one in one's determination never to underestimate life's manifold traps and treacheries; to be grateful for the simple absence of tyranny and terror; to count oneself fortunate to exist in the delight of the moment.

Cavafy provokes one to think about what truly matters in a life, and to brood on what remains when it is over. His poems cause one to consider which is more regrettable in one's life: the things done, or those left undone? Cavafy provides no answers to these questions. His achievement was to create out of historical particulars universal types who never let one forget the essential mystery of human nature. Cavafy admired those who could face this mystery without flinching, and his own poems lead one to think one has a chance to grasp that life truly is a mystery without necessarily making it any easier to face it on one's own. It was Henry James who said that "it is art that *makes* life, makes interest, makes importance . . . and I know of no substitute whatever for the force and beauty of its process." Constantine Cavafy might have said the same—in fact, his poetry says exactly that.

The Enduring V. S. Pritchett

Sooner or later, the great men turn out to be all alike. They never stop working. They never lose a minute. It is very depressing.
— V. S. PRITCHETT on Edward Gibbon

"The Age of Criticism," Randall Jarrell called the literary life of his own day, in an essay of that title written in the early 1950s. Jarrell used the phrase in derogation: there was too much criticism, from his point of view, and too much of it was extravagant in its pretensions. From the standpoint of today, however, that age is beginning to look more and more admirable. At the time T. S. Eliot, Edmund Wilson, F. R. Leavis, and Lionel Trilling were working at the critic's trade; so were John Crowe Ransom, William Empson, Yvor Winters, and Randall Jarrell himself, and to these one could, without too much strain, add another score or so of fairly impressive names.

Although born in 1900, and very much in his prime at the time of Randall Jarrell's essay, V. S. Pritchett's is not a name that many people would have included among the important figures from the Age of Criticism. For one thing, he didn't have a job at a university—he hadn't, come to that, even attended a university. For another, he had no interest in the theoretical or even disputatious aspects of literature: he wrote, that is to say, without an argument or a case to make. And for a third, he made his living from his writing, publishing (most frequently in *The New Statesman*) two-thousand-or-so-word book reviews every

54

week, supplementing these with a steady production of travel books, fiction, and biographical literary studies. In the Age of Criticism, Pritchett would have been called, with a slight air of put-down, a reviewer, or, only a touch more generously, a literary journalist.

Perhaps Pritchett's problem had to do with the fact that writing criticism, as practiced at the highest levels, is in some quarters regarded rather like making love: it is not thought quite proper to do it for money. V. S. Pritchett is a professional writer. At an earlier time, he would have been known as a man of letters, and John Gross, in the afterword to the new edition of his *Rise and Fall of the Man of Letters,* remarks that "no living man of letters had a better claim to be included" in his book than V. S. Pritchett. In fact, Pritchett was still very much in full sail when the first edition of Mr. Gross's book appeared in 1969. *A Cab at the Door,* the first of Pritchett's autobiographical volumes, had only just been announced—he would later write a second such volume, *Midnight Oil*—and much Pritchettian prose would flow under the bridge between then and now. The fluvial metaphor is perhaps allowable, since V. S. Pritchett has himself become something like the Ol' Man River of contemporary English literature: now in his early nineties, he jus' keeps rollin', he keeps on rollin' along. In the recently published second volume of his autobiography, *You've Had Your Time,* Anthony Burgess mentions seeing "an ancient but thriving Victor Pritchett." To put Pritchett's age in perspective, it helps to know that he read Virginia Woolf's books when they were just out.

To commemorate his achievement, perhaps also to mark his endurance, Pritchett's publishers, both in England and in the United States, have issued two thick volumes of his work: the *Complete Collected Stories* and the *Complete Collected Essays;* the latter, more precisely, turns out to be the collected literary criticism. Taken together, these two books run to nearly 2,500 pages and weigh in, on our family French cooking scale, at just over seven pounds. These books, neither of which comes with

an introduction or a prefatory word from their author or anyone else, are clearly meant as a tribute and one that provides
the occasion to consider the now rounded-out career of a remarkable writer.

V. S. Pritchett is both a throwback and an oddity. He is a
throwback to a time when, in England, one could write about
literature with the assumption that there was no need to teach
or preach to your readers, but as if one were merely holding
up one's end in an intelligent conversation. The assumption behind this seemed to be that your readers had of course read
the same books you had; and that, if a new book was under
discussion, they would soon read this book, too. Criticism in
America has generally had more to do with teaching one's
readers: introducing them to new subjects, straightening them
out on old ones. An element of unspoken condescension often
entered—and continues to enter—into the transaction. Criticism written by Americans has tended to be more thorough,
that written by Englishmen—or at least by some Englishmen—
more charming. V. S. Pritchett may be the last Englishman to
have worked under the splendid assumption that his readers
knew quite as much as he, were interested in pretty much the
same things, and operated at the same level of sophistication.

Victor (after Queen Victoria) Sawdon (his grandmother's
maiden name) Pritchett is an oddity—just how odd is explained
in his autobiographical volumes—in not being in any way to the
manner of literary culture born. To begin with a stark short-
story writer's fact that he supplies, he grew up in a home without a dictionary. His was a family, he wrote in *Midnight Oil,*
"where manners were unknown, where everyone shouted, and
no one had any notion of taste, either good or bad." His father,
a failed small business man, had greater powers of fantasy than
of imagination, and his mother's idea of jolly sport was changing the living-room furniture around. By the time he was
twelve, the family had moved something like a dozen times, each
move necessitated by his Micawberish father's having fallen

from yet another financial tightrope. Living on the economic edge, the family worked without a net. The cab was all too often at the door.

Along with these discouragements, Pritchett's father became an earnest Christian Scientist. Pritchett describes this religion, to which as a boy he was himself an adherent, as "notoriously a menopause religion," and one that, doubtless owing to its abstractness, "sounded better in German." Later in life he would describe it as "an enfeebled form of Emersonian metaphysics." In a story titled "The Saint," Pritchett remarks that "indeed our religion taught us never to believe what we saw"— not exactly the best training for a writer in the making. A religion of optimism, at least Christian Science didn't weigh a young man down with heavy notions of original sin. When he was young, Christian Science also provided Pritchett a social life through its Sunday school. In Paris, beginning to write, he early published in a Christian Science journal. He claimed that what finally allowed him to slip away from the religion was family egotism: "From our mother we had inherited an eye and ear for comedy; from our grandfather and father, a gift for irony and sarcasm."

Pritchett should by all rights have ended his days at a clerkish job of some sort—in a bank, perhaps, or a minor government department—for, as he says in the first volume of his autobiography, his grammar school was "intended to supply clerks for the boys who were going to public schools." He was a sometimes passionate but highly uneven student. He failed the one examination that might have provided him a chance to go to university. Had he not done so, he feels, he probably would have gone on to become a teacher or an academic. "I had had a narrow escape," he laconically notes. His grandfather, whom he describes as "looking like a sergeant major who didn't drink," upon one day inquiring after young Victor's age and being told he was fifteen, flatly stated to his father, "Put him to work." The sentence came down like the thump of a gavel. "My boyhood,"

Pritchett sadly remarks, "was over." He was sent out, wearing a bowler hat, to work in the leather trades.

How did Pritchett slog on through to achieve such considerable renown for literary achievement: from benighted to knighted in one generation, for he ended Sir Victor? As with many another writer, his natural disadvantages were a help. He hated dull work, he suffered from ennui, he had neither the taste nor the talent for making money. On the credit side of the ledger, he had an instinctive admiration for skill in any form; an aptitude for language, French and German being two subjects he had done well at in school and the sound of words being an obsession of his from childhood; and he felt a yearning toward art and culture and, to go along with it, a usefully nagging sense of his own inferiority. "Would I 'catch up?' " he asked himself, daunted as a boy by the books in a friend's father's library. (Decades later he would write: "I am appalled by the amount I have read.") Finally, his own homelife had distanced him from the world, and the seven years he would later spend in France, Spain, and Ireland made him feel a stranger at home and a foreigner even in his own country. What we have here, seen in retrospect, is the perfect combination of elements for a writer: a young man of intelligence, energy, and curiosity, mildly disaffected, and unfit to do anything else but write.

After a spell working in the leather trade in Paris, during which he attempted to paint, Pritchett began writing in earnest. His first publication was a joke he sold to *The New York Herald,* about which, in *Midnight Oil,* he notes: "It taught me one thing. If one had nothing to say one could at any rate write what other people said." (Writing what other people said—sounds rather like the perfect job description of the literary critic.) One minor publication led to another; soon he set to work on a travel book. He made a mistaken first marriage. (All Pritchett's subsequent books are dedicated to his second wife, Dorothy.) He worked as a correspondent in Ireland and then in Spain, a country with which he fell in love. (His dearest friend was Gerald

Brenan, author of *The Spanish Labyrinth*.) As a writer, he preferred to use the initials V. S. because he liked the impersonality of it, and, besides, "to have added the 't' of Victor to a name that already had three [t's], and was already made fidgety by a crush of consonants and two short vowels, seemed ridiculous."

Pritchett's first book, *Marching Spain,* a travel book, was filled, as he allowed more than forty years after having written it, with "exhibitionist prose" and errors of fact, but also with touches of originality and vigor. Not least among V. S. Pritchett's gifts is his ability to apprehend his own literary qualities. It is part of his talent for getting outside himself; a rare skill, it makes him in some ways his own best critic. In scattered comments in *Midnight Oil,* he limns his strengths and weaknesses, proclivities and antipathies with a nice detachment fitting to a writer who claims that "to strain after the essence of things has become a mania with me."

"I am no thinker or philosopher," Pritchett avers, truly enough. He knows that such truths as are available to him come through the impressions experience makes on him. He claims to have had a "vulgar instinct for survival." He also believes that "any originality in my writing is due to having something of a foreign mind," even though he is usually described as a traditionally English writer. "I have talent," he writes, "but no genius." That may well be true, but it has always seemed to me that the English language is deficient in not possessing a word that lies between the two; it would be a word that described how far talent, honed under the pressure of unrelenting hard work, can take one. This missing word would, I think, apply nicely to V.S. Pritchett.

Pritchett began writing for *The New Statesman* in 1928, when Clifford Sharp was editor and the charmingly indolent Desmond MacCarthy, who was rarely to be found on the premises, was literary editor. The weekly was dedicated to Fabian Socialism, but always allowed itself lots of latitude in the back of the book, as the pages given over to books and culture were called. Although his was a generation whose politics were formed by the Spanish Civil War, Pritchett reports that his own experience with so all-embracing a religion as Christian Science made it impossible for him to swallow Marxism, whose totalitarian consequences were repugnant to him. Besides, as he writes, "I was constitutionally a nonbeliever. Rarely have the active politicals had a deep regard for imaginative literature." And the political, it is true, has never been anywhere near the center of Pritchett's own writing, either as a critic or a storyteller.

Pritchett kept up his connection with *The New Statesman* through the years, all the while writing for other papers, but it was during World War II that the nature of his book reviewing there changed. Until then he wrote about new books, but, with the paper shortages owing to the war greatly curtailing the production of new books, and many other contributors to the paper off fighting the war, he was now called upon to write the leading literary article for each week's issue. It was usually an article dealing with a rereading of one of the classics. At a length of not more than two thousand words, he kept a flow of these articles coming: "one week the subject might be Walter Scott, the next Dostoyevsky, after that Benjamin Constant, George Fox, Zola, *Gil Blas,* and so on." This turned him from a reviewer with highbrow tastes into something much closer to a critic.

As Pritchett notes in *Midnight Oil,* he not only had no university training in any branch of literature, but "I had no critical doctrine—a shock later to the platoons of New Critics and later regiments—for critical doctrine is of little interest to the novelist, though it may mean something to the poet." He did avail himself of a few core notions: one was that the historical situation of the writer was always of interest; another that, as a practicing novelist and short-story writer himself, he often had keen and useful insights into the means and methods with which novelists worked; and yet another was that "literature grows out of literature as much as out of a writer's times," by which he

meant nothing so arcane as Professor Harold Bloom's "the anxiety of influence," but, as he puts it in an essay on Goncharov,
"literature had a double source: one in life, the other in literature itself."

Although early in his career Pritchett produced a few
novels, and he wrote more than one complete book on Spain,
his reputation today rests on his work as a literary critic and as
a short-story writer. Lucky is the writer who has found his
forms, and these have been Pritchett's. "I have had to conclude,"
he writes in *Midnight Oil,* "that I am a writer who takes short
breaths, and in consequence the story and the essay have been
the best forms for me." I have called Pritchett a literary critic,
but the term "literary essayist" perhaps makes a better fit. Unlike the great literary critics, Pritchett does not write out of a
moral or cultural program. Approaching the work of a writer,
often a writer of well-established reputation, Pritchett seems
instead keenest to understand why this writer exerts the powerful interest he does and whence his power derives. The place-
ment of a writer in his tradition and a judgment upon his work
finally do emerge in a Pritchett essay, but they tend to do so sub-
tly, by the way, almost as matters of subsidiary interest.

About his literary essays Pritchett has written: "I see myself as a practicing writer who gives himself to a book as he gives
himself to any human experience," which is reminiscent of Ana-
tole France's remark that "the good critic is he who relates the
adventures of his soul amongst masterpieces." Pritchett has not
written about poets. (In *A Cab at the Door,* he claims that the
forms of Protestantism in which he was brought up fertilized
neither sensibility nor the poetic imagination, but in prose he
"found the common experience and the solid worlds where
judgments were made and in which one could firmly tread.")
He occasionally writes about but is less than satisfactory on
books of limited subject (Malraux on Picasso), or books about
a single event or incident in literary history (the murder of
Lorca), or a historical work (Ladurie's *Montaillou*). He has writ-

ten preponderantly about novelists, where he is at his best, and he is especially good when presented with an opportunity to biograph, or draw a portrait of, the novelist through his work.

V.S. Pritchett is a critic without anger. He shows some mild animus against academic criticism, with its penchant for barbed-wire jargon, and in one of his essays notes that "literary criticism does not add to its status by opening an intellectual hardware store." He is also quite without snobbery, and can be amusing on other people's snobbery. Of Evelyn Waugh's auto-biography, *A Little Learning,* he writes: "Prep school, public school, university: these now tedious influences standardise English autobiography, giving the educated Englishman the sad if fascinating appearance of a stuffed bird of sly and beady eye in some odd seaside museum." Only rarely is he autobiograph-ical in his criticism, and when he is, he is rather touchingly so: "The last time I wept over a novel was in reading *Tess* when I was 18. Fifty years later Fortunata [a character in Peréz Galdós's novel *Fortunata and Jacenta*] has made me weep again."

That Pritchett would weep over the fate of a character in a novel is revealing of his method as a critic. For Pritchett takes characters in novels very seriously. He will write, devastatingly, of the characters in Samuel Butler's *The Way of All Flesh,* that But-ler "chose them for their mediocrity and then cursed them for it." Of *Middlemarch,* Pritchett writes that "the most moving thing in the book—and I always think this is the real test of a novelist—is given to the least likeable people." Characters do seem to have a life of their own for Pritchett, and part of the mystery of fiction is that novelists can on occasion create char-acters much more interesting than themselves. As a case in point, he adduces Oblomov so much more fascinating than the rather dull state official who was his creator, Ivan Goncharov. "From what leak in a mind so small and sealed," writes Pritch-ett, "did the unconscious drip out and produce the character of Oblomov, the sainted figure of non-productive sloth and inertia; one of those creatures who become larger and larger as we read?"

Pritchett's interest in both writers and the characters they create spares him, in most cases, the sleep-inducing burden of most critics of fiction, which is tedious plot summary. Writing about established masterpieces, Pritchett seldom has to take his readers by the hand and summarize the plot for them. At the same time, he understands that criticism, if it is to have a reasonably long life—and it is striking how readable so much of Pritchett's own criticism remains—must tell a story. The story that his criticism tells is about writers—their struggles, their creations, their uniqueness—so that, as Derwent May, writing in the *TLS,* has said, in a Pritchett essay we have not just the story of the novel but "the story of the writing and the reading of it as well." What Pritchett does, then, is tell us a story about the story.

Appreciation is at the heart of V. S. Pritchett's criticism. Appreciation provides a severe limitation on a critic, making him only as good as the work he is appreciative of. Perhaps this is why Pritchett seems best on nineteenth-century fiction, especially Russian and French fiction. He seems to me weakest on American writers: Mary McCarthy, Saul Bellow, John Updike, S. J. Perelman, all of whom, with his customary impulse toward appreciation, I believe he overrates. Part of his problem with these writers is that they haven't created strong characters of the kind that are best for Pritchett's particular kind of criticism or that are memorable for more than their muddle; or, to put it more precisely, their muddle, unlike that of the characters of Italo Svevo, a writer whom Pritchett adores, is without redeeming charms. It may well be that the quality of a nation's fiction during any particular period is best measured by the number of memorable characters that fiction collectively yields. American fiction of the past thirty or so years does not score high by this test.

Impressive though I remember many of V. S. Pritchett's essays being when I first encountered them in *The New Statesman,* these essays seem even more impressive when read in bulk. One of the reasons for this is that one discovers that Pritchett has the ability to write freshly on a subject one might have thought had already been quite exhausted through having been critically over-mined in the work of academics—strip-mined might be the better term. George Bernard Shaw qualifies as such a subject. In a few neatly formulated sentences, Pritchett can reinvigorate interest in him. Shaw's "own addictions," he writes, "were the Irish addiction to words and the Puritan's to work." A few paragraphs on, he adds: "The Irish are almost always shy, almost always trying to conceal, and they have notoriously been apt to produce a stage personality to do so." True, it seems to me, not only of Shaw but of Wilde, Yeats, Joyce, Beckett, and every other strong Irish writer.

Reading Pritchett in bulk, one is also reminded of his appetite for generalization and, what often comes to the same thing, aphorism. The generalization and the aphoristic formulation are the natural tools of the critic seeking essences. From the *Complete Collected Essays,* one could almost scrape out a slender volume of *Pritchett's Unfamiliar But Damn Good Quotations.* Allow me to offer a handful: "Travel is one of the great rivals of women." "Literature is made of the misfortunes of others." "There is more magic in sin if it is not committed." "The principle of procrastinated rape is said to be the ruling one in all the great best-sellers." "The peculiar power of American nostalgia is that it is not only harking back to something lost in the past, but suggests also the tragedy of a lost future." "The ecstasies of sexual sensation are no more to be described than the ecstasies of music they resemble." "Remove the vices of a novelist and his virtues vanish too."

In Pritchett's searching for writers' essences, his essays strike many such generalizations and cut many fine distinctions, while his own wide reading has given him the power to make endless comparisons between writers and between centuries and between national literatures. This is, after all, what a literary critic does, even though fewer and fewer practitioners are up to the job. But toward what end does he put on this display of a subtle and well-stocked mind in action? It is a pleasing enough game—and, for those of us who have a taste for it, splendid to watch—but when is the trophy awarded?

The answer, which will not come to everyone as good news, is never. Not only is there nothing definitive, nothing of the last word about any of Pritchett's criticism, but it is unlikely that he ever expected there would be. Reviewing a collection of Graham Greene's essays, Pritchett remarked that, in this particular book, Greene was "before anything a novelist-critic—that is to say he writes to discover something for *his* purposes which might not be ours. His reviews are an artist's raids." There is something of this quality in Pritchett's literary essays, too, except that he is interested in what we all ought to be interested in: the mysteries of literary creation and what writers can tell us about human nature.

Pritchett joins the overwhelming majority in not being able to say with precision what human nature is, but he does greatly admire those writers who accept, as he says the novelist Galdós does, "human nature without resentment." One of the reasons Pritchett is so taken with Italo Svevo is that Svevo had the courage and the comic gift not only to investigate the contradictoriness of human nature but come up laughing at what he found. Although he appreciates much, Pritchett admires above all those writers, Jane Austen and Henry Fielding among them, "who face life squarely." Of them he writes:

> They are grown up. They do not cry for the moon. I do not mean that to be grown up is the first requirement of genius. To be grown up may be fatal to it. But short of the great illuminating madness, there is a power to sustain, assure, and enlarge us in those novelists who are not driven back by life, who

are not shattered by the discovery that it is a thing bounded by unsought limits, by interests as well as by hopes, and that it ripens under restrictions. Such writers accept. They think that acceptance is the duty of a man.

Pritchett has written vast quantities of both criticism and fiction, but his personality comes through much more clearly in his criticism. He is, as usual, quite aware of this fact, even though he reports that writing stories has given him greater pleasure than writing criticism. "In my criticism, perhaps even more than in my stories, I am self-portrayed. When I reread those essays written in such number over the last thirty years, I am surprised to see how much they are pitted with personal experience, and how much reaction to life itself, either nettled or expansive, has been packed into an epigram or an aside." One of the problems with other critics who have written fiction—Edmund Wilson and Lionel Trilling come to mind—is that they sound quite the same in their fiction as they do in their criticism, so that fiction becomes, like war and diplomacy for Clausewitz, chiefly criticism by other means.

Nothing of the kind is true of Pritchett. Only rarely is the storyteller in him likely to be mistaken for the critic, so differently do the two sound. While a V. S. Pritchett literary essay has its author's fingerprints all over it, I am not so sure that I could recognize a V. S. Pritchett short story without its author's name atop it. "The creative writer must know his own mind," Desmond MacCarthy once remarked, "the critic must also know the minds of other people." As a storyteller there is something ventriloquistic about Pritchett. *Voice,* the current cant word in university creative writing programs to describe the distinctive way a writer sounds, is not strong in Pritchett's fiction. He does many voices: he does the lower-middle and working classes in a hundred different voices. His own sometimes gets lost in the cacophony.

Is this a bad thing? Does it matter if there is nothing distinctively Pritchettian about a V. S. Pritchett short story? Isn't the main thing that a fair number simply are good stories—and the hell with their fitting a pattern or dovetailing into something sufficiently uniform to be called an *oeuvre?* Writers of great contemporary reputation—Eudora Welty, William Trevor, Robertson Davies—have weighed in with testimonials about the pleasure Pritchett's stories give and compare them with those of Joyce and Chekhov. One understands their having done so; one wants to admire Pritchett's stories.

Something about the quietly sedulous way Pritchett has written his fiction is immensely attractive. There is an admirably selfless quality to his storytelling. For one thing, he has, in his fiction, taken up a people forgotten by literature: the English lower-middle class of shopkeepers, salesmen, dentists, minor manufacturers, publicans, clerks, antique dealers, and wives whose beauty and dreams have faded too quickly. What Pritchett once wrote about Gissing, may, in good part, also be said of him: "[His] discovery that in all character there sits a mind, and that the mind of the dullest is not dull because, at its very lowest, it will at least reflect the social dilemma into which it was born, is arresting." The point is connected with Pritchett's general view, set out in his criticism, that fiction ought not to disparage its characters or be written as if by foreigners living in their own country, which he believes a good deal of English and American fiction appears to have been.

Much of the program for Pritchett's own fiction seems to have been announced in his criticism. Apropos of Isaac Babel, Pritchett writes that "short story writers are poets," and that what the short story sets out to achieve is "an insight." Apropos of Borges, he notes that, "in the writer of short stories as in the poet, a distinctive voice, unlike all others, must arrest us," and he adds that the test of the artist is whether he can make his ideas walk, which is to say, come alive. Apropos of Kipling, he adds that the short story is "a form which depends on intensifying the subject, stamping a climate on it, getting at the essence of it."

Many of Pritchett's own stories exemplify these aesthetic axioms. Poetic though he may think the short-story form ultimately is or ought to be, his own vast output of stories includes almost every variety known to the form, and in my opinion his longer stories tend to be better than those in which he goes after more strictly poetic effects. "A short story," he writes in an essay on Flannery O'Connor, "ought to be faultless without being mechanical. The wrong word, a misplaced paragraph, an inadequate phrase or a convenient explanation, start fatal leaks in this kind of writing which is formally very close to poetry."

If Pritchett has a serious fault as a storyteller it is in his own impulse toward the poetic, which shows up in occasional small but disturbing touches. In one story a man sticks his hands in "his optimistic pockets"; in another a woman is wearing a "capable skirt"; another woman has "the disorder of a story"; a man is "as conceited as a gravestone"; another man has "an unreasonable chin and emotional knees"; yet another man stands "like a touchy exclamation mark"; and several clerks have "dejected buttocks," for which perhaps trousers with "optimistic pockets" ought to be recommended.

The stories are also sometimes studded with occasional aphoristic bits reminiscent of V. S. Pritchett's criticism. The narrator of "The Sailor" remarks: "Actually, I am in favour of snobbery, it is a sign of character. It's a bad thing to have, but it's a bad thing not to have had. You can't help having the diseases of your time." In the same story, the same character announces that "the secret of happiness is to find a congenial monotony." There are also numerous little touches straining after poetry and achieving it, such as a clergyman, in one story, comporting himself "like the actor walking in the sun of his own vanity"; or the man who, moving different parts of his body separately, "danced, as it were, in committee." Pritchett can be relied upon to have done his homework. If he writes about antique dealers, or window-washers, or bakers, he is always careful to get the niceties of these lines of work right. He often penetrates well beneath the surface of details to understand the drama playing there, a drama that is inseparable from a knowledge of such details. In "The Camberwell Beauty," a story about the obsession of antique dealing, Pritchett writes:

> Mrs. Price—August's woman—was living with a man exactly like the others in the trade: he hated customers and hated parting with anything. By middle age these women have dead blank faces, they look with resentment and indifference at what is choking their shops; their eyes go smaller and smaller as the chances of getting rid of it become rarer and rarer and they are defeated. Kept out of the deals their husbands have among themselves, they see even their natural love of intrigue frustrated. This was the case of Mrs. Price, who must have been handsome in a big-boned way when she was young, but who had swollen into a drudge.

If a poet can hit the gong six or seven times, leaving behind that number of great poems, his claim to immortality, it has been said, is assured. The same ought perhaps to be true of storytellers, except that, as has been noted countless times, not least by V. S. Pritchett in his criticism, "how little a novelist's [or short-story writer's] choice of story and character widens or changes between his first book and his last." This seems to be true, too, of Pritchett's own stories, eighty-two of which are included in his *Complete Collected Stories,* with the added oddity that one of his best stories, "Sense of Humour," is also among his earliest. Of these four-score and two stories, six or seven really are splendid. Among them I would include, along with "Sense of Humour," "It May Never Happen," "The Saint," "The Camberwell Beauty," "The Sailor," "The Skeleton," and "The Necklace." For really splendid stories, that's a lot.

In his fiction, Pritchett is thought to be a comic writer. "Class is a funny thing," says a character, double-entendrically, in the story "Noisy Flushes the Birds," and though Pritchett

wrings much humor out of the sometimes extreme social limitations that are locked in by social class in England, his stories
are more often striking in their darkness. Loneliness is the condition of so many of Pritchett's characters, who must make do
with a life that has disappointed expectations, where expectations even existed in the first place. "There is a loneliness in fat,"
he remarks of the two fat men in one of his stories. An elderly
homosexual, after tea and toast in the morning, "looked eagerly
to see what was annoying in the papers—some new annoyance
to add to a lifetime's accumulation of annoyances." "The Two
Brothers," another tale of loneliness, ends on the following sentences: "He took out a razor and became absorbed in the difficulty of cutting his throat. He was not quite dead when the
Guards broke in and found him." Life, in Pritchett's stories,
twists and breaks people apart.

The final story in the *Complete Collected Stories,* "The Image
Trade," which feels very autobiographical, is about an elderly
writer named Pearson who is being photographed by a fashionable photographer named Zut. As the photographer is setting things up, the writer thinks:

> Dozens of photographs of me have been taken. I could show
> you my early slim-subaltern-on-the-Somme-waiting-to-go-
> over-the-top period. There was my Popular Front look in the
> Thirties and Forties, the jersey-wearing, all-the-world's-a-
> coal-mine period, with close-ups of the pores and scars of the
> skin and the gleam of sweat. There was the editorial look, when
> the tailor had to let out the waist of my trousers, followed by
> the successful smirk. In the Sixties the plunging neckline, no
> tie. Then back to collar and tie in my failed-bronze-Olympic
> period. Today I fascinate archaeologists—you know, the bro-
> ken pillar of a lost civilisation. Come on, Zut. What do you
> want?

Later, when Pearson is presented with the finished photograph, he claims to see in its high-ceilinged, book-filled room

not a room at all but "a dank cistern or aquarium of stale water. No sparkling anemone there but the bald head of a melancholy frog, its feet clinging to a log, floating in literature." Quite an arresting, not to say devastating, little image, that, suggesting that a career soaked in literature can turn a man at the end of a long life into a saddened frog. Must be something to it, viewed from within, or else Pritchett would not have thought of it.

And yet how different Pritchett's career looks from outside that room! Brick by brick, essay by essay, story by story, he has over the years built a modest yet quite sturdy literary edifice. Writing for a small and probably diminishing audience, he has never lowered his standard or sullied his integrity. In an essay on the novelist Ada Leverson, Pritchett claimed that her career proved that one could be both a minor novelist and yet a considerable artist. To bring this off, he felt, one required a freshness of view without borrowing the courage of anyone else's convictions; skill in construction and distinction in style; and a delight in one's own limits, so that even when one was dealing only with what seemed the surface of life one's seriousness and life-enhancing quality shone through. Pritchett might, of course, have been writing about himself—a doubtless minor writer, but a true artist who has written an uncommonly high number of essays and stories built to last.

F. Scott Fitzgerald's Third Act

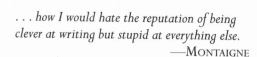

> *. . . how I would hate the reputation of being*
> *clever at writing but stupid at everything else.*
> —MONTAIGNE

Michel de Montaigne's dread has been F. Scott Fitzgerald's fate. As his reputation has filtered down through biography, memoirs of contemporaries, and posthumous publications of various sorts, Fitzgerald has been judged something like a lucky genius as a writer and an almost pure disaster as a man.

Officially, this unenviable reputation began with a remark by the poet Edna St. Vincent Millay which was picked up by Edmund Wilson, with whom Fitzgerald had gone to Princeton. In an essay of 1922, when Fitzgerald was himself only twenty-six and had just published his second novel, *The Beautiful and Damned,* Wilson, already an important critic, wrote:

> It has been said by a celebrated person that to meet F. Scott Fitzgerald is to think of a stupid old woman with whom someone has left a diamond; she is extremely proud of the diamond and shows it to everyone who comes by, and everyone is surprised that such an ignorant old woman should possess so valuable a jewel; for in nothing does she appear so inept as in the remarks she makes about the diamond.

Wilson went on to say that Fitzgerald was a clever enough fellow, but, nonetheless, "there is a symbolic truth in the description quoted above."

After this essay, Fitzgerald's reputation as the artistic equivalent of an idiot savant was firmly locked in place, so that Glenway Westscott, a much inferior novelist, could later call him "the worst-educated man in the world" and the poet John Peale Bishop, another Princeton contemporary, could remark that Fitzgerald had "left Princeton without a degree and without much of an education." More recently, Gore Vidal referred to him as "barely literate."

But, then, residing comfortably alongside the notion of F. Scott Fitzgerald as ignorant genius there is also the cult of Fitzgerald, which set in not long after his death at the age of forty-four. In this cult he is viewed as a tragic young god—tragic because much too soon dead. The spirit of the cult was nicely caught by the English critic Cyril Connolly, who in 1951, the year Arthur Mizener's biography of Fitzgerald, *The Far Side of Paradise,* appeared, wrote that "apart from his increasing stature as a writer, Fitzgerald is now firmly established as a myth, an American version of the Dying god, an Adonis of letters."

Dying young, leaving behind work unfinished and promise unfulfilled, Fitzgerald has become enshrined as a great failure. He had himself cultivated this reputation long before his death, beginning with the publication, in *Esquire,* of the essays that were posthumously collected by Wilson under the title of *The Crack-Up* (1945). Of the many differences between himself and his contemporary, Ernest Hemingway, Fitzgerald wrote in his notebook: "Ernest speaks with the authority of success. I speak with the authority of failure." But in literature and the arts, if nowhere else, the authority of failure sometimes proves the greater—so much so that one can sometimes say that here nothing quite succeeds like failure.

Which is not to say that Fitzgerald never enjoyed success

in the usual sense. On an imaginary graph, how wavy a line his reputation has ridden over the years! It begins headed straight up with the best-seller success of his first novel, *This Side of Paradise* (1920); it dips slightly with *The Beautiful and Damned* (1922); hits its artistic height with *The Great Gatsby* (1925); shows an eight-year gap between the publication of *Gatsby* and Fitzgerald's last completed novel, *Tender Is the Night* (1933); and then drops sadly, with all his books out of print and no one asking for or expecting more, which is where things stood at his death of heart failure in his Hollywood apartment in 1940.

At that point, Fitzgerald was broke and broken—as a man out of luck and as an author out of print. He had lived long enough to see his one unequivocal artistic triumph, *The Great Gatsby,* dropped from the Modern Library because it was not selling. He left his final book, *The Last Tycoon,* for which he had done the most meticulous planning, so incomplete that its potential quality was (and remains) difficult to judge. As a screenwriter, he had been dealt all the little humiliations Hollywood had to hand out. He had not had enough money to travel East to visit his daughter Scottie for more than a year, or to see his schizophrenic wife, the notorious Zelda, who would die eight years after him in a fire in an insane asylum of which she was an inmate. Debt and family obligations kept him on the griddle of hack production for the last decade of his short life.

A famous Fitzgerald tag line has it that "there are no second acts in American lives." Fine though the ring to that line is, it is not true when applied to Fitzgerald himself, whose literary life has had a powerful and continuing posthumous second and third act, and may even be in for an epilogue or two. For after his death there followed a slow rise in Fitzgerald's reputation, beginning with the publication of *The Crack-Up,* the return of all his books to print, the installation of the young-Adonis myth, and a steady flow of biographies and collections of letters.

True, there was the damage done in 1964 by the rivalrous

Hemingway, who in his memoir, *The Moveable Feast,* portrayed Fitzgerald as a weak, sexually insecure, hopeless drunk. But this was more than offset by the steady rise in his literary stock, combined with heavy academic attention. "Academic" may be imprecise, for *The Great Gatsby* is one of those books that most children are asked to read in high school and even in grammar school, and for all one knows by now in Montessori preschools. Along with *Huckleberry Finn,* it is one of the few books that is a common literary possession of middle-class American children in a less and less literary age. Teachers continue to milk it, often finding fresh and wonderful things, as does Ronald Berman in *The Great Gatsby and Modern Times,* who has discovered that the novel brilliantly foreshadows life in a mass society.

Yet even about *The Great Gatsby* there clings something of the quality of luck, of the one-shot deal, as if Beethoven had written the *Eroica* Symphony and otherwise only mildly interesting, largely botched, incidental music. How could this foolish, if not frivolous, young man, F. Scott Fitzgerald, ill-educated and not yet thirty, bring off so nearly perfect a book?

American literature has known other one-great-book authors—Mark Twain in some ways qualifies, and so, in others, does Melville—but none has quite the airy quality of Fitzgerald, who wrote two very boyish early novels that no one would bother reading today if their author had not also written *Gatsby;* a rich but perhaps overcooked fourth novel, *Tender Is the Night;* a handful of winning short stories; and an uncompleted final novel. Sometimes it seems as if Fitzgerald, in writing *The Great Gatsby,* had hit the lottery.

Especially does this seem the case when one totes up Fitzgerald's personal deficiencies. Raucous, often pathetic drunkenness is high on that list. Churchill once said that he always got the best of alcohol and alcohol never got the best of him. Not so Fitzgerald, who may have been an alcoholic as early as his college years. The Fitzgeralds, Scott and Zelda, were to drinking what Fred Astaire and Ginger Rogers were to dancing: the top, the colosseum, the Louvre museum, and so forth.

The Fitzgeralds achieved fame for jumping into the Pulitzer fountain near the Plaza Hotel in New York, which sounds relatively harmless and even came to symbolize the good times of the 1920's, the so-called Jazz Age. But while drunk, the Fitzgeralds' idea of amusing behavior was to collect everyone's watch and jewelry and boil them in a can over the stove; or to call out the fire department—upon the arrival of which Zelda, pointing to her left breast, would claim that that the fire was in her heart; or to destroy apartments, their own and other people's; or to insult servants, friends, and anyone else in sight, with Scott often ending an evening by getting into a fist fight, which he would inevitably lose. Not quite, the Fitzgeralds, what we should today call a "fun couple."

If Fitzgerald could not control his alcohol, he was not much better with money. Although he earned vast sums, money seemed to slip away from him like genial groups from a confident bore. He earned as much as $4,000 a shot for the many short stories he published in the *Saturday Evening Post* in the 1920's, a fee that would be roughly the equivalent of $40,000 in 1994. But this was sloshed away in boozy, sloppy living. In the mid-30's, he was getting at first $1,000, then $1,250 a week writing for the movies. But this went to pay off old debts and private-school bills for his daughter and private-sanitorium bills for Zelda. Public institutions, he judged, were not good enough for either.

Poor Fitzgerald, the man thought to be the great chronicler of the American rich—"Let me tell you about the very rich," he wrote in a famous short story, "They are different from you and me"—was never able to accumulate enough to provide himself with the time to write the serious books he was certain were in him. Like the solid reputation as an artist he so ardently desired, money, too, always eluded him.

As Fitzgerald would have been the first to tell you, he

botched it, and botched it badly. So do many of us, but what makes Fitzgerald's case poignant is, first, he really had something to botch; and, second, he was acutely, painfully aware of all that he had thrown away. To his daughter Scottie, to whom in her adolescence he regularly dispensed advice, he wrote in one of his last letters:

> What little I've accomplished has been by the most laborious and uphill work, and I wish now that I'd *never* relaxed or looked back—but said at the end of *The Great Gatsby:* "I've found my line—from now on this comes first. This is my immediate duty—without this I am nothing."

F. Scott Fitzgerald was a contemporary not only of Ernest Hemingway but of William Faulkner, who was probably the most complete and dedicated artist of the three. Faulkner's artistry has long been recognized, yet while he is established as an academic subject, people seem to read him less and less for pleasure. Hemingway's novels now seem slightly ridiculous, the ideas at their center hollow if not sentimental (Fitzgerald himself called *For Whom the Bell Tolls* "a thoroughly superficial book with all the profundity of *Rebecca*"), and it is mainly his short stories, which achieve the magical status of poetry, that today hold the attention of serious readers.

Faulkner and Hemingway each won the Nobel Prize, but Fitzgerald has probably had the greater influence on the general culture of America. More clear than the precise nature of this influence is its pervasiveness: the designer Ralph Lauren, with his fantasies of 1920's elegance, hardly seems possible without the precedent of Fitzgerald's novels. The (fictitious) novelist, Richard Caramel, a character in Fitzgerald's *The Beautiful and Damned,* remarks that "Everybody in the next generation will be named Peter or Barbara—because at present all the piquant characters are named Peter or Barbara." He then adds: "And then I'll come along and pick up the obsolete name,

Jewel, I'll attach it to some quaint and attractive character and it'll start its career all over again." Here is art as minor prophesy: consider all the young women named Nicole—after Nicole Diver in *Tender Is the Night*—currently in the world. Consider, too, all the boys named Scott, including the Scott Schwartzs, Feldmans, and Goldsteins. The writing of F. Scott Fitzgerald has always excited a yearning for elegance, perhaps because Fitzgerald himself so yearned for it.

Although Fitzgerald never graduated from Princeton—he did very badly there, and, technically, dropped out—his is the name more strongly associated with the school than any other, even that of Woodrow Wilson, once its president. Whereas the Princeton he entered was considered lazy and aristocratic, its characteristic note one of indolent elegance, its reputation that of "the pleasantest country club in America," after and because of Fitzgerald it has been thought of as literary and exclusive and in the snobbery sweepstakes an even better buy than Yale or Harvard. While he did not strike his contemporaries at Princeton as a powerful personality—"Fitzgerald," John Peale Bishop wrote about him, "was pert and fresh and blond, and looked, as someone said, like a jonquil"—the impression he has made on posterity continues to be enormous.

When the young *Paris Review* crowd—George Plimpton, William Styron & Co.—went off to Paris in the 1950's, they did so in emulation of Fitzgerald as much as of any other writer. They were not alone in this. When I was an undergraduate at the University of Chicago in the 1950's, there was an entire fraternity—Beta Theta Pi—that seemed to be living on an F. Scott Fitzgerald script of stylish partying and heavy drinking. One of its members had published a story in *New World Writing,* an impressive accomplishment for a boy not yet twenty, and I remember him, drunk in his room, telling me before passing out that he could imagine the floor covered wall to wall with martinis and Anchor Books (the most elegant of highbrow paper-backs of the time). The performance was pure Fitzgerald.

Such extra-literary adoration—the Fitzgerald phenome-non—has complicated a clear view of Fitzgerald's talent. Per-haps no other American writer has so trickily presented the problem of separating the work from the life. Cyril Connolly, who as a reviewer wrote a great deal about him, concluded that "Fitzgerald is overrated as a writer, that his importance, apart from *Gatsby* and a few stories, lies in his personality as the epit-ome of a historical moment." Yet that historical moment seems to live on and with an interest that is more than historical. Books about, books studying, and books recalling Fitzgerald continue to appear. Can it be that there is something about him that transcends both his writing and his life—something cen-trally human that sustains our fascination?

In his collection of Fitzgerald's letters, Matthew J. Bruc-coli maintains that "the dominant influences on F. Scott Fitzger-ald were aspiration, literature, Princeton, Zelda Fitzgerald, and alcohol." If those were the influences, Fitzgerald's real *subjects* were ambition, snobbery, loss, and self-pity—the subjects both of his books and of his life. His depths, as Fitzgerald's own pro-tagonist, Dick Diver, says of the young movie actress Rosemary Hoyt in *Tender Is the Night,* were "Irish and romantic and illog-ical." Fitzgerald was not least Irish in his concern with social sta-tus; from Henry James through John O'Hara, the Irish, once much contemned in American life, were sensitively attuned to the horrors of snobbery and stimulated by the delights of so-cial attainment.

In good part, behind the continuing attraction of Fitzger-ald is his style, his lush, lovely style, style to the highest power, which is style not merely as pretty writing—though Fitzgerald was able to produce vast quantities of that—but as an attrac-tive way of viewing the world. Style of this power, style this per-vasive, is otherwise known as charm. Raymond Chandler, who thought Fitzgerald "just missed being a great writer," maintained that charm was the quality Fitzgerald had in superabundance—charm, he added, as Keats would have used the word: "a kind of subdued magic, controlled and exquisite, the sort of thing you get from good string quartets."

What made Fitzgerald a considerable artist was that he was able to get this charm into his writing—much more into his writing, one gathers, than into his life, which at times could have served as a reverse Dale Carnegie course. But if he was himself a living, breathing version of How *Not* to Win Friends and Influence People, in even the least of his stories one finds the magic, the fine touches, that seem to heighten life's possibilities.

The Fitzgerald charm does not disarm everyone. It has distinctly not disarmed Jeffrey Meyers, Fitzgerald's newest biographer. Meyers, though an academic by paycheck, is by vocation a professional biographer who works in a manner with which I am in great sympathy. He writes biographies that do not seek to be definitive but instead to revitalize the discussion about particular twentieth-century writers. He tends to be more interested in the life of a writer than in his work—or, perhaps more precisely, in relating the life to the work. He produces books of fewer than 400 pages—rare in contemporary literary biography—does not spend a decade or more on a book, and never pauses long enough between books to set up shop as the great expert on a single writer, in the manner of the late Richard Ellmann (James Joyce) or Leon Edel (Henry James). One assumes that he writes a book because an author has, at one time or another, actively engaged his passions as a reader.

F. Scott Fitzgerald is hardly a fresh subject. At least six full-blown biographies have preceded Meyers's, not to mention many critical studies and a biography of Zelda. The Fitzgerald turf has been pretty well worked, which means that the time for revisionism has arrived. When literary ground has been thoroughly plowed, someone is sure to come along and attempt to blow it up. This, in part, is what Meyers has done.

Meyers's is not an entirely destructive work. No previous biographer, for example, has shown how heavily Fitzgerald drew upon aesthetic notions learned from Joseph Conrad. Meyers is excellent on the partly rivalrous, partly, one has to say, sadomasochistic relationship with Hemingway. By way of original research, he has tracked down a late-life love of Fitzgerald's named Bijou O'Conor.

Meyers's biography also comes, to return to my agronomic metaphors, after much spade work has been done by others, and so he is in a position to clear up matters of controversy. One such has to do with a story told by Hemingway in *A Moveable Feast.* According to Hemingway, Fitzgerald once approached him to ask whether he thought his, Fitzgerald's, member was too small to give Zelda satisfaction; Hemingway thereupon took Fitzgerald into the men's room for an inspection, pronounced nothing wrong with him in that department, and said the whole thing was Zelda's way of trying to destroy him. In connection with this episode, Meyers is able to write, in a sentence whose ramifications I, for one, find depressing in the extreme: "There is a surprising amount of evidence about Fitzgerald's sexual organ and sexual performance." Meyers's own conclusion is that the Hemingway story is itself highly dubious—that Hemingway probably made it all up.

Yet, on the whole, so unsympathetic is Meyers to Fitzgerald that one wonders if he ever felt the attraction of his writing. Or might it be that he finds the chasm so great between the charm of the writing and the squalor of the life that he has felt the need to provide mainly a chronicle of the chasm? Whatever the case, the spirit of Meyers's biography tends to be prosecutorial. He does not forgive Fitzgerald much, and uses everything at hand against him.

Right out of the gate, we learn that "Fitzgerald inherited his elegance and propensity to failure from his father, his social insecurity and absurd behavior from his mother." Witnesses are brought in to testify that the young Fitzgerald was egotistical, solipsistic, undisciplined, a lightweight, a bad hat in almost every regard. "Fitzgerald joined the army for the same reasons that he went to Princeton," Meyers writes characteristically. "It was the fashionable thing to do."

As the chronicle continues, wherever possible Meyers underscores Fitzgerald's imperceptiveness, and he was, true enough, a young man on whom much was lost. Meyers also stresses Fitzgerald's irresponsibility, his obtuse politics, his selling-out to the temptation for easy money, his pathetic masochism when among men he took to be his betters (chiefly Wilson and Hemingway), his need for approval, his selfishness, his failure as a parent (the Fitzgeralds "had very little to do with Scottie's day-to-day life"), his infidelities, his endless dramatization of his own self-pity, and, to round things off nicely, his anti-Semitism (deployed when he was drunk, against his last lady friend, Sheila Graham).

Meyers's bill of complaint could be extended; and none of it, even an admiring reader of Fitzgerald is bound to allow, rings entirely false. Yet though Meyers has shown the depth of the discrepancy between the man and the work, he has not been able to account for the attraction of that work.

Writing in his later days to the young novelist and screenwriter Budd Schulberg, Fitzgerald said of himself that he "used to have a beautiful talent once," adding that even now "nothing I ever write can ever be completely bad." He was right about that—just as he was right when, sadly, he told Joseph Mankiewicz, the Hollywood producer (who rewrote Fitzgerald's first and only credited screenplay, *Three Comrades*): "I'm a good writer—honest." And he was right, too, when, in the year of his death, he wrote to Maxwell Perkins, his editor at Scribner's, that "even now there is little published in American fiction that doesn't slightly bear my stamp—in a *small* way I was an original."

I used to think Fitzgerald was a writer best read when young, but now, having reread him, I find myself newly impressed with the quality of his prose, the acuity of his generalizations, his ability to create great lyrical moments through dialogue and description. He knew how to do purple in many different, splendid shades. He can put one on the French Riviera in a single sentence, as here, from *Tender Is the Night:* "They drank the bottle of wine while a faint wind rocked the pineneedles and the sensuous heat of early afternoon made blinding freckles on the checkered luncheon cloth." Sex in a Fitzgerald novel has a crisp, clean quality, and is left to the imagination of the reader, which is where it must remain if it is not to dominate a novel. The consummation of the flirtation between Rosemary Hoyt and Dick Diver, in *Tender Is the Night,* is handled with admirable economy: "She wanted to be taken and she was, and what had begun with a childish infatuation on a beach was accomplished at last."

Read alongside Jeffrey Meyers's biography, Matthew Bruccoli's collection of letters reminds us that the saving remnant in Fitzgerald was the part of him that was always the artist. He once declared that he "had done very little thinking, save within the problems of my craft." But about his craft he really did think long and deeply. "I honestly believed," he wrote to his daughter toward the end of his life, "that *with no effort on my part* I was a sort of magician with words—an odd delusion on my part when I had worked so desperately hard to develop a hard, colorful prose style." Not only did he come to understand that the lesson of the artist was effort, unremitting effort, but he understood quite well that the nature of his own talent was poetic, and what it required to come to fruition in prose was "assimilation of material and careful selection of it, or more bluntly: having something to say and an interesting, highly developed way of saying it."

Fitzgerald was a true artist, both by gift and by desire. This may be why he was such a bust in Hollywood. He wrote to

Maxwell Perkins that "I just couldn't make the grade as a hack—that, like everything else, requires a certain practiced excellence." But perhaps more convincing is the reason he gave to his wife: "As soon as I feel I am writing to a cheap specification, my pen freezes and my talent vanishes over the hill." His own most cherished hope was that "some day I can combine the verve of [*This Side of*] *Paradise,* the unity of *The Beautiful & Damned* and the lyric quality of *Gatsby,* its aesthetic soundness, into something worthy of the admiration of those few" people who knew what true literary art looks like.

No one reading Fitzgerald's letters, or his novels, or the pieces in *The Crack-Up* can think him unintelligent. He was, for example, deft at reading other people's novels, and he could be penetrating about his friends. Already in his twenties he had Edmund Wilson's psychological number, writing to an acquaintance that Wilson "appreciates feeling after it's been filtered through a temperament but his soul is a bit *sec* [dry]"—which seems to me bang on about Edmund Wilson.

At the same time, one recognizes that Fitzgerald's intelligence was of a particular kind, being almost wholly at the service of imagination. Take the following lengthy passage about Dick Diver at a psychiatric congress in Munich:

> He had no intention of attending so much as a single session of the congress—he could imagine it well enough, new pamphlets by Bleuler and the elder Forel that he could better digest at home, the paper by the American who cured *dementia praecox* by pulling out his patients' teeth or cauterizing their tonsils, the half-derisive respect with which this idea would be greeted, for no more reason than that America was such a rich and powerful country. The other delegates from America—Schwartz with his saint's face and his infinite patience in straddling two worlds as well as dozens of commercial alienists with hangdog faces, who would be present partly to increase their standing, and hence their reach for the big plums of the crim-

inal practice, partly to master novel sophistries that they could weave into their stock-in-trade, to the infinite confusion of all values. There would be cynical Latins, and some man of Freud's from Vienna. Articulate among them would be the great Jung, bland, supervigorous, on his rounds between the forests of anthropology and the neuroses of schoolboys. At first there would be an American cast to the congress, almost Rotarian in its forms and ceremonies, then the closer-knit European vitality would fight through, and finally the Americans would play their trump card, the announcement of colossal gifts and endowments of great new plants and training schools, and in the presence of the figures the Europeans would blanch and walk timidly. But he would not be there to see.

Fitzgerald picked up such rich material through the years that his own wife spent in and out of insane asylums in Europe and America. But he knew how to use it—to integrate it beautifully into the thought of a character, a practicing psychiatrist, Dick Diver, considered by many critics to be more intelligent than his creator, F. Scott Fitzgerald. This is what I mean by intelligence at the service of imagination. Dumb like a fox, they used to say; Fitzgerald was dumb like a writer.

But what chiefly continues to make Fitzgerald's writing of enduring interest is his great theme: loss. Only once did he find the perfect objective correlative—the perfect relation between theme and concrete case—and that was in the fantast Jay Gatsby, whose extravagant aspirations include buying back the past. Of course, Fitzgerald was more than a bit of a fantast himself, with a past he would himself spend many years wishing to recapture. "I remember riding in a taxi one afternoon between very tall buildings under a mauve and rosy sky," he once wrote about his early success in Manhattan; "I began to bawl because I had everything I wanted and knew I would never be so happy again." This was after his first novel had been established as a best-seller, he had won the hand of his beloved Zelda, and the future looked to be all caviar and champagne and beaches on the Riviera.

As everyone knows, it did not quite turn out that way. Fitzgerald's drinking quickly got out of control, Zelda broke down in a permanent way, and to keep his shaky but expensive ship afloat, he began writing things for which he had not much respect. As usual his own best analyst, Fitzgerald, in an essay entitled "Early Success," makes the case with penetrating precision:

> The man who arrives young believes that he exercises his will because his star is shining. The man who only asserts himself at thirty has a balanced idea of what will power and fate have each contributed, the one who gets there at forty is liable to put the emphasis on will alone. This comes out when the storms strike your craft.

Although nothing Fitzgerald wrote was utterly without interest—his winning style saw to that—he would never again, after *The Great Gatsby,* write anything that altogether pleased him. This, too, was part of his sadness. "I am not a great man, but sometimes I think the impersonal and objective quality of my talent and the sacrifices of it, in pieces, to preserve its essential value has some sort of epic grandeur," he wrote to his daughter near the end of his life, adding: "Anyhow after hours I nurse myself with delusions of that sort."

Too rarely did Fitzgerald hit this impersonal and objective quality in his fiction. So we are left with this Midwestern Irishman, who claimed to have "a two-cylinder inferiority complex," and who seems to have spent at least a third of his adult life drunk and another third recovering from drunkenness or fighting to stay away from drink. With the last third, he wrote a handful of memorable stories, one slender, nearly perfect novel, two gallant fictional failures, and some confessional writing that brilliantly dramatized his own self-pity. Why does he continue to fascinate?

Some would read in Fitzgerald's life a cautionary tale. But what is its moral? If you drink, stay home? Don't marry a maniac? Be careful how you handle success, remembering, as he wrote in *The Beautiful and Damned,* that "the victor belongs to the spoils"? Not very edifying, any of this.

What is impressive is that, even after Jeffrey Meyers has reported the worst about Fitzgerald, he remains a poignant figure. There was no meanness in him; for a writer, he was singularly unmalicious. "I have honestly never gone in for hating," he wrote to Hemingway, attempting a rapprochement in their relations. One cannot even blame Fitzgerald for being a bad husband or father. For one thing, he beat us to the punch by asserting it himself; for another, it really was not quite true, because by his own lights, and under his own crippling difficulties, he did all he could, financially and spiritually, for his wife and daughter, even sacrificing his talent for them.

No, the interest in F. Scott Fitzgerald is that he felt so deeply, and, when he was going well, expressed so beautifully, so many things that other Americans have felt but have not been anywhere near so able to express: social unease in his own country, a yearning for an elegant and orderly life, and an inner sense (which in a letter to his daughter he ascribed to all great men) that life "is essentially a cheat and its conditions are those of defeat, and that the redeeming things are not 'happiness and pleasure' but the deeper satisfactions that come out of the struggle."

It was in *The Crack-Up* that Fitzgerald wrote that "the test of a first-rate intelligence is the ability to hold two opposed ideas in the mind at the same time, and still retain the ability to function." Even though Fitzgerald could not always do this in his own life, he posed precisely this problem in his best fiction, where classic (one is tempted to call it American) optimism and yearning are countered by the tragic truth that, as he once put it, "the natural state of the sentient adult is a qualified unhappiness." These two opposed notions were at the heart of his fiction. They remain at the heart of not only American but all human life. That F. Scott Fitzgerald picked up on this contradiction in the human spirit as early as he did, and worked it as richly as he did, is the reason that he was perfectly justified in thinking that "in a *small* way I was an original."

Wise, Foolish,
Enchanting Lady Mary

Once, and but once, his heedless youth was bit,
And liked that dangerous thing, a female wit.
                                        —ALEXANDER POPE

"**A** passionate man," said Stendhal, "is seldom witty." Building on that aphorism, one might go on to say that a witty man is rarely handsome. A beautiful woman who, along with being witty, is also commonsensical is rarest of all. They do, however, turn up, perhaps every century or two. Such a woman was Lady Mary Wortley Montagu. She lived (1689–1762) in a cold and hard age, where beauty helped immensely, wit was a useful weapon, common sense a necessity, and only passion an embarrassment.

Lady Mary was born with every advantage, real and artificial, and a number of true disadvantages. One distinct advantage was that she was an aristocrat, the daughter of Evelyn Pierrepont, Marquis of Dorchester, afterwards Duke of Kingston. Her secure place among the well-born was a fact she never forgot, nor was she above using it against her social, if not intellectual, inferiors. Of Alexander Pope and Jonathan Swift, with both of whom she had had a falling out, she remarked that they were "entitled by their birth and fortune to be only a couple of link-boys"—that is, boys hired to carry torches to light the way for others.

In later years, writing to her daughter, Lady Bute, whose husband was prime minister under George II, she noted that English writers, being generally low-born themselves, attempt to "represent people of quality as the vilest and silliest part of the nation." In her own experience, she added, "the greatest examples I have known of honour and integrity has been amongst those of the highest birth and fortunes." Gardening with Italian peasants, chatting with innkeepers, befriending women in Turkish harems, Lady Mary could be charmingly old shoe, but she always kept nearby a high horse for mounting when it pleased her to do so.

As for disadvantages, the full consequences of the chief one to befall her, the loss of her mother when Lady Mary was only four years old, shall never be known. It shall never be known because she only once, in a youthful autobiogrpahy, wrote of it. Availing herself of the third person and more than a little romantic melodrama—she was a reader of bad novels her life long—she wrote: "Her first misfortune happened in a time of life when she could not be sensible of it, though she was sufficiently so in the course of it; I mean the death of a noble Mother, whose virtue and good sense might have supported and instructed her youth." She goes on to say that this support and instruction was left to "the care of a young Father, who, tho' naturally an honest man, was abandoned to his pleasures, and (like most of those of his quality) did not think himself obliged to be very attentive to his children's education."

The other disadvantage, Lady Mary herself would have maintained, was to have been brought up a woman in the age of Queen Anne. In one of her more famous mots, she wrote that "my only consolation for being of that gender, has been the assurance it gave me of never being married to any one among them." In fact, she not only made the best of having been dealt this card, but, on occasion, turned it into a trump.

The eldest of four children, alternately pampered and neglected by her father, raised by a superstitious governness,

Lady Mary, at an early age, presided at her father's table, which meant, among other things, being put in charge of carving various joints of meat, the task assigned to the woman of the house. She also had the run of her father's rather impressive library, of which she made good use. She began to write poetry, and, at thirteen, she repaired to her father's library, where, with the aid of a dictionary and a grammar, she began to teach herself Latin, which she did well enough to undertake translations of Ovid and, some years later, Epictetus's *Enchiridion,* which she showed to Bishop Burnet, who is said to have been much impressed. Of her intellectual attainments, Robert Halsband, Lady Mary's biographer and editor, writes: "She tended to be a blue-stocking proud of her erudition, though she later regarded a reputation of learning as a misfortune in a woman."

Lady Mary's father was a Whig, which she herself remained all her life, and a member of the Kit-Cat Club, that London gathering place for artists, intellectuals, and aristocrats interested in politics and culture, and among his friends were Addison, Steele, and Congreve. All accounts of Lady Mary include the story of her father nominating his then not yet eight-year-old daughter as the candidate for the Club's annual beauty, to be toasted by all the members, holding that she was more beautiful than anyone else nominated that year. To make good his claim, he had the child brought to the Club, all the members agreed on her beauty, and she was declared winner and passed from lap to lap, roundly praised, and toasted straightaway.

Recounting this story, her granddaughter, Lady Louisa Stuart, reports in her "Introductory Anecdotes" to her own son's nineteenth-century edition of Lady Mary's letters: "Pleasure, she said, was too poor a word to express her sensations; they amounted to ecstasy: never again, throughout her whole future life, did she pass so happy a day." Lady Mary's father afterwards commissioned a painting of her, so that the painting itself could regularly be toasted, which it was. This was but the first of many occasions on which she would play the happy role of cynosure. Although she would in later years refer to herself in her letters as a mere "spectatress," lime was the light she bathed in most happily.

Few people can have contained within themselves more contradictory qualities than Lady Mary. She was detached and highly observant, yet loved, indeed craved, attention; she was cynical yet romantic, informal yet snobbish. "Lady Mary is one of the most extraordinary shining characters in the world," wrote the English anecdotist Joseph Spence, after meeting her in Rome; "but she shines like a comet; she is all irregular and always wandering. She is the most wise, the most imprudent; loveliest, disagreeablest; best natured, cruellest woman in the world."

In describing her conduct during her courtship by Edward Montagu Wortley, Leslie Stephen, writing in the *Dictionary of National Biography,* remarks that she showed "masculine sense rather than tenderness." Lady Mary may have been that entity for which many men are said secretly to yearn but perhaps none has ever discovered: someone with a masculine mind and a feminine body. The largely epistolary courtship between Lady Mary and Wortley was carried on, from her standpoint, as a great seduction of common sense, difficult as that may be to imagine. Her father disapproved the marriage, principally because Wortley would not agree to his insistence on an arrangement whereby all his estates would be entailed to his and Lady Mary's first-born son. Lord Dorchester, as he then was, ordered his daughter to marry another man, a gentleman with the wonderfully Wodehousian moniker of Clotworthy Skeffington. Engaged to Skeffington though she formally was, she nonetheless kept up negotiations with Wortley. (Wortley's father, though named Montagu, agreed to call himself by his richer wife's family name of Wortley, a practice his son tended off and on to continue.)

"I never speak but what I mean," Lady Mary wrote to him,

"and when I say I love, 'tis for ever." Wortley, from all accounts a rather humorless man and from his portraits a very handsome one, was obviously smitten. "I know how to make a man of sense happy," she wrote to him, "but then that man must resolve to contribute something toward it himself." She told Wortley that she didn't quite believe in his love. She threatened to cut off correspondence with him. When she picked it up again, she informed him that her ideal of marriage is to be found in friendship. "By friendship," she wrote, "I mean an entire communication of thoughts, wishes, interests, and pleasures, being undivided; a mutual esteem, which naturally carries with it a pleasing sweetness of conversation, and terminates in the desire of making one or another happy." Wortley, suffering jealousy and doubt, continued to waver. Lord Dorchester now really put the screws to Lady Mary about marrying Skeffington—a case, in the old-fashioned and most precise sense, of genuine peer pressure.

Finally, the deal was done. An elopement was planned; Lady Mary would be Wortley's, but without dowry. "I shall come to you," she wrote in August of 1712, "with only a nightgown and a petticoat and that is all you will get with me." Toward the close of the same letter, she adds: " 'Tis something odd for a woman that brings nothing to expect anything; but after the way of my education, I dare not pretend to live but in some degree suitable to it." By which she meant that, though she may come to him a pauper, she didn't for a moment expect to live like one.

Lady Mary was twenty-three, Wortley thirty-four, when they married. In Lady Mary, Wortley got both more than he bargained for and less than she promised. Before their marriage, she had written to him: "I am determined to think as little of the rest of the world—men, women, acquaintance and relations—as if a deluge had swallowed them. I abandon all things that bear the name of pleasure but what is to be found in your company. I give up all my wishes, to be regulated by yours, and I resolve to have no other study but that of pleasing you." Could Wortley have believed this? If he did, he was not only unimaginative but a fool. His wife was inveterately the most social of beings.

Wortley was a man of some worldliness. He had the interests of a gentleman of his time in amateur scholarship, which included a fair amount of learning in foreign and ancient languages. Joseph Addison was his close friend. He was not yet rich when he married, but, a man who looked after his business, he died leaving an estate of more than £800,000, along with an annual income of £17,000 from his lands—at that time, as the old joke has it, a lot of money.

Lady Mary was peremptory and, though otherwise splendidly imaginative, was unable to imagine herself wrong. At twenty-four she wrote out a correction of *Cato,* Addison's famous play, correcting it as if it were the work of child. Addison, *mirabile dictu,* not merely accepted but acted upon many of these corrections. Such a woman was not to be set aside like a trophy or a lap dog, which Wortley, early in his marriage, attempted to do, leaving his wife—soon his wife and infant son— stranded in the country while he sat in Parliament in London. This arrangement, she made plain to him, was intolerable and, under the barrage of constant criticism, he moved her to London.

Before she married, Lady Mary, who was determined not to be a spinster, shared a secret code with her friend Philippa Mundy, in which the two young women referred to marriage to a man one loved as Paradise, to a man one detested as Hell, and to a man one merely tolerated at Limbo. Lady Mary's marriage all too quickly slid from Paradise to Limbo, and what caused her and Wortley's marriage to become hollow is a matter of some controversy. Those who have written about Lady Mary's life, in deciding who was responsible for the dissipation of feeling between them, have cast votes on different sides.

Marrying a genius is probably always a mistake. Those of

us who are not ourselves geniuses will feel a certain sympathy for Wortley. Leigh Hunt, writing more than a century after the fact, cited Wortley's inattentiveness for the breakdown of his marriage, yet nonetheless thought "the lady, in all respects, was too much for him,—had too much fondness (if he could but have responded to it), too much vivacity of all sorts, and even too much of his favorite 'good sense.' " Joseph Walter Cove, another of Lady Mary's biographers, remarks that "husbands are not, as a rule, fond of being outshone by their wives," as Wortley clearly was by his. Yet Wortley remained steadfast, even in the long years when he and his wife were separated, she living alone in Italy and in France. During this later period, Lady Mary wrote to her daughter of Wortley that she "knew him to be more capable of a generous action than any man I ever knew."

The first of Wortley's generous actions was to give his wife, once she had moved with him to London, the widest possible berth in her own social trafficking. With her good looks, her intellectual ebullience, her eye for scandal and talent for spreading it, she took London in her early years the way Grant took Richmond—her social conquest, that is to say, was complete. Wortley, in the words of Robert Halsband, "conceded that since no one could match her intelligence, he would never contend with it."

At the court of George I, the fifty-four-year-old Hanoverian king who spoke very little English, Lady Mary throve. Positioning herself in a way that she hoped would redound to her husband's political success, she became a friend of the Princess of Wales, who would one day be Queen Caroline; the king, a man with an eye for female beauty and charm, took note of the striking Lady Mary. She took rather different, cooler note of him, later describing him thus: "The king's character may be comprised in a very few words. In private life he would have been called an honest blockhead; and fortune, that made him a king, added nothing to his happiness, only prejudiced his honesty and shortened his days." Lady Mary understood the uses and pleasures of power and thoroughly grasped that, then as now, imbeciles were frequently found in high places.

In London she not only kept up a regular social round amongst her own class, but also cultivated many of the capital's literary men: Congreve, John Gay, John Arbuthnot, the painter Charles Jervas, and, most fatefully, the brilliant little hunchback of Twickenham, Alexander Pope. She was quick-witted, perceptive and penetrating both, with a ready supply of that malice in which the age may be said to have specialized. Walter Bagehot is excellent on the social scene that Lady Mary found in London, at a time when aristocrats were undeterred in their behavior by the not-yet-invented social brake that today we call public opinion:

> The aristocracy came to town from their remote estates—where they were uncontrolled by any opinion or by any equal society, and where the eccentricities and personalities of each character were known and fostered and exaggerated—to a London which was like a large county town, in which everybody of rank knew everybody of rank, where the eccentricities of each rural potentate came into collision with the eccentricities of other rural potentates, where the most minute allusions to the peculiarities and the career of the principal persons were instantly understood, where squibs were on every table, and where satire was in the air.

All this provided a perfect field of operations for Lady Mary, with her wit and lively sense of the grotesque: she once described the marriage between a rheumatic woman and a man who had the use of only one arm as "curious as that between 2 oysters, and as well worthy the serious enquiry of the naturalists." She not only had the temperament necessary to satire, the reigning tone of the time, but showed a ready literary talent, being able to shape comic couplets, the chief form of the time, with such an effortless aplomb that her verse was often thought to have been composed by Pope, much to the latter's consternation. Of the Princess of Wales, who had befriended her, she wrote:

> Ah! Princess, learn'd in all the courtly arts
> To cheat our hopes, and yet to gain our hearts.

Such versifying was not published, at least not under her own name, especially by an aristocrat such as Lady Mary, in whom publication itself would have been construed as vulgar in the extreme. But it was passed round around to all the right—that is to say, the malicious-minded—people. Lady Mary was clearly among the right people—she was very much, as we should nowadays say, in the loop.

The interconnections, the intertwinings, among the social, the literary, and political in eighteenth-century England are a good part of what gives the period its brilliance and fascination. In what other period could a man such as Joseph Addison become an important secretary of state; or Edward Wortley Montagu find favor at court because he could communicate with his king in French; or Horace Walpole later hold a grudge against Lady Mary (he referred to her as "Moll Worthless") because she was a longtime friend of the woman, Molly Skerrett, who became his father's mistress and thus the enemy of his mother. How delightfully intimate this world was, how perfectly vicious!

Life, for Lady Mary, was always to be taken as it was, not as one wished it might be. In her letters, she was amusing about the vanities and foibles—especially sexual foibles—of others, but rarely was she censorious. She had a clear sense of what it took to get on in a less-than-perfectly-just world. She urged the perhaps too passive Wortley to greater heights through impudence. " 'Tis necessary for the common good for an honest man to endeavor to be powerful when he can be the one without losing the first more valuable title," she wrote to her husband. Later, she added: ". . . as the world is and will be, 'tis a sort of duty to be rich, that it may be in one's power to do good, riches being another word for power, towards the obtaining of which the first necessary qualification is impudence, and (as Demosthenes said of pronunciation in oratory) the second is impudence, and the third, still impudence." She reminded her husband that every man who early attained to high place had this quality. "A moderate merit with a large share of impudence is more probable to be advanced than the greatest qualification without it."

In 1715, when she was twenty-six, Lady Mary was afflicted with small pox, which caused the loss of her eyebrows and left her skin pitted and pocked. Although she retained her large, almond-shaped eyes—without eyebrows, they took on a startled, staring quality—her slightly acquiline, slender nose that gave her face a permanent refinement, her small soft mouth with its full, slightly pouting lower lip, a great beauty was ruined by this arbitrary turn in her fortune. "I am," she later wrote, "of the opinion that it is extremely silly to submit to ill-fortune. One should pluck up the spirit, and live upon cordials when one can have no other nourishment." Yet, when she grew older, she claimed no longer to look into mirrors.

The following year, 1716, Wortley was appointed Ambassador Extraordinary to the Court of Turkey. Caught up in the most intricate diplomatic negotiations among Austria, France, Turkey, and England, Wortley, who expected his appointment to last no fewer than five years, was dismissed, at the insistence of Austria, whose diplomats thought him acting in the interest of Turkey, after little more than a year. But the trip proved the making of his wife's reputation. Her *Turkish Embassy Letters* along with her pioneering work in England on spreading the use of small-pox inoculation, which she had learned about in Constantinople, lifted her above being a mere clever woman to being a figure of permanent interest.

With an entourage of twenty servants in tow, Lady Mary, her husband, and child passed through Holland, Germany, Austria, Hungary, and the Balkans—with a long stop in Adrianople, where the Sultan had arranged lodgings for the new English Ambassador and his family—before arriving in Constantinople. Under conditions of early-eighteenth-century travel, the trip took roughly eight months. Lady Mary had prepared herself for this adventure by attempting to learn Turkish; in Adrianople, she went about in Turkish costume as she would later do in Constantinople. Many later portraits show her in this same get-up.

In Turkey and in the countries she visited along the way, she revealed herself an excellent ethnographer, one of the participatory kind, falling in with local customs, broadly tolerant of other ways of living, and endlessly curious about the different cultures in which she found herself. "Thus you see, my dear," she wrote to an English friend, apropos of the ritual of taking a second husband—"one that bears the name, and another that performs the duties"—at certain German courts, "gallantry and good-breeding are as different, in different climates, as morality and religion. Who have the rightest notions of both, we shall never know till the day of judgment." For a woman certain of her own judgment at home, she was splendidly broad-minded in foreign lands.

The prose pictures Lady Mary sent back from Turkey left a permanent impress on European culture: Ingres is said to have made use of her description of a Turkish harem for *Le Bain Turc,* his painting of 1862. The most carefully prepared of her literary productions, these letters were clearly composed with later, most probably posthumous, publication in mind. In their day, Smollett, Voltaire, Johnson, and Byron expressed admiration for them. Gibbon, upon finishing them, noted: "What fire, what ease, what knowledge of Europe and Asia!" Dr. Johnson is supposed to have said that Lady Mary's letters were the only book he ever read for pure pleasure.

A curious and lively mind, exercising itself in a careful

style upon an exotic subject, retains an eternal interest. In her letters from Turkey, Lady Mary described the limitless power of the Turkish janissaries, who, in effect, held the Sultan and everyone else captive. She is splendid in her descriptions of Turkish women and their elaborately bedizened dress. "As to their morality or good conduct, I can say like Harlequin, ''Tis just as 'tis with you'; and the Turkish ladies don't commit one sin the less for not being Christians." Like every good writer, she knows that the larger subject of the travel writer is human nature in a fresh context, but considered in a way that never scamps the delights of cogently observed particulars. She understands, too, that one of the benefits travel confers is that of providing silken thread for spinning endless fine distinctions. She herself, we learn from her letters, prefers Italian to French music, French to English acting, and English to French women.

While in Turkey Lady Mary learned about inoculation as a defense against small pox, a disease "so fatal and so general amongst us," as she wrote to her friend Sarah Chiswell, and she claimed that she planned to allow her own son to undergo inoculation by Turkish methods. "I am patriot enough," she wrote, "to take pains to bring this useful invention into fashion in England." When the time comes to make the attempt, she predicted, she is almost certain to be opposed by English doctors, who are unlikely to have sufficient virtue "to destroy such a considerable branch of their revenue for the good of mankind, but that distemper is too beneficial to them not to expose to all their resentment the hardy wight that should undertake to put an end to it."

Four years later, in 1721, when a small-pox epidemic struck England, all that Lady Mary had prophesied turned true. When a London physician attempted to explain, in a pamphlet, how inoculation worked, there was an unwillingness to believe him. Lady Mary, who had already had her son inoculated, now offered her second child, a daughter born in Turkey, to be inoculated as a matter of public record. The Princess of Wales, much impressed by this, determined to widen the tests for inoculation. General interest, and soon widespread participation, in inoculation followed, so that Lady Mary was able to write to her sister: "I suppose the . . . faithful historians give you regular accounts of the growth and spreading of the inoculation of the small-pox, which is become almost a general practice, attended with great success."

Now returned to England, Lady Mary required an inoculation of another kind—that against scandal. Unfortunately, in the circles in which she traveled, none was available. She took up her turn in the elaborate dart game of insult that was the amusement of choice of the brightest figures of the age. She could cast as cold an eye as any among them. When Pope wrote some sentimental verses about two rustic lovers struck by lightning who were joined forever in eternity, Lady Mary set out, in a letter to Pope, rather a different script for their likely future; her version ends on the following lines:

> A beaten wife and cuckhold swain
> Had jointly cursed the marriage chain.
> Now they are happy in their doom,
> For Pope has wrote upon their tomb.

Life in England was far from smooth for Lady Mary. Her marriage seemed to turn permanently cold; Wortley, concentrating all his attention on business and sitting in Parliament, receded into the dim background. (She, from all reports, was technically faithful to him—that is, there is no evidence that she ever took a lover.) Her young sister died and so did her father, who, true to his word when she married against his wishes, left her nothing. Her young son began to show first signs of his lifelong delinquency by running off to sea at the age of thirteen: he would later scandalize her in various ways, and later in life became a Mohammedan. Her other sister, Lady Mar, after many signs of losing her grip, lapsed into insanity, and Lady Mary had to battle her brother-in-law for custody of her.

Earlier, acting on a tip from Pope, Lady Mary had given financial advice to a Frenchman named Rémond, who had powerfully flattered her, to invest in South Sea stock. At the bursting of the South Sea Bubble, he wanted his money back. He claimed she had duped him, and threatened to expose her to Wortley, who would not have been pleased. She was perfectly innocent, but in a society where scandal was the standard, truth was no fit defense. Besides, as Lady Mary was attracted by gossip, so quite as much did she attract it. This incident with Rémond would later be used against her by her enemies Horace Walpole and Alexander Pope.

Pope was not always her enemy. Quite the reverse. In his letters, he was rapturously in pursuit of her, so much so that she had delicately to defuse his epistolary passions by never answering them in kind. For a time, it appeared as if the two were in satirical cahoots. Not long after Lady Mary and Wortley returned from Constantinople, they acquired, along with their London place, a house in Twickenham, where Pope lived and where, as Peter Quenell writes in his life of Pope, "he had planned his gardens as a kind of decorative trap, a labyrinth of alleys and avenues in which he had hoped that Lady Mary might consent to lose her way."

And then, in a complication of ways that has never been made clear, it all exploded. The various stories set out in explanation of the break run, at the most trivial level, to Pope's once loaning Lady Mary some sheets, which she returned to him unwashed; to, in one of his versions, his unwillingness to write a satire on someone at her and her friend Lord Hervey's insistence. Some held that he harbored resentment about her criticism of his poem about the lovers caught in the thunderstorm. Her granddaughter reports Lady Mary recounting to her that Pope had declared his love to her, which "in spite of her utmost endeavours to be angry and look grave, provoked an immoderate fit of laughter; from which moment he became her implacable enemy." (Unrequited love, to Pope, far from being a bore, was a license to kill.) Maynard Mack, Pope's excellent biographer, thinks this last story possible but unlikely. He thinks it more likely that Pope convinced himself that Lady Mary was somehow behind a number of public attacks on him, for he reported to Robert Walpole that she was blackening his own name as she one day would his, Walpole's.

Pope was not a good man to have as an enemy. His was the sharpest pen in England, and when he unsheathed it he intended not to wound but to kill. In the *Dunciad* as well as in other poems, Lady Mary appears as Sappho. In another of his poems, he refers to a "hapless Monsieur"—this would of course be Rémond—who

> much complains at Paris
> Of wrongs from Duchesses and Lady Maries.

Before he was done, Pope accused Lady Mary of being personally filthy, treacherous, having a venereal disease, and being a whore. In his "Imitation of the First Satire of the Second Book of Horace," he describes victims of Sappho as "Poxed by her love, or libelled by her hate." She fired a few good shots of her own across his bow, including the following from "Verses Addressed to the Imitator of the First Satire of the Second Book of Horace":

> Then whilst with coward hand you stab a name,
> And try at least t'assassinate our fame,
> Like the first bold assassin's be thy lot,
> Ne'er be thy guilt forgiven, or forgot;
> But as thou hat'st, be hated by mankind,
> And with the emblem of thy crooked mind
> Mark's on thy back, like Cain by God's own hand,
> Wander, like him, accursed through the land.

Along with Pope's enmity came, rather like a package deal, that of Swift and Bolingbroke. It could not have been pleasant for Lady Mary to have been the public target of some of the meanest hit men in England. Her marriage was deadened if still legally intact. She had been put through Rémond's blackmail. Her son was a permanent disappointment, her daughter made a financially disappointing marriage that she could not know would later turn out to be a politically advantageous one. England must, in every way, have seemed stale to her.

In 1740, then, Lady Mary expatriated herself, to France and to Italy, where she would remain until the final year of her life. Some have argued that she made a deal with Wortley, who felt she was disgracing him, to live abroad at his expense. A more reasonable conjecture about her abrupt flight to Europe is offered by Bagehot, who speculated: "She turned abroad, not in pursuit of definite good, nor from fear of particular evil, but from a vague wish for some great change—from a wish to escape from a life which harassed the soul, but did not calm it; which awakened the intellect without answering its questions."

Four years earlier Lady Mary had met and become infatuated with a young man named Count Francesco Algarotti. Part of her plan in departing England was to live in Italy with Algarotti. A man still in his twenties, a natural philosopher interested in Locke and Newton, who had put the latter's *Optics* in the form of a dialogue, Algarotti was a real piece of work. He was, as Robert Halsband quietly puts it, "a handsome man of great charm and androgynous tastes, capable of love affairs with either sex." Frederick II, King of Prussia, with whom Algarotti settled in for a good spell, called him "the Swan of Padua" and recalled him, in his memoirs, as "a man of taste, of gentle mind, keen, shrewd, supple, but a great wheedler, and above all very selfish." (One admires the diminution of virtue in that description.) Lady Mary was nearly twice Algarotti's age, and Robert Halsband doubts whether there was any element of sexual passion in her feelings for him. For him she was probably no more than, in the modern term used by gigolos, just another "old hide," or wealthy woman who might prove useful.

Although they exchanged many letters and both lived in Turin at the same time, Algarotti is significant chiefly in being the last disappointment in Lady Mary's life. She lived more than twenty-two years in self-imposed exile in Italy and France, and, no longer fortified by the illusion of hope, grew more and more impressive. She lived on an allowance of £1,200, generously supplied her by Wortley, sufficient to sustain a decent margin of luxury, with enough left over to make her an interesting target for various Italian confidence men and assorted hustlers. Living alone, occasionally visited by Englishmen abroad, she lived, as she once claimed to her sister she lived in England, endeavoring "to make the world as agreeable to me as I can, which is the true philosophy; that of despising it is of no use but to hasten wrinkles."

Away from London and its school for scandal, Lady Mary became deeper in her isolation. Writing from Brescia, in Italy, she claims to be as much removed from the world as it is possible to be "this side of the grave, which is my own inclination." At her villa outside Brescia, she writes to her daughter that "I enjoy every amusement that solitude can afford." She cultivates her garden and her own mind, and, as she notes, "whoever will cultivate their own mind will find full employment."

During this portion of her life, Lady Mary is living, in effect, in a monastery of her own devising, and thinks of herself as a "lay nun," if not quite the abbess that in childhood she once imagined herself. In solitude, the world begins to fall into place for her. She comes to understand what is important—that a cook who makes a fine pudding and keeps a clean kitchen is as valuable as a genius; that a country doctor who trudges selflessly on his long rounds is a true hero. Abroad, she obtains that fine distance that goes by the name of perspective. To Lady Bute she writes: "I know now (and alas, have long known) all things in this world are almost equally trifling, and our most serious projects have scarce more foundation than those edifices that your little ones raise in cards."

As she grows older, Lady Mary believes less and less in free will. Liberty, she holds, is chimerical, and, she avers toward the end of her life to her friend Sir James Steuart, "I am afraid we are little better than straws upon the water; we flatter ourselves that we swim when the current carries us along." None of this, however, gets her in the least down. If we travail without anything like free will, so be it: "let us sing as cheerfully as we can in our impenetrable confinement and crack nuts with pleasure from the little store that is allowed us."

In her sixties, her spirit seems to deepen without her wit or energy abating. She dispensed advice to her daughter on the education of her granddaughters, raised poultry, kept bees and silk worms, taught the Italians who lived nearby to make English puddings and custards, read works both serious and frivolous in her lush garden. "Those who can laugh and be diverted with absurdities are the wisest spectators, be it of writing, actions, or people," she held. She also held—and there is no reason to disbelieve her—that "I now find by experience more sincere pleasure with my books and garden than all the flutter of a court could give me."

In 1761, at the age of seventy-two, just after the death of Wortley, she decided to return to England. "I am dragging my ragged remnant of life to England," she wrote. After an expatriation of nearly twenty-three years, she arrived in England in January 1762, was discovered to have cancer of the breast in March, and on August 21, lulled by hemlock, was swept off the board of life. "And so farewell," writes Leigh Hunt in the final paragraph of his essay, "poor, flourishing, disappointed, reconciled, wise, foolish, enchanting Lady Mary!"

Lady Mary had a second life through posthumous publication. Knowing that her daughter, Lady Bute, and her son-in-law with their aristocratic horror of publication would not be in favor of any of her works seeing print, on her return to England Lady Mary left a copy of her letters from Turkey with a Reverend Benjamin Sowden in Rotterdam, "to be disposed of as he thinks proper." She had to have known that he would have thought it proper to have them published, as he had already strongly suggested she do herself. The published letters were an instant success. "The publication of these letters," wrote Smollett, "will be an immortal monument to the memory of Lady Mary Wortley Montagu, and will show, as long as the English language endures, the sprightliness of her wit, the solidity of her judgment, the elegance of her taste, and the excellence of her real character." Although Lady Bute burned her mother's diary, she did not destroy her mother's other papers, and some forty years after Lady Mary's death a collection of her works, including the verse and the few essays she wrote under pseudonyms, was published. It added further luster to her reputation.

But it is Lady Mary's letters, chronicling fifty-four years of her life, that constitute her true achievement. When she read Madame de Sévigné's letters, she wrote to her sister, Lady Mar, that "very pretty they are, but I assert that mine will be fully as entertaining forty years hence. I advise you, then, to put none of them to the use of waste paper." Excessive humility was never Lady Mary's long suit, but in this instance, I believe, she was correct. Her letters cut through empty formality and false sentiment, from neither of which Madame de Sévigné was wholly free, and reveal a splendid healthiness of mind pondering a world it never finds devoid of interest. Within her letters one discovers literary criticism, a mother lode of novelistic material, a brilliant eye for and witty response to human foible, and an almost complete absence of depression, even when, one might have thought, depression was well warranted.

Lady Mary's letters contain little of great events, not a vast amount about famous persons, and a paucity of personal confession. They are relentlessly interesting because, as a writer, dullness was simply not available to her. The best method for writing letters that will retain eternal interest is never to be boring. Always on the intellectual *qui vive,* she was never for a moment bored by life, the reward for which was that she was incapable of writing boringly about it. This is why, despite her many faults, for all who enjoy the grand spectacle of a lively mind in perpetual motion, Lady Mary Wortley Montagu will always be a minor classic.

Kenneth Tynan,
The Unshy Pornographer

Be an empiricist
In socialism and sex!
Read Wilhelm Reich
And remember the Czechs!
—KENNETH TYNAN, in a birthday poem to
his daughter Tracy

In a letter written to the agent Irving "Swifty" Lazar proposing an autobiography strong on name-dropping—a "conglamouration of stars," as John Gielgud once put it in a slip of the tongue while acting in a Congreve play—Kenneth Tynan described himself as a talent snob. Quite accurate, too. Right out of the gate the young Kenneth Tynan was a fan—fanatically worshipful of athletes, of musicians, and above all of actors—and fanatical worship easily elides into snobbery.

Later, Tynan was snobbishly pleased at his connections with the talented and greatly acclaimed. ("Last year," he wrote to friends in 1980, "met Cary Grant. Top that.") "In our teens," Tynan wrote at forty in a profile of Duke Ellington, "we make hero-lists of those we worship and intend one day to meet. Mine when I was thirteen included a cricketer, a stripper, a painter, a drama critic, several actors, a film director, and a jazz musician. I crossed them off as I met them, either socially or professionally, but until recently only one name remained unblotted." This was of course Ellington's. Cross another name off.

Arranging his life around his enthusiasms, Tynan became a drama critic—the drama critic of his age, in fact—thus finding a way to obtain a good seat for every show in town and entrée to friendship with nearly every interesting figure of his day connected with the stage or movies. Whom Ken Tynan didn't know wasn't worth knowing. Michelangelo Antonioni claimed that he got the idea for his movie *Blow-Up,* about swinging (read: decadent) London, from a party he attended in the middle 1960's at Tynan's Mount Street apartment.

Every critic, no matter what his subject, is, one supposes, something of a talent snob. What is the point of criticism beyond that of making those distinctions—between the unacceptable and the acceptable, and between the better and the best—that are at the heart of all acts of criticism and snobbery alike? I discriminate, the unspoken credo of the critic in the arts runs, therefore I am. For Kenneth Tynan discrimination was never a problem. Authority in discrimination, that mysterious yet central element in the make-up of the good critic, came to him early, really quite startlingly early. Tynan looked for magic in theatrical performance—for, as he once described his own theater-going in the 1940's and 1950's, the chance "of seeing outsize personalities operating at full blast." Full blast—in and for the moment—was also the way he wished to live his own life, and for the most part he did.

As a theater critic, Tynan provided his own kind of magic. Simon Callow, the actor and biographer of theatrical personages, in a preface to a collection of Tynan's magazine profiles, wrote that the theme of Tynan's profiles "is always Life as Performance, embodied in prose which is Writing as Performance." *Brilliant* was the word most regularly applied to Tynan's drama criticism. A Tynan review was smart, penetrating, persuasive, entertaining. One wanted to read it almost as much as one might want to see the play under review, and it may not be going too far to say that frequently it was a good bit better than that play.

As is well enough known, musicians show early brilliance, so do mathematicians, so sometimes do actors and (even though less often) poets, but critics almost never. Or if they do it tends to be brilliance of a flashy kind unlikely to endure. Critical intelligence takes time to develop: for learning to be acquired, judgment to form, perspective to broaden. Kenneth Tynan is a glittering exception. He seemed to come into the world with vast reserves of theatrical knowledge. The theater was in his bones, his flesh quivered at any hint of theatrical excitement, his mind was handsomely stocked and ready for any critical contingency.

Tynan was a man marked for success. He was in that line of extremely clever young men come down from Oxbridge and straightaway given important jobs, it being understood that they need not make the vulgar climb implied in starting at the bottom. A partial roster of their names includes J. C. Squire, Desmond MacCarthy, and Cyril Connolly. "We are both admirably successful failures," Squire said to MacCarthy toward the close of their careers. Connolly, too, made a nice success out of failure. But Kenneth Tynan—"Ken" to Katharine Hepburn and Orson Welles and Johnny Carson and many another name of not lesser magnitude—had larger things in mind.

At the end of his short life—he died at the age of fifty-three—Tynan must have known he had blown it, and though failure may from a certain jaded point of view seem more elegant than success, it could never have seemed so to Kenneth Tynan, who worshiped success. "I see no point in an avant-garde which has no ambitions beyond a tiny minority," he once said. And of him his wife, the late Kathleen Tynan, who was also his biographer, wrote: "He believed in joining the Establishment to change it from within." A statement that may be decoded to mean that he, Tynan, wanted everything and he wanted it every which way.

Kenneth Tynan was raised in one of those extraordinarily complicated domestic arrangements in which the English seemed for a time to specialize. He was illegitimate. His father, a successful merchant whose name was Peter Peacock, kept up businesses and lives in both Birmingham and Warrington. One is reminded here of J. R. Ackerley's father, who kept up two households in two different parts of London, each unknown to the other. (The sun never sets on British polygamy.) In Tynan's case, it was only he, the son, who didn't know that his father, whose name he thought was Peter Tynan, was actually Sir Peter Peacock, and he only discovered it at his father's death, when he, Ken, was twenty-one. Only then, too, did he learn that he had five half-brothers and sisters, whom he never met nor, after this discovery, ever attempted to meet.

As a boy, Tynan collected autographs, came early to confidence in his own views, and was indulged by his mother and usually given way to by his father. His father wanted Ken to go to Rugby, for example, but his mother thought it a bad idea, for outside Birmingham he might have discovered the scandalous circumstances of his birth. The chief influences in his life came from outside his home: from movies, from magazines, from friends. A cousin once said of Kenneth Tynan that he went about as a young man like the peacock he didn't know he was. He wore flamboyant clothes and carried strong opinions. At the age of ten, in 1938, he wrote a letter to the editor of *Film Weekly* staking out the claim that Humphrey Bogart was a great actor. He was a great show-off. "He had to take your breath away, he just couldn't resist it," a school friend later noted, adding: "And it went right through his life."

By the time he went off to Oxford at eighteen, Tynan had read *Ulysses,* taken his personal philosophy from D. H. Lawrence—including the notion that "sex is the supreme mystical emotion"—and worshiped Orson Welles. He worried about whether "I am really a repulsive character—whether my pose is exorcising the real Me." He had begun to sign off his letters, in imitation of Sarah Bernhardt, *Quand même,* "in spite of everything."

He went to Oxford on a scholarship, and his success there was predictable in everything but its magnitude. Between the institution and the boy, it was love at first sight. "God," he wrote to a Birmingham friend, "how magnificent and mellow it all is; the very stones seem lambent." Twenty years further on, he would write of his Oxford days: "Nothing can ever top the sense of privileged exhilaration I felt then." And so it must have been.

Tynan's talent was as ubiquitous as his position as, in the words of a classmate, "a licensed shocker." Paul Johnson, who was at Oxford at the same time, remembers Tynan "fighting a little lone war all on his own, to bring glamour back to Oxford." He became the drama critic of *Isis,* the leading student magazine. He directed and acted in plays. He specialized in going too far. He dressed quite as extravagantly outside the theater as on its stage, going about in bottle-green or purple suits, gold satin shirts worn with gold velvet bow ties, cloaks with red linings, and green suede shoes. He smoked Russian cigarettes through a black-and-white cigarette holder. He sometimes wore makeup. He was doing an Oscar Wilde. In her biography of Tynan, his wife remarks that he "even encouraged the rumour that he was homosexual," which makes for a historically interesting first: someone trying to pass not as hetero- but homosexual.

Tynan early had the ability of impressing whomever he felt required it. C. S. Lewis, his tutor at Oxford, whom in a schoolboy letter he described as "terribly sound and sunny," said of his, Tynan's, early essays that if Lamb and Gibbon had been the same person, they would when young have produced student essays like Tynan's. Lewis taught him much about prose style. He won academic prizes for essays on Milton and Shakespeare. Not yet twenty, he had no hesitation about writing on Orson

Welles or Arthur Koestler or a Laurence Olivier performance of *King Lear* or the American theater in an *ex cathedra* manner. As an undergraduate, he wrote for *Vogue*. "Oxford gave me a superiority complex," he would later aver. "I think it ruined me."

Charm, he knew, was his trump card. "I would rather write amusingly and inaccurately than correctly and tediously," he wrote to a friend. To the same friend he wrote, after meeting Stephen Spender, "He reminded me of the title of Mr. Sinatra's latest song: 'My Nancy with the Laughing Face,' " and described a waitress "with a strong resemblance to Virginia Woolf (or a depressed turkey)." He had no compunction about approaching the celebrated. Even before going up to Oxford, he arranged to meet James Agate, the leading drama critic of the day, who made a pass at him. As an undergraduate, he wrote confidently to John Gielgud. Later, when his daughter was about to be born, he asked Katharine Hepburn, whom he had just met, to be the child's godmother. Great celebrity seems never to have daunted him. And why should it, for he planned on acquiring it himself.

Tynan took a second-class honors degree in English, which disappointed him, but which didn't really matter, for he had otherwise sufficiently established his brilliance. He was clearly a man in a hurry, someone on a schedule, as all the passionately ambitious are. Not long before he left Oxford, he declared that he wished to direct plays, and noted that Peter Brook, at twenty-three, was already far ahead of him in this line. He also thought he might achieve a career as an actor. He planned a collection of his theater pieces, which he actually did bring out (*He That Plays the King*, 1950) when he was only twenty-four. Still, he had premonitions of an early death, encouraged somewhat by the discovery of weakness in his lungs. He allowed to his first of four different fiancées that the word *waste* troubled him more than any other.

Writing to an actress in 1951, Kenneth Tynan remarked

that "a lot of stories become more effective if the audience knows the ending, and becomes absorbed by *how* things happen, rather than by *what* things happen." In good part, Tynan himself predicted the course his own life would take. Not yet twenty-one, writing to one of his fiancées—Tynan's chief method of seduction as a young man seems to have been to propose marriage—he noted: "My attempt to live *in the moment,* looking neither forwards nor backwards, has led me to absorb myself completely in the things going on immediately about me. I feel more poignantly the implications of circumstances because I have made it my credo to do so." Even earlier, in 1945, at eighteen, in boyish lower-case lettering, he noted: "i have never written a book. i have begun many, and finished none. i write quickly, but polish slowly. i shall never write a sustained novel or critical essay; my critical works will bulk small but precious." And that is pretty much how Kenneth Tynan lived his life: for the moment, in journalism, leaving a small body of work behind.

Freshly down from Oxford, the most famous undergraduate of his day—"The Golden Age is finished, gone the grace / Who now so fit to fill Ken Tynan's place," ran a poem in *Isis* upon his departure—journalism welcomed him. He began writing drama criticism for *The Spectator,* went from there to the *Evening Standard,* the *Daily Sketch,* the *Observer,* and, beginning in 1958 until his death in 1980, off and on for *The New Yorker.* (In 1965, he turned down an offer by *The New York Times* to become its drama critic.) As he remarked in the preface to *Curtains* (1961), a collection of his theater pieces: "Long before I became an undergraduate I enjoyed setting down my impressions of plays in performance; it seemed to me unfair that an art so potent should also be so transient, and I was deeply seduced by the challenge of perpetuating it in print." He puts the same point slightly differently fourteen years later, in his introduction to *A View of the English Stage* (1975), where, after noting that the theater he knew as a boy and young man belonged to the actors, he writes: "What turned me into a critic was the urge to commemorate these astonishing men and women, whose work would otherwise die with the memories of those who saw it."

When Kenneth Tynan came on the scene as a drama critic, the English theater was perhaps as rich in actors as it would ever be in its history. How they did please their audiences, let us count the names: John Gielgud, Ralph Richardson, Edith Evans, Margaret Leighton, Paul Scofield, Margaret Rutherford, Michael Redgrave, Anthony Quayle, Cyril Ritchard, Charles Laughton, John Plowright, Agnes Moorhead, Alec Guinness, Donald Wolfit, Maurice Evans, Peggy Ashcroft, Rex Harrison, and (the younger generation now) Peter O'Toole, Richard Burton, Albert Finney, Nicol Williamson, Alan Bates—and, above all, Laurence Olivier, the actor of actors and easily the actor of the era of great actors, whom Tynan returned to again and again in his criticism, and under whom he served as literary manager of the National Theatre from 1963 until 1973.

The young Kenneth Tynan was, in his drama criticism if not in his life, Henry James's young man on whom nothing was lost. In a theater, his antennae twirled at a furious pace: nothing got by him, he picked up everything, he was a being organized for writing about the theater. "He writes about acting and the theater," noted Simon Callow, "as if he were a sports commentator." That is quite good, giving as it does the sense of excitement that Tynan brought to his critical response to stage performance, except that no sports commentator was ever quite so alive to all that was going on before him as Tynan was in a theater or able to report his response so felicitously as he in his reviews.

Young as he was when he set out his ambitions, Tynan quite achieved them, at least those having to do with preserving extraordinary performances upon the stage. Early in his career, he was pre-eminently the enthusiast, the critic as appreciator, and he handed out charming bouquets: "This is the best Hamlet I have seen. . . . I think, in fine, that we can speak of Paul Scofield as 'Scofield' and know whom we mean." Frederick Valk in *The Master Builder* "seemed an Alp." After a Danny Kaye performance, "you are left panting but relaxed, as dogs always seem to be." Of Richard Burton: "at twenty-five he commands repose and can make silence garrulous." And of Peter Brook's staging of *King Lear:* "Writing about this incomparable production, I cannot pretend to the tranquility in which emotion should properly be recollected."

Along with handing out bouquets, Tynan also had a winning manner of allowing the plays under review to issue in *aperçus,* about the theater or about life in general, that convinced one that a great deal more was going on onstage than one might have thought. Reviewing Congreve, whom he calls the "only sophisticated playwright England has ever produced," he adds: "By sophisticated I mean genial without being hearty, witty without being smug, wise without being pompous, and sensual without being lewd." Sometimes he operated on forced cleverness. "If prose styles were women," he writes apropos Orson Welles's adaptation of *Moby-Dick,* "Melville's would be painted by Rubens and cartooned by Blake: it is a shotgun wedding of sensuousness and metaphysics." On a good night, though, his powers of formulation banged the gong resoundingly: "Samuel Beckett's new work, the latest bulletin from the Arctic latitudes of his particular hell, the starkest portrait he has yet drawn of the slow burial that begins with birth, is called *Happy Days.*" Shaw's *The Millionairess* "contains hardly any of those somersaulting paradoxes with which, for so long, Shaw concealed from us the more basic gaps in his knowledge of human nature."

Tynan could be most amusing on the attack. He called the imitators of Harold Pinter the "Pinteretti." Of Ionesco, whose politics and aesthetics he disliked, he wrote: "When you've seen all of Ionesco's plays, I felt at the end, you've seen one of them." He referred to Graham Greene's *The Potting Shed* as "not a whodunit but a Goddunit." Dame Beatrice Lillie's title "sits drolly on her head, like a tiara on an emu." In a Jean Giraudoux play, he describes an actress "got up in what I can best describe as a Freudian slip." It was in the form of a theater review of the staging of Faulkner's *Requiem for a Nun* that he wrote his two-for-the-price-of-one parody of Faulkner and Thornton Wilder's *Our Town,* which begins:

> Well, folks, reckon that's about it. End of another day in the city of Jefferson, Yoknapatawpha County, Mississippi. Nothin' much happened. Couple of people got raped, couple more got their teeth kicked in, but way up there those faraway old stars are still doing their old cosmic crisscross, and there ain't a thing we can do about it. It's pretty quiet now. Folk hereabouts get to bed early, those that can still walk. Down behind the morgue a few of the young people are roastin' a nigger over an open fire, but I guess every town has its nightowls, and afore long they'll be tucked up asleep like anybody else. Nothin' stirring down at the big old plantation house—you can't even hear the hummin' of that electrified barbed-wire fence, 'cause last night some drunk ran slap into it and fused the whole works. That's where Mr. Faulkner lives, and he's the fellow that thought this whole place up, kind of like God. Mr. Faulkner knows everybody round these parts like the back of his hand, 'n' most everybody round these parts knows the back of Mr. Faulkner's hand.

Neither an immitigable highbrow nor a Little Englander, Tynan's theatrical tastes were usefully catholic. He had bred-in-the-bone knowledge of Shakespeare, yet also loved British vaudevillians. He took great pleasure in things American—our musical comedy, movies, jazz as well as Jack Benny, Danny Kaye, and other of our comedians—at a time when many English intellectuals were strongly anti-American. "If latter-day

English drama is serious in intent, contemporary in theme, and written in rasping prose," he wrote in 1959, "Broadway and Hollywood are part of the reason." He also wrote well about French, German, and Russian theatrical performance. He was always keenly on the search for the new note in drama.

Lively though Tynan's reviews were, filled with enthusiasm, comedy, and sharp observations, his great success in good part came through his thrusting himself on the stage and somehow making himself part of the show. Through his writing, he was able to come across as if he were in a continuous, high-stakes battle—the battle to bring good and serious theater to England. "As a critic," he said, "I had rather be a war correspondent than a necrologist." It turned out that he was more than a war correspondent, for the latter does not create campaigns, plot strategy, regularly fire with the intent to kill at the opposing side. The extent of Tynan's influence on British theater may be argued, but that it was considerable, I think, cannot.

What also cannot be argued is the extent of Kenneth Tynan's personal ambition. Before long it became clear that it was too grand to limit itself to criticism merely. In a brief piece in the *Observer* in 1955 Tynan wrote about the severe French theater critic Paul Leautaud, who ended his days a man living among his cats, and who, when called upon at his Paris apartment, emits "a strangled cry of grief. . . . It is the sound made by a critic at the end of his life." Alone, sour, petulant, such is the fate of the critic. "Logically," adds Tynan, "for his kind, there is no other. You would become a critic? Consider M. Leautaud: and think again."

Such thoughts must have been much on Tynan's mind as he began to expand his own operations. Early in 1956, he was asked to be a script editor at Ealing Studios, the then successful British movie production company. He had planned a book on the subject of genius-watching. At the age of thirty-one, he was invited to write his autobiography by an editor at Jonathan

Cape, who wrote to him: "Quite frankly, I cannot think of anyone else of your age in England to whom I would or could make such a suggestion." In 1958, Wolcott Gibbs, *The New Yorker*'s theater critic, died, and William Shawn invited Tynan to replace him, which Tynan agreed to do, though on a part-time basis. (He would keep his *New Yorker* connection for the remainder of his life; and he ended as a writer of profiles for the magazine.) Later, in 1963, he signed on as a regular contributor to *Playboy*, for which he did interviews and was to write three pieces a year for $7,000, in those days a handsome fee.

Nineteen sixty-three was the year that Tynan ceased to function full-time as a theater critic, for that year he signed on as dramaturg and literary manager of the new National Theatre in England under the artistic direction of Laurence Olivier. In his own drama criticism, he had been plugging away at the idea of a National Theatre for many years. ("There is little wrong with the production [of *Henry V* at the Old Vic]," he wrote, "that a National Theatre and a more experienced company could not cure.") When he wrote to Olivier suggesting himself for the job—this not long after attacking Olivier's directorship of the Chichester Theatre Festival—the actor is said to have remarked to Joan Plowright, his wife, "How shall we slaughter the little bastard?" After in fact hiring Tynan, Olivier added, "Anything to get you off that *Observer*." Tynan took the job at well under his salary as a theater critic, and clearly put a great deal of his energy into it.

Kathleen Tynan, who edited her husband's letters, notes that of the seventy-nine plays produced during Kenneth Tynan's ten-year tenure at the National Theatre, more than half were "undisputed critical and box-office hits" and that "thirty-two of these were Ken's ideas; twenty were chosen with his collaboration." Some of the most interesting letters in *Kenneth Tynan: Letters* have to do with Tynan's counsel, to Olivier and to other directors, about staging plays for the National Theatre. They reveal how he knew the theater from the inside (he is very good on matters of production) and from the out (he retained a fine sense of what does and does not stir an audience). He knew what makes a play work; he operated well as a play doctor.

He also had a program, a not-so-secret agenda, in mind for the National Theatre. "I once defined a critic as a man who knew the way but couldn't drive the car," he wrote. "As a back-seat driver at the National Theatre, I am putting that maxim to the test." He once said that a serious writer can adopt one of three attitudes toward the world: he can mirror its sadness and sickness; he can withdraw from it; or he can seek to change it. The third attitude was the only one he could countenance. In a then-novel twist on government support for the arts, he wrote to Laurence Olivier: "Subsidy gives us the chance—denied to movies and TV—of staking a line of our own, with no commercial pressures and without the neutralizing necessity of being 'impartial.'"

Tynan seemed for the most part to have a decent working relationship with Olivier, but his real problems were working with the government, specifically with the Lord Chamberlain, who functioned as the official censor of theatrical production, a job that went back as far as 1737 and Robert Walpole. Tynan argued with the Lord Chamberlain not only over what language could be used onstage but also over what plays could be staged. *Kenneth Tynan: Letters* provides a lengthy account over his wishing, in 1966, to stage Rolf Hochhuth's *Soldiers,* a play that more than suggested that Winston Churchill not only sanctioned a large number of civilian deaths by approving bombing of civilian targets by approving bombing of civilian targets but conspired to assassinate one Colonel Wlyadyslaw Sikorski, who, the play posited, was a reminder that Churchill had sold out the Poles in order to achieve his wartime goals.

The Lord Chamberlain argued that there was no authoritative evidence for any of this, and Tynan took the view that none was required—that a playwright could interpret history as he wished. The Lord Chamberlain countered that he would not permit the slandering of recent historical figures, at least under the auspices of a state-run theater. In Tynan's view, *Soldiers* is "the kind of play that can help the theater in general to fulfil its role as a public forum where history, art and morality are brought into one focus." The Lord Chamberlain and the view of the government's National Theatre Board, however, prevailed, though two years later, in 1968, the play was privately produced in Toronto, New York, and London, where it received good reviews but had only short runs.

But this incident was only further evidence of the politicization of Kenneth Tynan. From the outset, he was turned off by the inanities of English drawing-room comedy, and as early as 1958, in an attack on Eugene Ionesco, he went on record as looking for "evidence of the artist who is not content with the passive role of a symptom but concerns himself, from time to time, with such things as healing." He had gone from an art-for-art's-sake to an art-for-our-sake man—and in a big way. He became the great proponent and exponent of Bertolt Brecht and the Berliner Ensemble, and, along with Eric Bentley, probably did more than any single critic to advance Brecht's reputation in the non-Communist world. "I have seen *Mother Courage* and I am a Marxist," he declared. Brecht's best plays, he announced in *The New Yorker,* "all deal with the tension between instinct, love, and emotion, on the one hand, and, on the other, a society that perverts or exploits all three." More and more, capitalist society, repressive and cruel, became the great villain for Tynan. In the words of an old Broadway musical comedy song, "Put the blame on Mame, boys."

It did not take Tynan long to join the herd of independent minds. His crowd in New York included Lillian Hellman, Richard Avedon, Dwight Macdonald, Jules Feiffer, and Norman

Mailer, who admired him for his "extraordinary ability to get what he wanted out of the establishment without ever compromising himself fatally." He was among the signatories for the Fair Play for Cuba Committee. He marched in the Campaign for Nuclear Disarmament at Aldermaston (to which, his wife notes in her biography, he took a cab). Obsessed by the prospect of nuclear war, he was a better-red-than-dead man, and during the Cuban missile crisis, so nervous was he in the service of his beliefs, he actually purchased a single ticket for Australia. He was on the Who Killed Kennedy Committee. He became a regular letter-to-the-editor writer on behalf of all left-wing causes, including an attack, if you can fancy it, on the Common Market, a subject he must have thought about for a full ten minutes.

But Kenneth Tynan as a revolutionary, or even as a political intellectual, was never really very convincing. He liked success too much: large, naked, gaudy success. Even as a young man, as Kathleen Tynan notes, "he insisted on the best restaurants, the best tickets, and was rashly generous." Later in his life he wrote admiring *New Yorker* profiles on Johnny Carson, Mel Brooks, and Tom Stoppard, and what came through in these pieces above all was that these men had done it, had made it, had broken the bank. He, too, would have loved such a success, no doubt about it, but it was never to be available to him. He was instead condemned to live perpetually on the wharf, always hoping his ship would soon come in.

The closest shot Tynan had to a big score was with *Oh! Calcutta!* The idea for this revue of skits based on sexual fantasies was Tynan's and so was the organization and production of it. *Oh! Calcutta!* was the entering wedge of pornography onto the stage of what was once known as the "legitimate theater." Porno, slick and alluring, but porno pure and less than simple was the end and the intention of this revue. When Tynan wrote explaining it all to the late Terry Southern, whom he asked to contribute a sketch to the show, he added that there was to be "no crap about art or redeeming literary merit" about it, either. *Oh! Calcutta!*—after the French phrase *Quel cul t'as* (What an arse you have!)—was a New York, London, and indeed international hit and a part of the social history of the 1960s. Owing to a bad contract, over the years Tynan made only roughly a quarter of a million dollars on *Oh! Calcutta!,* peanuts when one comes to consider that the show is said to have grossed—just the right word, I believe—some $360 million.

Yet there is something appropriate about Kenneth Tynan's being the impresario of *Oh! Calcutta!* He was, after all, the first man to say "fuck" over the BBC. The occasion for his having done so was a discussion, with Mary McCarthy, about the censorship of *Lady Chatterley's Lover.* It is sad to think that this, in the current cliché, defining moment may define a talented man down into posterity. Yet it was as a sex provocateur that Tynan came to be best known during the 1960s. When asked by Dick Cavett on his television talk show to define sexual decadence, Tynan replied: "It is whatever makes a man who thinks his ideas of sexuality are liberal, wince."

Kathleen Tynan refers to her husband's romantic socialism, but what he really wanted to be, one supposes, was a Marxist of sex. It is of course an absurd thing to wish to be. Leaving aside here the question of who owns the means of production and the fact that in this realm the class struggle is a rather difficult thing to make out, all that is left is the notion of "to each according to his needs." Tynan's own needs were a bit odd. His taste ran to spanking girls, which is coming to seem *le vice anglais.* (Philip Larkin was also an enthusiast.) Kathleen Tynan tells of cleaning out her husband's things, after their separation, and discovering a Pandora's box of porno, which makes one think that perhaps having one's wife write one's biography isn't always a smashing idea.

For writers of Tynan's generation, sex was rarely viewed

as a pleasant (chiefly) indoor sport. Instead it became half an ideology, and something like an alcohol substitute. As a way of clouding one's mind and destroying one's life, sex is nowhere near as efficient as alcohol. It can, however, make one look even more ridiculous. And the older one gets, the more ridiculous one begins to look. The young drama critic Kenneth Tynan once congratulated the actor Gerald Teale for portraying Mark Antony with "all the sadness of middle-aged lust, [but] without a vestige of its repulsiveness." Poor Tynan, in playing himself as the great sexual liberator of the age, was able to communicate only the repulsiveness of middle-aged lust and damned little of its sadness.

Tynan was planning a biography of Wilhelm Reich and a sequel to *Oh! Calcutta!* called *Carte Blanche.* He was one of those who goaded on the comedian Lenny Bruce with exaggerated praise for his putatively revolutionary comedy. "We miss him," Tynan wrote after Bruce's appearance in England, "and the nerve-fraying, jazz-digging, pain-hating, sex-loving, lie-shunning, bomb-loathing life he represents." Sex and politics, as in that quotation, washed together in Tynan's mind in the way they did in the 1960's generally. Logic, consistency, proportion, common sense didn't really matter. The sixties, for Tynan, were, in a phrase of the day, "a gas."

Alas, lots of noxious fumes and debris were left when the party was over: broken marriages, regrets for work not done, self-recriminations for wretched political judgments (not many of these). In Tynan's case, there was the additional difficulty of his fragile health. The congenital weakness of the lungs, much worsened by his heavy smoking, resulted in a strong case of emphysema, which eventually killed him. In his later years, he had to seek out dry climates. Money was another problem. Life-long, Tynan also smoked what Balzac, referring to plans for books that would never get written, called "enchanted cigarettes." Along with the autobiography he never got round to writing and for which he was accepting publishers' advances right up to the end, he failed to finish his book on Reich as well as another book on why certain plays have survived, a pornographic book, an anthology of masturbation fantasies, a book about Olivier, a play, an erotic movie, and a great many other writing projects. The end of his life was a shambles. Living in Los Angeles, locked in a wheel chair, lashed to an oxygen tank, a bit player on the periphery of a world of show-business celebrities, he sat in the sun reading, his wife informs us, *The Fetishist Times.*

In a review of the play *Becket,* Tynan called Jean Anouilh "a quick but shallow thinker." Might not the same be said about him? Tynan, too, was wonderfully bright and quick, but did his culture, outside of the theater, run very deep? Was he in any way genuinely thoughtful? He had all sorts of opinions, but there is no evidence that, taken together, they added up to anything like an interesting point of view. He was talented, immensely talented, without being in the least original. In the end, he was a man of his time, and it was a low, dishonorable time.

Tynan might have ended a great drama critic, but there was a problem: a great drama critic needs great drama. The absence of a sustained serious drama is why there have been no truly great American drama critics. Almost by main force, Tynan tried to create a great drama out of the early work of John Osborne, Arnold Wesker, and above all Bertolt Brecht, to whom he wished to play the same cicerone's role that Shaw played for Ibsen. Perhaps he saw it couldn't be done and moved on.

So much did Tynan's ambition go beyond mere criticism that, late in life, he confessed that he hated writing. Pity, because it was the thing he did best. Such ideas as he had now seem less than hopeless, yet his accounts of actors in performance still hold up. What we know about the great actors of any age, we owe to the great drama critics: Hazlitt, Shaw, Beerbohm, Agate, and now Tynan. Writing about actors, Tynan still catches and keeps one's attention. His prose has the magic that genuine style makes manifest. Forty and more years after the fact, he can be read with pleasure on performances long stilled. Style, that great preservative, may in the end save Kenneth Tynan, even from the sad damned fool who had the good luck to possess it.

Elizabeth Bishop:
Never a Bridesmaid

*If a poet praises another poet's verses, you may
wager that these are slight and worthless.*
                                    —LA BRUYÈRE

In the history of modern literary reputation, the career of
Elizabeth Bishop makes an extraordinary chapter. Miss
Bishop was, in her lifetime, one of the most relentlessly praised
and handsomely rewarded of poets. The Pulitzer Prize, the National Book Award, the Book Critics Circle Award, the special
publishing arrangement with *The New Yorker,* the Consultantship
in Poetry at the Library of Congress, the international prizes,
the various grants and fellowships, the teaching job at Harvard,
the honorary degrees—like late autumn leaves on a gently
breezy day, all these and more floated down onto Elizabeth
Bishop's lap. What made all this so remarkable is that some of
these rewards came so early and on the basis of so little actual
poetic achievement. "Always the bridesmaid, never the bride,"
she commented one year when it was rumored but it turned
out she didn't win the National Book Award. Not to worry,
though, for she won it soon thereafter. In her case, "Always the
bride" might have been closer to it.

    Elizabeth Bishop was born in 1911, which puts her at the
senior end of the generation of poets—Lowell, Jarrell, and

Berryman chief among them—who, for their combined ré-sumé, might have availed themselves of Wordsworth's couplet: "We poets in our youth begin in gladness; / But thereof comes in the end despondency and madness." *Poètes maudits* though they sometimes thought themselves and indeed may have been—they did lots of boozing, wore out their hearts too early from bad living, suffered insanity and often ended in suicide—theirs was also a generation ignited by calculation and on fire with ambition. When you read their correspondence and the biographies and memoirs about them, you can scarcely miss how careful they were, all of them, in their own ways, most meticulous caretakers of their careers. It was only about that larger entity, their lives, that they were heedless.

But, then, a modern poet unmindful of his career is rarer than a pinto flamingo. In the twentieth century, where to be even a greatly gifted poet guarantees nothing, attention to matters of career must be paid. When in 1953 Elizabeth Bishop learned of the death of Dylan Thomas, she wrote to a friend: "Dylan made most of our contemporaries seem small and disgustingly self-seeking and cautious and hypocritical and cold." One thinks here of that antithesis to the oh-screw-it, let-'er-rip spirit of Dylan Thomas, the still young T. S. Eliot, writing in April 1919 to J. H. Woods, his former philosophy professor at Harvard:

> There are only two ways in which a writer can become important—to write a great deal, and have his writings appear everywhere, or to write very little. It is a question of temperament. I write very little, and I should not become more powerful by increasing my output. My reputation in London is built upon one small volume of verse, and is kept up by printing two or three more poems in a year. The only thing that matters is that these should be perfect in their kind, so that each should be an event.

Elizabeth Bishop was not quite so careful a caretaker of her career as Jarrell or Lowell or Delmore Schwartz—all of whom seemed to calibrate the effect on their reputation of each book review, reading, anthology appearance, blurb—but she, too, knew that to these things attention must be paid. The three testimonials for her successful application for the Houghton Mifflin Literary Fellowship for poetry, the first of many such awards she would win, came from Marianne Moore, Edmund Wilson, and John Dewey—the first two names are impressive, but that last name, it seems to me, is the real kicker. Living in Brazil between the ages of forty-one and fifty-six, she may have seemed, as we nowadays say, out of the loop. But she wasn't, not really, for she never lost important touch with Randall Jarrell and Robert Lowell, both of whom did much to advance her cause. When it came to looking after her own career, there was nothing loopy about Miss Bishop.

Elizabeth Bishop was famous for the paucity of her production. This at first flush might seem as if she were on the T. S. Eliot success plan: ". . . printing two or three more poems in a year . . . these should be perfect in their kind. . . ." In fact, she was, for the better part of her life, something very close to a blocked writer, and one may be sure her perfectionism was no help here. One could extract from her letters an impressive threnody of self-incrimination about her inability to get her work done. Two or three poems a year, à la Eliot, would to her have seemed positively Balzacian production. Innumerable were the delays she caused in publication of her books because she wasn't able to complete enough poems to comprise a volume of sufficient thickness. Of her first book, *North & South,* she wrote to Marianne Moore: "The book seems so thin and says so very little, actually." Beyond innumerable were the self-lacerating comments she made about her own inability to finish a poem. When she won the Pulitzer Prize in 1956, she wrote to her New York physician and friend Anny Baumann: "I'm sure it's never been given for such a miserable quantity of work before." The Bishop *oeuvre,* though one hesitates to use so grand a word for so slender a body of work, small as it is—a slender volume of prose, a *Complete Poems* filled out by adolescent verse and translations, a book-length translation from the Portuguese—nonetheless still feels a bit padded.

Although there was no shortage of despondency and madness in Elizabeth Bishop's life, the early portion given over to gladness was itself all too brief. By the age of five she was, for all practical purposes, an orphan. Her father died, of the kidney complication called Bright's Disease, when his only daughter was eight months old. The shock was one from which her mother, then thirty-two, never recovered; and when Elizabeth was five, Gertrude Bishop, after bouts of hallucinatory and even violent mental illness, entered a public sanatorium in Dartmouth, Nova Scotia, from which she never emerged—she died in 1934, just before her daughter was graduated from Vassar College—and in which her daughter never saw her. To lose a father to an arbitrary illness before one's first birthday and to lose a mother to madness at five—that, surely, is enough to keep a lifelong therapeutic conversation going.

Such psychologically cataclysmic events set strict and disabling conditions on the remainder of Elizabeth Bishop's life. After her mother's departure into madness, the young girl lived at various times with her two sets of grandparents as well as with aunts and uncles in Boston and Worcester, Massachusetts, and in Nova Scotia. She was always treated kindly, but in the nature of the case felt dislocated and separated from normal family life. As a child, she suffered eczema and asthma; the latter remained a problem lifelong. Religious belief was not available to her, and for sustenance of the spirit she early retreated into the aesthetic. As a young girl, she did watercolors and won school essay prizes, but it was poetry that early lit her fire: she read Whitman at thirteen, George Herbert at fourteen, and Gerard Manley Hopkins at sixteen.

Plump, not especially pretty, she must have seemed an odd

girl: shy yet in the realm of culture authoritative. At Vassar, she was called by her ecclesiastical surname, Bishop, in recognition of this authoritativeness. The writer Eleanor Clark, a classmate, said that Elizabeth Bishop could be "quite authoritative in class without saying a word"—so much so that she could make young teachers nervous. She entered Vassar in 1930, the year after the beginning of the Depression and the year, too, after the class of Mary McCarthy, the school's most notorious graduate. Her fees were paid by her Bishop grandparents, and, at the age of twenty-one, she came into a small inheritance from her father's estate. Although she never had a lot of money, Miss Bishop, apart from two short-term jobs—doing correspondence at a bogus writing school in New York, working a mere five days cleaning binoculars in Key West during World War II—never held a regular job until she was in her fifties, when she began teaching, first at the University of Washington, later at Harvard, and briefly at M.I.T. and N.Y.U.

At Vassar, she wanted to major in music, later regretted not having majored in classics, and did in fact major in English. She was among the inner circle of literary young women who were stirred by the poetry of Eliot, Auden, Stevens, and Hopkins. In the classroom, she acquired admiration for the poems of George Herbert, Richard Crashaw, and other seventeenth-century English poets. One of her teachers described her as "egocentric—aloof—responds to beauty in any form." Another said that she was "doomed to be a poet." She contributed poems, stories, and essays to campus publications, including one, *Con Spirito,* she helped found. She began sending poems to little magazines, with occasional successes, and won an honorable mention when she submitted poems to the young Lincoln Kirstein in a contest he held for young writers at his magazine *Hound & Horn.* At Vassar, she was notable for taking serious things seriously, and about nothing was she more serious than about poetry.

Elizabeth Bishop had friends at Vassar, but these friendships, one assumes, must have been considerably qualified by three secrets she had had to keep to herself. The first was that her mother was in an insane asylum. As an orphan, the young Elizabeth had more freedom than most Vassar girls, and spent most of her summers not with family but with classmates. Some classmates knew that her mother was still alive but not under what conditions; certainly, she never featured this particular item of permanent sadness life had placed on her menu.

The second was that she had what is euphemistically called a drinking problem. One definition of a drunk is someone who, in his thirties and forties, drinks as much as he drank in college. How much Elizabeth Bishop drank at Vassar is not known, though Brett C. Millier, her biographer, writes that "Elizabeth drank destructively from that time onward, and her life by 1939 was dominated by her need for alcohol and by the effects of heavy drinking on her body, mind, and relationships." She had the bad luck to come into her maturity when Prohibition was still intact and alcohol had the added thrill of being illegal; and, possibly, the even worse luck to have inherited alcoholism, for her Uncle Arthur and other members of her family were notable boozers. She fought alcohol all her life, and frequently lost. No sedate tippler, when she drank, she was a three-sheets-to-the-wind, fall-down-the-stairs, break-your-collarbone, blue-eyed, hide-the-hair-tonic drunk.

Elizabeth Bishop's third secret was that she was homosexual, though it is not altogether clear the extent to which she was herself then in on the secret. She had the occasional date when at Vassar, among them with the then young poet Donald Stanford. Later, she went out with a literary-minded man four years older than she named Robert Seaver. He worked in a bank, had literary interests, and, owing to polio, walked on crutches. She turned him down when he proposed marriage to her, and not long afterward he committed suicide. Two days after his suicide she received a note from him that read "Go to hell!" In *Remembering Elizabeth Bishop,* Frank Bidart, who was later to be among her confidants, claims that Miss Bishop told him, Bidart, she was then in love with a Vassar roommate named Margaret Miller, a painter who lost an arm in a car accident when travelling with Elizabeth Bishop and another friend in France.

Even less is known about the origins of female than is known about male homosexuality. Is it caused genetically, by environment, by the brutishness of men, by conscious preference? Brett Millier, in considering Elizabeth Bishop's lesbianism, remarks that in her, as in most people of her historical time, "the pressure to conform was great, and the dream of a 'normal' life died hard." Later in her life, her fame already secured, Miss Bishop was still not ready publicly to own up to her homosexuality, even though everyone seemed to know about it. When Frank Bidart wrote candidly about his own homosexuality, Elizabeth Bishop worried that it might be used against him professionally, and she told him that she herself "believed in closets, closets, and more closets."

Lesbian relationships, of which Miss Bishop had a number, must have been most comfortable for her. She was someone who couldn't bear to be alone; she couldn't take too much in the way of pressure; complicated sexual involvement was not her idea of a jolly time. In any relationship she entered into, it had to be understood that she was the vulnerable one, the one who needed to be looked after. She once remarked that she wished she had had a child, but, with all her problems, it could only have been a disaster. (Robert Lowell later avowed he regretted never asking her to marry him. What a marriage made in hell that would have been!) She herself needed a mother, and this seems to have been the part that many of her lovers, even ones much younger than she, played in her life. Lota de Macedo Soares, the Brazilian aristocrat who made a home for her during the happiest period in her life, seems to have functioned as both her mother and father. All her days, Elizabeth Bishop, this seemingly calmest of calm poets, was a woman terribly in need.

An insane mother, an incipient drinking problem, worry about her own sexual proclivities—this was rather heavy baggage for a young woman to carry around. How Elizabeth Bishop would hate having this baggage opened by the customs officials of literary criticism (in this essay, I am, alas, acting as one). She is on record as deploring the "confessional" in poetry. She had a falling-out, though not a rupture in relations, with Robert Lowell for his late poetry, which was full of personal revelations, a subject on which Lowell thought her the victim of "extreme paranoia." She didn't like poets washing their linen in public; and having others wash hers for her would doubtless have galled her all the more. "I just hate the level we seem to live and think and feel on at present," she wrote to Lowell on this matter in 1972. "Stick around, baby," Lowell, had he a gift for prophecy, might have replied, "you ain't seen nothing yet."

Other people—editors, friends, former pupils—have been doing the confessing for Elizabeth Bishop. For the most part, it has been done gently, without malice. In Brett C. Millier, Miss Bishop has found a sympathetic biographer; in Robert Giroux, with whom she dealt first at Harcourt, Brace and then at Farrar, Straus & Giroux and who has brought out the edition of her letters, an understanding editor; and in Gary Fountain, who finished the job Peter Brazeau had begun in *Remembering Elizabeth Bishop,* a careful chronicler. (Things could have been much worse: the letters she wrote to Lota de Macedo Soares, in which she must have had to fend off suspicions about her drinking and jealousies about other lovers, were burned by Miss Soares's friends and family.) But the cumulative effect of all this biographical material has been to reveal a poet who lived the better part of her life psychologically *in extremis,* with sad squalor and ample anxiety her regular companions. This isn't the picture that this most refined and coolly distant of poets herself wished to present to the world.

Yet without these revelations it is far from clear that Elizabeth Bishop's poetry would have been as accessible as it now seems. She herself wrote almost no criticism after her student days. Her letters only occasionally touch on literary matters, though when they do, these often seem splendid, little morning sunrises of pure insight. When Robert Lowell sent her, in typescript, many of the poems that would later appear in *Life Studies,* for example, she replied by recalling those wonderful moments when artistic creation lights up the entire world:

> If only one could see everything that way all the time! It seems to me *it's* the whole purpose of art, to the artist (not to the audience)—that rare feeling of control, illumination—life *is* all right, for the time being. Anyway, when I read such an extended display of imagination as this, I feel it *for* you.

Yet, now that the revelations have been made, the milk spilt, the linen aired, the gossip all gushed, one suddenly realizes that many of Elizabeth Bishop's poems are made simultaneously more penetrable and a little less impressive with the addition of biographical information. Not least of the ironies here, of course, is that this woman, who was always careful to separate her life from literature—"You felt with Elizabeth," Clement Greenberg said, "life came first"—who fancied herself the most private of poets, produced poetry of a kind that was finally inseparable from her own life. To the critic Jerome Mazzaro she wrote:

> Well, it takes an infinite number of things coming together, forgotten, or almost forgotten, books, last night's dream, experiences past and present—to make a poem. The settings, or descriptions, of my poems are almost invariably just plain

facts—or as close to the facts as I can write them. But, as I said, it is fascinating that my poem ["Crusoe in England"] should arouse in you all those literary references.

That was written in 1978. Now, after the publication of Elizabeth Bishop's letters, a biography, and a book of reminiscences by friends and acquaintances, after reams and reams of critical attention, we know a great deal more about what went into the making of those poems. The price to be paid, the terrible trade-off that has been made, is that the poems cannot be read in isolation any longer. Once one might have said that these refined, rather pure poems, difficult though they may be to crack for ultimate meanings, have their own splendor. Once one might have said—as Howard Moss did say—that "Miss Bishop is completely sane" and "she has made sanity interesting without lecturing us about it." No longer. Now one more readily picks up interior meanings in her poems and understands that behind these often cool and well-made verbal contraptions, villanelles, sestinas, and the rest, the poems of Elizabeth Bishop, lie the themes of dispossession, loss, withdrawal, remorse, isolation, consolation sought but never found—more sadness, really, than any one human being should have been asked to bear—and that they represent the ruins shored up from a hard and often horrifying life.

On one reading, one might say that, given all that Elizabeth Bishop had gone through, the achievement that is her poems is all the more impressive. On another reading, knowing all that she went through, one can just as easily read into these poems all the evasions, scamping of difficult truths, and thinness that biographical knowledge, that snake in the literary Garden of Eden, makes all too plain.

Elizabeth Bishop has been treated very kindly by criticism. "The reviews [of *Geography III*] so far have been embarrassingly good," she wrote to Anny Baumann, "but of course someone is bound to *attack,* sooner or later." That was in 1977. Twenty-one years earlier, having been told that there was a stringent review by Edward Honig of the combined volumes *North & South* and *A Cold Spring* in *Partisan Review,* she writes to her friend Pearl Kazin: "I've never minded criticism a bit, strange to say—but what if this review (I haven't seen it yet) says the TRUTH?—does point out all the awful faults I know are there all right?"

The first line in Honig's review pointed up the influence on Elizabeth Bishop's poems of Marianne Moore: "Elizabeth Bishop's poetry aspires to a very high order of craft and sensibility—to a perch, say, which only Marianne Moore, among living women poets, precariously occupies." Miss Moore was twenty-four years older than Elizabeth Bishop when the two women met in 1934, the same year Miss Bishop's mother died. The meeting was brought about by the librarian at Vassar College, where Miss Bishop was still a student. They met outside the reading room of the New York Public Library, a possible getaway strategy for Miss Moore if this Vassar student, like so many she had met before, turned out to be a clucking bore. In fact, the two women clicked straightaway. David Kalstone, who in *Becoming a Poet* has written at length about their relationship, remarks that Elizabeth Bishop "enjoyed playing her role of forward niece" to Marianne Moore. Miss Moore, for her part, must have taken pleasure in so attractive and talented an acolyte.

Marianne Moore became not only Elizabeth Bishop's teacher but also, in effect, her editor and agent. Along with heavily editing the younger woman's poems and prose, she sent off her work to magazine editors she knew; on occasion, when Miss Bishop had already sent the same poem off to another editor, this caused a contretemps. Miss Moore became Elizabeth Bishop's sponsor, at one point introducing her work in *Trial Balances,* a volume of poets under twenty-five, each introduced by an older, established poet. No influence without anxiety, as Professor Harold Bloom never tires of telling us, and Elizabeth Bishop found she had at times to struggle free of Miss Moore's attempts at total management, choosing to ignore her editing or publishing work she knew Miss Moore would disdain.

Marianne Moore struck a nice balance with Elizabeth Bishop of helpfulness, praise, and criticism. She told Elizabeth Bishop that she had "a precise and proportioning ear" of a kind rare in contemporary verse. Of some of the young Miss Bishop's poems, she said that they "are so fine, and dart-proof in every way—especially 'The Weed' and 'Paris, 7 A.M.'—that they shame my impulsive offer of helpfulness." But she could also say that Bishop was "menaced by the goodness of your mechanics," adding that, "When I set out to find faults with you, there are so many excellences in your mechanics that I seem to be commending you instead and I wish to say, above all, that I am sure good treatment is a handicap unless along with it, significant values come out with an essential baldness." What I take Marianne Moore to be saying here is that, in the end, content, the true meaning of a poem, must come through strongly and that Elizabeth Bishop, so sound in so many ways, had not yet in her poems achieved this.

What Miss Bishop gained from the relationship with Marianne Moore, apart from endorsement and the delight of being in the fairly regular company of a genuinely eccentric woman with an authentic commitment to art as a way of life, was a method of poetic creation. Twenty years after they met, Elizabeth Bishop wrote to Marianne Moore to tell her that her poetry "opened my eyes to the possibility of subject-matter I could use and might never have thought of using if it hadn't been for you.—(I might not have written any poems at all, I suppose.)" She also learned from Miss Moore the art of accuracy of observation. She learned a useful realism, too, a realism for aesthetes of the kind that Miss Moore applauded in Wallace Stevens, who showed that "realism need not restrict itself to grossness." It made a firm impression on Elizabeth Bishop that when two young men took Marianne Moore to see Eisenstein's

Potemkin, Miss Moore responded by saying, "Life is not like that."

David Kalstone writes that Miss Bishop "adopted Moore's methods but learned to use them in different ways." That method was to make pure description do the work of narrative. Description, in this wise, becomes not so much a method as a principle of composition. Henceforth her poems would be attempts to capture recognitions that came about through meticulous observation and description of landscapes, animals, objects, places, stop-action moments of travel—almost never of persons or of dramatic situations. When she came to review Elizabeth Bishop's first book of poems, Marianne Moore gave her review the title "A Modest Expert." More than twenty years later, Howard Moss picked up this notion when, in a review of Miss Bishop's *Questions of Travel,* he wrote that "these poems are profoundly modest." Others have referred to her "modest masterpieces."

Another thing Elizabeth Bishop learned from Marianne Moore, or so Miss Bishop tells us in "Efforts of Affection," her portrait of Miss Moore, was "not to worry about what other people thought, never to try to publish anything until I thought I'd done my best with it, no matter how many years it took— or never to publish it at all." This, sensible lesson though it may seem, was, as advice goes, a mixed blessing.

Costiveness of publication was for Elizabeth Bishop an endless problem. A red thread—rope is perhaps more like it— that runs through her letters has to do with the endless regret about her inability to produce more work, which brought on depression, which often erupted into a bout of alcoholism, which ended in humiliation and shame, which increased her deep insecurity, which led to her ever greater dependence on the women who took it upon themselves to look out for her. She produced four slender volumes of verse at roughly ten-year intervals: *North & South* (1946), *Poems* (1955), *Questions of Travel*

(1965), and *Geography III* (1976). She did her translation of *The Diary of "Helena Morley"*; she turned out a quite small body of journalism and eight chiefly autobiographical sketches that are assembled under the rubric "Stories" in *The Collected Prose*. For a woman who had no serious job until her middle fifties, nor any of the domestic cares of being either wife or mother, who garnered all the available grants and fellowships (*Partisan Review*, Guggenheim, Rockefeller, Ingram-Merrill, and so on), this was disappointing, not least to Elizabeth Bishop herself.

The one place where her writing seemed to flow was in her letters. *One Art*—the title comes from her poem about the art of accepting loss in her own life—shows this flow at flood-tide. Miss Bishop's letters, like her poems, tend to be chiefly descriptive; she arranged much of her adult life so that she lived in exotic backgrounds—Key West, Florida; Petropolis, forty or so miles from Rio de Janeiro, where her friend Lota had built a home, with an outbuilding that was a separate studio for Elizabeth—from which she could report on the flora and fauna (much of it human fauna) surrounding her. Cool-eyed, she described human beings, in Florida and in Brazil, as if they were herons or some rare sort of mango.

Elizabeth Bishop's letters are chatty and tactful, yet, despite the pleasant fumes of intimacy they give off, except for those to Dr. Anny Baumann and to Robert Lowell, they don't give too much away. We learn of all the books she planned but never got around to writing—Balzac called plans for such unwritten books smoking "enchanted cigarettes"—among them, a book of travel essays on South America, a collection of short stories, a play ("of all things"), another book of pieces about Brazil. Tidbits of backflesh—my own menu prose for minor backbiting—from time to time creep in: a letter to Lowell puts down a Jarrell poem recently published in *Partisan Review* (Jarrell later writes to Lowell saying he doesn't think much of Bishop's long poem "At the Fishhouses"), a put-down of Marianne Moore's translation of La Fontaine, unkind words for William Carlos Williams, Richard Eberhart, and Robert Frost, and for Richard Wilbur's poetry.

But the note of sadness rings insistently. After drinking up all the booze in a friend's apartment in Washington, she writes to say that "I get along better on boredom and adversity than on gaiety and, relatively speaking, success." Many are the reports of falls off wagons, of little breakdowns, of asthma and allergy attacks, of every kind of anxiety (about doing poetry readings, lecturing, meeting certain people), of suicidal thoughts: "I don't want to be this kind of person at all," she writes to her friend the painter Loren McIver, "but I'm afraid I'm really disintegrating, just like Hart Crane, only without his gifts to make it all plausible."

Reading along in these letters, one soon comes to feel that the end cannot be far off—except that one feels in one's hand the heft of another 440-odd pages to go—for poor Miss Bishop, when she is rescued by Lota de Macedo Soares. In the winter of 1951, she set out for a trip to South America, and when staying with Lota, a trilingual Brazilian whom she had met in 1942 in New York, she developed a violent allergic reaction to the fruit of a cashew tree. Lota nursed her during her illness and invited her to stay on in Brazil as long as she liked. Miss Bishop was swept away by the sweetness and generosity of the offer and stayed on for no fewer than fifteen years.

These years, with only brief interludes of sadness, were the happiest years of Elizabeth Bishop's life. A year after settling into Brazil, she writes to Robert Lowell that "I am extremely happy, for the first time in my life." She is given—"my lifelong dream"—a toucan, whom she names Sammy. She learns to drive and acquires, from the proceeds of the sale of her story "In the Village" to *The New Yorker,* an MG, something to write about to Randall Jarrell, another car enthusiast. She has a vegetable garden, orchids grow outside the studio Lota has built for her—"things couldn't be better." She discovers cortisone, which inhibits her asthma, makes her euphoric, and, for once, literarily productive: along with her translation, during these years she turns out a dozen poems, the stories about her childhood, and a book on Brazil much rewritten by the editors at Time, Inc., who commissioned it.

Yet, sad to report, as the old maxim has it, Anywhere you go, there you are. Which is to say that even in Brazil, where the clouds came into the house, where the landscape was permanently lush, and the living was easy, old problems arose. Elizabeth Bishop suffered setbacks on the booze front. The thinness of Brazilian culture and the maddening lackadaisicalness of South American ways—"no one *ever* learns *anything,* and a 'habit' is unheard of"—began to get to her: the flora turns out to be much more impressive than the fauna, which, even for a writer whose subject is nature, can after a while be tiresome.

But saddest of all, her relationship with Lota, the love of her life, began to go sour. Lota, a woman of extraordinary energy, became caught up in Brazilian politics while put in charge of creating a grand people's park in Rio de Janeiro. Lota was apparently a high-energy melancholic, and when things began to go bad with her park project, she sank into depression and then breakdown. When Elizabeth Bishop decided to aerate the relationship a bit by taking the recently dead Theodore Roethke's teaching job at the University of Washington, things did not get better but rapidly worse.

"Lota has been simple hell to live with for the past five years," Miss Bishop writes to Dr. Baumann, adding in another letter that "well, we were happy for ten years or so," and then again: "it has been the worst stretch of my life except maybe the first eight years." Later, in the autumn of 1967, when Miss Bishop went to New York, Lota, not yet recovered from a breakdown, joined her and their first night together overdosed herself with Valium, lapsed into a coma, and died a week later.

Poor Elizabeth Bishop, ejected from the only paradise she had ever known. Although she would live another twelve years and would go on to even greater poetic fame, the remainder of her life after Lota has finis written all over it. She lived in San Francisco: attempted to live in Ouro Prêto, the highest point in Brazil, where she had acquired and attempted to rehabilitate an eighteenth-century house; lived for a while in Cambridge, then settled into an apartment at Lewis Wharf in Boston. As always, there were women who were ready to live with her, travel with her, clean up after her. She would climb on and slip off the wagon, and had now reached the stage in her drinking at which broken bones seemed to be part of the regular protocol.

Elizabeth Bishop was never for long without money worries, and these increased as she headed toward old age. The only solution, a most imperfect one, was teaching. Robert Lowell, who had sponsored her for so many grants and prizes, arranged for her to take up his post teaching the writing of poetry at Harvard. She detested the snobbery and one-upmanship of Harvard, and felt herself, as every honorable teacher must, something of a fraud in taking money for teaching students to write: "These things shouldn't be *taught*—I'll be relieved and have a moral load off my mind when I sell my house [in Ouro Prêto] and my papers and don't have to do this any more." Out of the need for money, she gave up her compunction about giving poetry readings. The time of honorary degrees had arrived. When elected to the then fifty-member American Academy of Arts and Letters, she accepts but cannot help remarking to an old college friend that there are so many *"creeps"* among the members.

Here is the winning Elizabeth Bishop—the figure who must be set next to the tragic Elizabeth Bishop if anything like a complete portrait is to emerge. Dana Gioia, who was her pupil at Harvard, has remarked upon the admirable way "in which the best parts of the bohemian and the bourgeois naturally co-existed in her character without affectation." This is the woman who, after being interviewed for the *Vassar Quarterly,* discovers that an interview with the very political Muriel Rukeyser appears in the same issue, making her, Miss Bishop, "sound like Billie Burke." (Her own politics, of the standard-issue Nixon-hating kind, were never central to her character.) This is the woman who can describe the novels of Robert Penn Warren as "just like *Gone with the Wind* with metaphysical footnotes." This is the woman who refers to a Brazilian friend "wearing a blue shirt and purple trousers, looking like a large bunch of violets." This is the woman who is amused by being referred to, in Brazil, as "the famous American poetess," and remarks that she likes the word "poetess," which "I think is a nice mixture of poet and mistress."

A leitmotif in Elizabeth Bishop's letters is her distaste for being segregated as a woman poet. "Perhaps I shouldn't say this—but it antedates Female Lib-ism by 40 years," she wrote to Robert Lowell, "I'd rather be called *'the 16th poet'* with no reference to my sex, than one of 4 women—even if the other 3 are pretty good." She was distrustful of women writers—Virginia Woolf, Rebecca West, Elizabeth Bowen—who always made one aware of their social origins, calling them the " 'our beautiful old silver' school of female writing." She told May Swenson that she would never agree to appear in anthologies of women poets, because "literature is literature, no matter who produces it . . . [and] I don't like things compartmentalized like that."

Miss Bishop came of age before the universities had so badly colonized and bollixed up literature into little ethnic and sex subgroups. She grew up admiring the last generation of poets who didn't earn their livelihood in universities: Stevens, Eliot, Marianne Moore, and Robert Frost—non-blue-jean-wearing, which is to say altogether adult, poets. She believed that writers were chiefly of two kinds: good and bad. She knew, in her heart she knew, how difficult it was to be really good. As for her own standing, she told Wesley Wehr, a painter and paleobotanist in Seattle: "Oh, it's not that I think I'm all that good a poet, but I look around at the other poems being written by my contemporaries, and I think, maybe I'm not so bad."

On the other hand, being Elizabeth Bishop, she much more frequently must have thought, "maybe I'm not so good, either." Not much could quell the self-doubt that ran so deeply in her. The same year, 1956, that she won the Pulitzer Prize she also won a *Partisan Review* fellowship underwritten by the Ford Foundation. "Never has so little work dragged in so many prizes, I'm afraid," she wrote to her friend Pearl Kazin, "and I catechize myself minutely, worrying about *why*."

As for the quality of her work, Bishop was even less than confident about it. When Isabella Gardner compliments her on "Visits to S. Elizabeths," her poem about Ezra Pound, she replies that she herself "really couldn't tell much myself whether it conveyed my rather mixed emotions or not." After praising Robert Lowell for some of his *Life Studies* poems, she remarked: "Oh heavens, when does one begin to write the *real* poems? I certainly feel as if I never had." Earlier she had written to Lowell: "On reading over what I've got on hand I find I'm really a minor female Wordsworth—at least I don't know anyone who seems to be such a nature lover."

What was the quality of Elizabeth Bishop's poetry? In *Remembering Elizabeth Bishop,* Joseph Frank says that "she seemed to be one of the few poets about whom there was very little disagreement." In her lifetime, she had first Marianne Moore behind her, then Randall Jarrell and Robert Lowell and James Merrill. After her death, fellow poets praised her even for what one might have thought weaknesses. Thus, Frank Bidart, on the matter of the paucity of her production, remarks that "one of the great things about her work is that she *didn't* write too much. . . ." Marianne Moore, in her 1946 review of *North & South,* proclaimed that Elizabeth Bishop is "spectacular in being unspectacular." After this she was fixed forever into being Our

Lady of the Understated Emotions. "The quiet exactitude of her work," said Dana Gioia, "showed that emotions didn't have to be screamed to be genuine." Howard Moss, who was her editor at *The New Yorker,* in one of three different full-court praising pieces he wrote about her, writes that "she has taught us without a shred of pedagogy to be wary of the hustling of emotions, of the false allurements of the grand." How tired Elizabeth Bishop must have been reading yet again about her bloody restraint and freaking modesty! As she wrote to James Merrill, "I don't get much criticism. . . ."

Since her death, of course, Elizabeth Bishop has received a vast quantity of criticism, almost all of it approving. Always a poet's poet, she has, in death, become a critic's poet as well. Yet the quality of this criticism is on the whole disappointing. Even in the hands of such intelligent critics as Helen Vendler and the late David Kalstone, there is very little in the way of strong formulation of what, exactly, Elizabeth Bishop's poems are really about and why they are important. Apropos of her writing in Brazil, for example, Kalstone wrote: "Did the disparate poems and stories she was writing cohere, in their own way, as self-presentation? Did her work in these years amount to something as sustained as Lowell's recent work appeared to be?" That is a good question that Kalstone, in *Becoming a Poet,* a book unfinished at the time of his death, never quite got around to answering. Nor, insofar as I am aware, has anyone else.

The general critical procedure in dealing with Elizabeth Bishop's poetry is to assume that she is, in her understated, modest way, a genius—"genius tries to pass itself off as less than it is," wrote Howard Moss—and go on from there to attempt to tease out the meaning of her individual poems. "These poems," Moss wrote, "strike me as ageless; there are no false starts, no fake endings." Moss does acknowledge that "these poems, so easy to read, give up their secrets slowly."

I should myself put this last proposition rather differently: Elizabeth Bishop usually achieves an impressive line-by-line lucidity without this lucidity necessarily yielding a final, or higher clarity. Although Miss Bishop went to the precisionist school of Marianne Moore, her description is far from infallible. Is the cold sea, as she writes in "At the Fishhouses," really "like what we imagine knowledge to be: / dark, salt, clear, moving, utterly free"? Knowledge, as Miss Moore might say, is not like this. In "Cape Breton" we are presented with "little white churches [that] have been dropped into the matted hills / like lost quartz arrowheads." This, too, doesn't quite ring the gong, at least not for me. Neither does the thunder, in "Electrical Storm," "Personal and spiteful as a neighbor's child"; nor, from "The Riverman," does the moon "burning bright / as the gasoline mantle with the flame turned up too high, / just before it begins to scorch." Whenever Miss Bishop avails herself of personification—as in the lighthouse in "Seascape" who thinks "he" knows what heaven and hell are—it is almost always disappointing.

A large number of Miss Bishop's poems, well-made and mechanically sound though they may be, do not, as she writes in her letter about Robert Fitzgerald's poems, "ignite." She wrote a number of splendid poems: "The Fish," "Filling Station," "First Death in Nova Scotia," "Crusoe in England," and "One Art" would be among my Bishop selections were I the anthologist charged with filling an ample volume. But the case for her being a major poet, the modest genius of American poetry, seems to me not easily made.

Elizabeth Bishop's very method—that of careful description, the "perfectly useless concentration" that she saw as at the heart of poetic creation, out of which a deeper truth would presumably flow—too often failed to work the magic it sometimes can. She was committed to steering clear of the personal in her poetry, which, with only occasional exceptions, she did, the most notably successful exception being the poem "One Art."

The art in the title of that poem is the art of loss, which, she came to understand, was the theme pervading her own life. To have dwelt on it, to have written endlessly about her personal losses, would only have demeaned her. With all its nightmares, her life was a full-time struggle, from which her writing gave some relief but no real solution.

Richard Wilbur, in *Remembering Elizabeth Bishop,* recounts, apropos of his going off to church one morning in Maine, Elizabeth Bishop saying to him, "You don't really believe all that stuff. You're just like me. Neither of us has any philosophy. It's all description, no philosophy." Wilbur goes on to say that at this point "Elizabeth shifted to talking about herself and lamenting the fact that she didn't have a philosophic adhesive to pull together an individual poem and a group of poems together, but she was really quite aggressive at that point." Neither did she have any interest in moral complication. "For Bishop," Helen Vendler has written, "the charm and interest of life was that it was as it is; she believed in no religion, no afterlife, no external sanctions or morality."

Precise description has its own morality; some might argue, its own theology: God, it has been said, is in the details. But without a larger vision than Elizabeth Bishop was able to acquire, major literature may not be possible. Certainly, it prevented her from ever producing those large philosophical poems—"The Wreck of the *Deutschland,*" "Sunday Morning," "The Waste Land," "Two Tramps in Mud Time"—that are at the center of every major poetical corpus in our century. Critics have tried to inflate the importance of such poems of Miss Bishop's as "The Moose" or "Filling Station" (with its ending line, "Somebody loves us all"), turning them into theologico-philosophical statements. They are lovely poems—good, nice, really quite swell poems—but they just cannot carry the weight of critical significance assigned to them.

Forced to play a bad hand through life, Elizabeth Bishop

played it as well as she could. At her best, she seems a winning woman: amusing, brave, without either exhibitionism or complaint. Her small but genuine achievement marks her as too good a poet to fail to understand that, despite the claims made on her behalf, she was a long way from great.

Life Sentences,
The Art of Joseph Conrad

> *Mr. Conrad has no ideas, but he has a point of view, a "world"; it can hardly be defined, but it pervades his work and is unmistakable.*
>
> —T. S. Eliot, "Kipling Revividus"

> *He [James] had a mind so fine no idea could violate it.*
>
> —T. S. Eliot, "On Henry James"

From T. S. Eliot, no praise for a novelist could be higher, one must conclude, than to be found without ideas. These two Eliotic quotations, along with manifold affinities, lash Henry James and Joseph Conrad together. As for their affinities, both James and Conrad were precursors of modernism in their profound contemplation upon the endless questions of form in literary creation. In the work of each writer, plot never supersedes artistic purpose and artistic purpose is never separated from moral vision. James invoked one to be a person on whom nothing was lost and, what comes close to the same thing, Conrad affirmed that, in the moral realm, ignorance is no excuse. James loved complication, and Conrad seemed unable to avoid it. Both would be out of business without the extensive use of irony. So many qualities do the two writers share that it is possible to think of Joseph Conrad as

Henry James for people who prefer to read about the out-of-doors.

Neither James nor Conrad was unacquainted or unconcerned about ideas, but both felt that the important truths for artists occurred above, beyond, in any case well outside the realm of ideas. "It is impossible to know anything," wrote Conrad to his friend Cunninghame Graham, "though it is possible to believe a thing or two." James chimed in with his own negative but nonetheless equally ardent artistic credo: "never say you know the last word about any human heart," implying, what is perfectly true, that no one after all does. Both novelists swam best in the murky waters of the morally questionable. Despite their different ways of approaching their tasks, each man understood that it was the scrupulous investigation of moral questions that gave the novel both its power and its grandeur. Each was tireless in his own investigations.

"All novelists since Conrad are cads," said George Macaulay Trevelyan. One has to assume he meant by this not only that Conrad was a gentleman to the manor (and manner) born, but that he did not feel it incumbent upon him as a novelist to do boudoir patrol as the Bloomsbury writers and those who came after them had done. Something to it, perhaps, but not much more than there is to calling Conrad a great sea-writer, a reputation he labored under for many more years than he himself wished. What Joseph Conrad was was an artist to the bone, possessed of the instincts of an artist and in search of an artist's truths.

Joseph Conrad was born in 1857, the year of the publication of *Madame Bovary,* and died in 1924, two years after the publication of *Ulysses.* As a novelist, he sat astride two traditions, the nineteenth-century tradition of the thickly plotted novel anchored in action and adventure and the twentieth-century tradition of the novel with its emphasis on irony, on analysis, and on psychological depth. Yet Conrad insisted on his modernity.

Attempting to account for the commercial failure of his early fiction to the magazine publisher William Blackwood, he wrote:

> I am *modern,* and I would rather recall Wagner the musician and Rodin the sculptor who both had to starve a little in their day—and Whistler the painter who made Ruskin the critic foam at the mouth with scorn and indignation. They too have arrived. They had to suffer for being "new." And I too hope to find my place in the rear of my betters. But still—my place.

That Conrad has arrived as a classic of English literature is nowadays scarcely cause to hold the presses for the Long Island edition. But what, precisely, his place might be has not been clearly worked out. A Pole who wrote in English, a modernist artist who believed in the most old-fashioned way in duty and honor, Joseph Conrad is the great anomaly of modern, perhaps of all, literature, the exception who proves no rule. In one sense, Conrad's place is in the line begun by Flaubert and ending with Joyce—the international line of the perfectionists and experimentalists. But Conrad is also among the chief moralists of the novel. He preferred to put his characters—and his readers—in situations of ethical bafflement and then watch to discover if their moral compasses will help them find their way home. This, too, was Henry James's *modus operandi.* Reading both writers provides superior entertainment as well as a strenuous test of one's own equipment for moral navigation.

The only child of Polish aristocrats, of the class in Poland known as the *szlachta,* that combination of nobility and gentry that made up the ruling class, Conrad was born Józef Teodor Konrad Korzeniowski. His mother died when he was seven, his father when he was eleven. Conrad's father, Apollo Korzeniowski, a translator, poet, and essayist, was also a great Polish patriot, which meant, in the nature of the case, a great enemy of Russia, which held Poland under its thick and brutal thumb. Owing to his father's politics, the Korzeniowskis were sent into exile in the northern part of European Russia in 1862. This exile was especially hard on Conrad's mother, who became tubercular; Conrad's father also acquired tuberculosis, and only because of his extremely poor health was he allowed to return to Poland for the last eighteen months of his life. When he died, he was given a hero's burial, with several thousand people following the cortège to the cemetery outside of the medieval city of Cracow.

Conrad grew up under the watchful eye of his uncle, his mother's brother, Tadeusz Bobrowski, a man of much more conservative bent than his father, both politically and temperamentally, who attempted to steer the boy unto a safer path than that chosen by his father. Conrad's orphaned youth was jittery and erratic. He was an uneven student, given to illness, fits of anxiety, rebellion, cigar smoking, and awkward adolescent amorous passions. He spoke about one day becoming a great writer, a boast his classmates found laughable.

Perhaps only because the young Korzeniowski—he would change his name to Joseph Conrad in 1894—seemed such a hopeless misfit was he permitted to take the extraordinary leap, for a Polish aristocrat, of joining, at the age of seventeen, the French merchant marine. In *A Personal Record* (1912), Conrad writes that "I verily believe mine was the only case of a boy of my nationality and antecedents taking a, so to speak, standing jump out of his racial surroundings and associations [to go to sea] . . . the truth is that what I had in mind was not a naval career but the sea."

In fact, the truth in this matter is in flux of controversy. When Conrad first presented his notion of going to sea, his tutor called him "an incorrigible, hopeless Don Quixote." Some thought that a life at sea would teach him much-needed discipline; others that it might be good for his health. His Uncle Tadeusz, according to Zdzislaw Najder, Conrad's best biographer, saw in his going to sea the prospect for his nephew of a career combining "maritime skills and commercial activities—better still as a middleman in the huge agricultural products trade." It is known, too, that his uncle wanted him to obtain another citizenship, so that he should be out of the legal clutches of Russia. Early attempts at acquiring Austrian and Swiss citizenship both came to nought, and Conrad was eventually granted British citizenship, in 1886, when he was twenty-nine.

Joseph Conrad's career at sea spanned twenty years, from 1874 to 1894, though during this period he was actually assigned to ships for only ten years and eight months, and of this time he spent, according to Najder, "just over eight years at sea, nine months of this as a passenger." Taking a succession of maritime examinations, he rose through the ranks from second mate to captain, though he only served briefly in the latter capacity, including a crucial six-month stint in command of a steamer on the Congo that resulted in a near fatal case of fever and dysentery and the masterpiece novella "Heart of Darkness" (1899).

A most odd figure the young Conrad must have cut among his fellow seamen. Small, dandiacal in his dark suits, bowler hat, and gold-knobbed walking stick, formal, taciturn, speaking a greenhorn's English, a reader of books, obviously a man of wide culture, Conrad commanded the hard drinkers, vagabonds, and thuggish sailors who signed on for long international voyages on merchant ships. (The better class of sailor joined the Royal Navy.) Other captains and officers referred to him as "the Russian Count."

"No," Conrad would write in retrospect, "perhaps I should say that the life at sea—and I don't mean a mere taste of it, but a good broad span of years, something that really counts as real service—is not, upon the whole, a good equipment for a writing life." Yet without his years at sea, Conrad's later literary life is difficult to imagine. Life at sea, and in the ports and places to which the sea took him, furnished the perfect subject matter for a writer born to a life of permanent exile. (As Henry James wrote to Conrad: "No one has *known*—for intellectual use—the things you know.") Life at sea was the only society that he would ever really know from the inside.

Conrad tended both to demean and to idealize his time at sea, though at no time did he consider it permanent. In later life, whenever he compared life on land and life at sea, the latter was always made to seem simpler, more manly, better. At the same time, from letters and from reports of people who remembered him during his time at sea, Conrad was among his maritime colleagues a misfit, lonely and cut off from the larger European culture into which he was brought up and for which he yearned.

The incipient writer in Conrad must have felt deep frustration aboard ship. He claimed to have begun his writing life in 1890, when, at the age of thirty-three, he started writing the novel that was to be *Alymayer's Folly*. But there is reason to believe that, four years earlier, he had entered a short-story contest sponsored by the magazine *Tit-Bits* with a story called "The Black Mate." In Conrad's own, so to say approved, version, he one day spotted from the deck of his ship an outcast named Charles Olmeijer on an island in the Malay Archipelago, and four years later began, as a way to while away a holiday, his novel based on this character. Some time later he showed pages of the far from complete novel to a young, educated English passenger on a ship on which Conrad served as a mate, and because this fellow found Conrad's pages readable and interesting, he determined to persist. The writing of this novel, Conrad wrote, "was not the outcome of a need," but "the necessity which impelled me was a hidden, obscure necessity, a completely masked and unaccountable phenomenon." With the writing of the first page of *Almayer's Folly*, Conrad wrote, "the die was cast."

More likely it was cast well before. Given Conrad's background—a greatly admired father with belletristic interests, an early dreaminess that found an outlet in reading, a youthful rebelliousness that precluded his learning a profession, the condition of exile, a dark moodiness of temperament that issued in deep reflection—there probably wasn't much else he could have done but write. Conrad would never for a moment have suggested that his becoming a writer was a matter of conscious decision or free will. "I like the worthy folk who will talk to you of the exercise of free will, 'at any rate for practical purposes,' " he wrote. "Free is it? For practical purposes! Bosh!" Then, again, Conrad's becoming a writer may have been as simple as Desmond MacCarthy once put it: "I think it was because he had seen so many things in human nature and the world that he did not wish to be forgotten or to forget, that Conrad, to our great gain, became a writer." *Almayer's Folly* was begun when Joseph Conrad was thirty-three and published when he was thirty-eight. Although Conrad would become both a smoother prose writer and one more accomplished at organizing and orchestrating his novels and stories, his view, his outlook, his vision was settled from the first. It was never to be changed, only tested, amplified, and exfoliated to its full, immensely rich complexity. This was the advantage in his beginning to write only after coming to maturity.

H. L. Mencken, an early admirer, said that, in reading Conrad, a reader "must bring something with him beyond the mere faculty of attention. If, coming to Conrad, he cannot, he is at the wrong door." To grasp anything like the full power of Conrad's fiction, one must, I think, at some point in one's life have been impressed with the utter indifference of the universe to even the most grand of human plans. One must have felt the brute fact that we both come into and go out of this world alone—and, however much surrounded by other people, nonetheless spend much time in between in spiritually this same condition of loneliness. However great one's love of justice, one must know that it is not evenly meted out in this world, nor is it ever likely to be. One must understand that good frequently goes without reward while at the same time evil is never justified and always brings its own punishment. Life must be considered a struggle, a battle, a riddle to which it may well be that nothing resembling a persuasive answer is available.

Conrad never posited any of this directly, but one can scarcely conclude otherwise from his stories and novels. Although he often alluded to his true purpose as an artist, the two most famous of his statements on the matter come from prefaces, the first to his novel *The Nigger of the Narcissus* and the second to *A Personal Record*. In the former, Conrad wrote:

> My task which I am trying to achieve is, by the power of the written word to make you hear, to make you feel—it is, before all, to make you *see*. That—and no more, and it is everything. If I succeed, you shall find there according to your deserts: encouragement, consolation, fear, charm—all you demand—and, perhaps, also that glimpse of truth for which you have forgotten to ask.

As for that glimpse of truth, in the preface of *A Personal Record*, Conrad wrote:

> Those who read me know my conviction that the world, the temporal world, rests on a few very simple ideas; so simple that they must be as old as the hills. It rests notably, among others, on the idea of Fidelity.

So there it is, Conrad's artistic credo, to make his readers hear, feel, and see, and after that to make plain to them, through the exempla of stories, that the world rests on a small number of ideas, fidelity notable among them. It explains everything and yet stated baldly it explains nothing. As Marlow, Conrad's narrator in "Heart of Darkness," says, "Droll thing life is—that mysterious arrangement of merciless logic for a futile purpose. The most you can hope from it is some knowledge of yourself—that comes too late—a crop of unextinguishable regrets." And knowledge of yourself, self-knowledge, seems to be only available in Conrad through traumata brought about by extreme moral tension. In Conrad's fiction, characters meet the problems that moral tension sets them and through doing so acquaint themselves with glimmerings of the larger significance of life; or they avoid these problems—through insensitivity, through ignorance, through removing themselves from life—and live, outside the realm of self-knowledge, in degradation or ignominy or triviality.

For Conrad "imagination, not invention, is the supreme master of art as of life." Imagination is inseparable from language, and not the least interesting of Conrad's choices—if choice it was—was to write in English, the third of his languages in order of acquisition. He claimed himself "adopted by the genius of the language, which directly I came out of the stammering stage made me its own so completely that its very idioms I truly believe had a direct action on my temperament and fashioned my still plastic character." He went on to say that "if I had not written in English I would not have written at all."

Whatever the inevitability of Conrad's writing in English, the language was never easy for him. To add to his torments, he was a writer in the *mot juste* tradition. One must imagine in operation here the perfectionism of a Flaubert but perfectionism sought in a language not one's own. In making the corrections for *Almayer's Folly,* Conrad is said to have made more than eight hundred changes that had to do with the replacement of one word by another. His wrestle with English was endless. Everyone who met Conrad seems to have remarked on his punctilious manners and his difficult English. E. V. Lucas, the English essayist, noted that Conrad "spoke with a very strong foreign accent and in sentences not too well constructed." Edward Garnett, who was most helpful to Conrad in his dealings with publishers and editors, reported that Conrad, when reading from the manuscript of *An Outcast of the Islands* to him, "mispronounced so many words that I followed him with difficulty. I found then that he had never once heard these English words spoken, but had learned them all from books!"

One can see—one can feel and hear—Conrad's struggle with English in these two separate passages from *Almayer's Folly*:

> While the sun shone with the dazzling light in which her love was born and grew till it possessed her whole being, she was kept firm in her wavering resolve by the mysterious whisperings of desire which filled her heart with impatient longing for the darkness that would mean the end of danger and strife, the beginning of happiness, the fulfilling of love, the completeness of life.

> Dain Maroola, dazzled by the unexpected vision [of Almayer's daughter Nina], forgot his brig, his escort staring in open-mouthed admiration, the object of his visit and all things else, in his overpowering desire to prolong the contemplation of so much loveliness met so suddenly in such an unlikely place—as he thought.

That the author of these awkward sentences would go on to become a master of English prose is part of the measure of Joseph Conrad's achievement. His struggle with English would never end, never get easier, but, over the years, as he got better and better, it took place on higher and higher ground. His prose was distinctly his own; he struck a note that sounded like that of no one else. But then great masters—the name of Henry James once again comes to mind—teach us not only to accept but to love their original, their absolutely characteristic no matter how idiosyncratic, note. Max Beerbohm, who held both James and Conrad in the greatest regard, wrote his two best parodies of these writers. Here, from Beerbohm's *Christmas Garland,* is the perfect first paragraph from his Conrad parody:

The hut in which slept the white man was on a clearing between the forest and the river. Silence, the silence murmurous and unquiet of a tropical night, brooded over the hut that, baked through by the sun, sweated a vapour beneath the cynical light of the stars. Mahamo lay rigid and watchful at the hut's mouth. In his upturned eyes, and along the polished surface of his lean body black and immobile, the stars were reflected, creating an illusion of themselves who are illusions.

Like the prose on which it was modeled, this passage, capturing Conrad exactly, is slightly awkward and out of beat ("The hut in which slept"), laced with surprising juxtapositions ("the cynical light of the stars"), oddly placed adjectives ("lean body black and immobile"), and impressive portentousness ("an illusion of themselves who are illusions"). Easy enough to mock, Conrad's prose became more and more elegant—and, when needed, eloquent—over the years. The opening paragraph of *Nostromo* (1904), for example, shows Conrad writing prose of a pellucidity any native-born writer of English would envy:

In the time of Spanish rule, and for many years afterwards, the town Sulaco—the luxuriant beauty of the orange gardens bears witness to its antiquity—had never been commercially anything more important than a coasting port with a fairly large local trade in ox-hides and indigo. The clumsy deep-sea galleons of the conquerors that, needing a brisk gale to move at all, would lie becalmed, where your modern ship built on clipper lines forges ahead by the mere flapping of her sails, had been barred out of Sulaco by the prevailing calms of its vast gulf. Some harbours of the earth are made difficult of access by the treachery of sunken rocks and the tempests of their shores. Sulaco had found an inviolable sanctuary from the temptations of a trading world in the solemn hush of the deep Golfo Placido as if within an enormous semi-circular and unroofed temple open to the ocean, with its walls of lofty mountains hung with the mourning draperies of cloud.

Writing in a language he never spoke with ease, Conrad really did make us, his readers, see—and from this all else followed. As he himself put what he took to be both his problem and his task, he had "to make unfamiliar things credible. To do that I had to create for them, to reproduce for them, to envelop them in their proper atmosphere of actuality. This was the hardest task of all and the most important in view of that conscientious rendering of truth in thought and fact which has been always my aim."

Note that it is both thought and fact that interested Conrad. Perhaps this is why so much of his fiction seems, as V. S. Naipaul once remarked, "like a simple film with an elaborate commentary." By the early 1920's, Conrad, always in need of money, sold the film rights to all his novels; and many of these have been made into movies or done on stage or on television. But none has been anywhere near successful, chiefly because in Conrad it is the thought accompanying the fact that makes him—as it makes James and Proust—a great writer; and it is the thought, precisely, that the movies cannot accommodate.

In creative-writing courses, young students are regularly exhorted to show and not to tell. But the great writers have always been splendid tellers, and Conrad has been the among the best of them. "What men wanted was to be checked by superior intelligence," Conrad writes in his story "The End of the Tether," "by superior knowledge, by superior force, too—yes, by force held in trust from God and sanctified by its use in accordance with His declared will. Captain Whalley believed a disposition for good existed in every man, even if the world were not a very happy place as a whole." As Naipaul rightly notes, "by his sheer analytical intelligence, Conrad holds us." Naipaul adds: "For Conrad, though, the drama and the truth lay not in events but in the analysis: identifying the stages of consciousness through which a passionless man might move to the recognition of the importance of passion."

Most of Conrad's characters begin in a state of passionlessness. It is their want of passion that often puts them beyond the pale of normal humanity. Beyond that pale they indubitably are. Conrad gave his second novel the title *An Outcast of the Islands,* and at the center of nearly all of his fiction is an outcast of one sort or another. Sometimes one is made an outcast by conditions beyond one's control (as in "Amy Foster" or *Under Western Eyes*); sometimes one is made an outcast by greed, fantasy, or laziness *(Almayer's Folly, The Secret Agent),* sometimes by a will to power or pride *(Nostromo),* sometimes by moral purpose gone madly awry ("Heart of Darkness"), sometimes by deliberate philosophical decision *(Victory),* sometimes by too great reliance on irony (*Nostromo,* again).

Conrad was especially sensitive to this condition of being an outcast, for he was himself not so much an outcast by conscious decision as he was cast out of normal life by the harsh political and autobiographical conditions of his early life. V. S. Pritchett has noted that "before anyone else . . . Conrad the exile foresaw that in half a century [after he wrote] we should all become exiles, in a sense." It is by no means clear that Pritchett understood what this sense was, for in his fiction Conrad is dealing with matters much deeper than the sense of feeling like an exile inherent in the alienation, however vague or specific, that many people have come to feel at the end of the twentieth century toward their family, or culture, or country. In good part Conrad's genius resides in his taking particular cases of outcasts, specifying their situations until they become crushingly real, and while doing so—here the magic of art comes into play—elevating these particular cases into a universal condition.

The solitariness, the absolutely devastating aloneness, of so many of Conrad's central characters can send a shudder through one's soul. To be an outcast means, in the root sense, to be cast out from the wider community. In good measure, the sadness at the heart of so much of Conrad's fiction is that the surrounding community comes itself to resemble an abyss of self-deception and self-seeking. Perhaps the only relief from this loneliness in Conrad's books comes, oddly enough, in that loneliest of settings, where the universe itself seems most cruelly indifferent, the sea.

In many of Conrad's sea stories, men pull together, not merely for a common but usually for a crucial goal, as in the horrendous storms in "Typhoon" or *The Nigger of the Narcissus,* where life itself is at stake, and emerge heroic in blending their lives into a larger common purpose. As Conrad wrote in *Lord Jim:* "we exist only insofar as we hang together." I earlier quoted Conrad remarking that notable among the ideas on which the world rests is that of Fidelity. In his fiction, Fidelity is often another word for duty. Those who understand their work, stay on the job, ever faithful to their duty, these are the characters Conrad seems most to admire. As Conrad puts it in *Youth,* where his narrator attempts to grasp the reasoning behind the dutifulness of the English seaman:

> They didn't think their pay half good enough. No; it was something in them, something inborn and subtle and everlasting. . . . There was a completeness in it, something solid like a principle, and masterful like an instinct—a disclosure of something secret—of that hidden something, that gift of good or evil that makes racial difference, that shapes the fate of nations.

Among the more sentient of Conrad's characters, self-knowledge is crucial to any chance not for happiness, a quality that doesn't seem to enter into Conrad's figurings, but for measured contentment. Self-knowledge, in Conrad, does not have necessarily to do with high intelligence. Once again as in the novels of Henry James, so in Conrad, great intelligence is as likely as not to lead a character to disaster: to make him more manipulative, greedy, cruel. No, what is wanted is not so much intelligence as moral sensibility. The quality of moral sensibility determines one not to harm others but also to understand, if not quite one's exact place in the larger, otherwise utterly mysterious scheme of the world, at least to understand that one can never for a moment pretend that one is a free agent, unbounded by the legitimate claims of others. The one piece of clear, cautionary advice on this point in Conrad is given to us through the mouth of Axel Heyst, the lonely hero of *Victory,* who emerges from the philosophical nihilism taught him by his father, to report from the depths of his soul: "Ah, Davidson, woe to the man whose heart has not learned while young to hope, to love—and to put its trust in life."

Conrad meant love not in the sexual or even the romantic but in the larger sense of love of life itself. Although *Victory* is in good part a love story, and so, too, is *Almayer's Folly* a love story, while *The Secret Agent* may be the most powerful anti-love story ever written, Conrad was not a writer whose own passions were greatly engaged by the erotic. Conrad refused to read Freud, saying, "I do not want to reach the *depths.* I want to treat reality like a raw and rough object which I touch with my fingers." Zdzislaw Najder is surely correct when he writes: "I believe that Conrad opposed the emphasis on erotic themes in literature because he was convinced that it would overshadow more vital and serious problems. Among the subjects that concerned him most—responsibility, sense of duty, guilt, justice, freedom, honor, solidarity, anarchy, order—masculine-feminine affairs were not in the forefront."

Conrad was, in brief, after larger game. He sought to comprehend humankind in all its grandeur, pathos, enigmas, contradictions, and irreconcilable qualities. While sticking strictly to the particular—the true realm of fiction—he sought the highest generality. The kind of human mystery that engaged Conrad's interest as a novelist is formulated in the following, from a letter to a friend: "Egoism, which is the moving force of the world, and altruism, which is its morality, these two contradictory instincts, of which one is so plain and the other so mysterious, cannot serve us unless in the incomprehensible alliance of their irreconcilable antagonism."

An interest in the larger questions is also useful in being one sure way of escaping the entrapments of personality. "When once the truth is grasped that one's own personality is only a ridiculous and aimless masquerading of something hopelessly unknown," Conrad wrote to Edward Garnett, "the attainment of serenity is not far off." Conrad would not himself ever attain much in the way of serenity, but his wanting to escape personality is reminiscent of nothing so much as T. S. Eliot, in "Tradition and the Individual Talent," remarking that poetry—and by extension all art—"is not the expression of personality, but an escape from personality. But, of course, only those who have personality and emotions know what it means to want to escape from these things."

Joseph Conrad was among those who knew. Through the publication of letters and of much biographical study, it has become evident that Conrad was what we should nowadays call a depressive. Conrad's own statement of the case for personality, handsomely stated to his friend Marguerite Poradowska, is itself put with the dark force of the depressive: "We must drag the chain and ball of our personality to the end. This is the price one pays for the infernal and divine privilege of thought; so in this life it is only the chosen who are convicts—a glorious band which understands and groans but which treads the earth amidst a multitude of phantoms with maniacal gestures and idiotic grimaces. Which would you rather be: idiot or convict?"

Conrad's view of his own writing, set out in letters to friends, publishers, and his agent (J. B. Pinker), is that of a man serving a life sentence—sentenced to the endless making of sentences. His complaints about the difficulty of composition make Flaubert's seem as cheerful as a Doris Day song. In 1894, in a letter to Marguerite Poradowska, he writes: "I am completely stuck. I have not written a single word for a fortnight. It's all over, I think. I feel like burning what there is. It is very bad! Worse than bad." And, to the same correspondent: "I work a little. I agonize, pen in hand. Six lines in six days." To Cunninghame Graham he wrote: "I am like a tight-rope dancer who, in the midst of his performance, should suddenly discover that he knows nothing about tight-rope dancing. He may appear ridiculous to the spectators, but a broken neck is the result of such untimely wisdom." But then most of his comments about his writing are of this tenor, ending with his comment, near the close of his life, to Jacob Epstein, who was doing his bust, that he, Conrad, "was finished." "I am played out," Epstein remembers him saying, "played out."

His own past achievements seemed to offer Conrad scarcely any solace at all. Mentally, he allowed himself no time off for work well done; there was only the torture of books still to do, prose perpetually owed to magazines and agents. "I do not dream of making a fortune," he wrote to a childhood friend in Poland, "and anyway it is not something to be found in an ink-well. However, I must confess that I dream of peace, of a little recognition and of devoting to Art the rest of a life that would free me from financial worry."

All this might have been easier had Conrad not been so wreckless with money. As a born aristocrat, he felt that he must live, even in his adopted country of England, in the expansive manner of the aristocracy, which meant living in too large houses, driving too large cars, and racking up too large bills. "I can't exist very long in this penury," runs a fairly standard Conradian *cri de poche,* "I've got some small liabilities to attend to. . . . And besides. . . ." Besides, besides, besides—there was always a besides: his wife's poor health, his children's school bills, his need to find a better place to write.

Great difficulties with writing and genuine ineptitude with finances do not generally guarantee a jolly outlook. But Conrad would probably have been depressed even without these serious barriers to contentment. The commercial success that came with his novel *Chance* (1913) did not much lessen it. His depression was not merely a habitual gloominess or a variant of the blues. It came closer to lapsing into insanity. To his agent, Pinker, he writes: "Really all these anxieties do drive me to the verge of madness—but death would be the best thing." To a friend he writes: "I must go through these depressing periods; there is no cure for them apparently"; and to another friend he adds: "Half the time I feel on the verge of insanity." To John Galsworthy, he writes: "I am trying to put off this horrid dread of the future which oppresses me. I am dispirited by that feeling of mental exhaustion of which I cannot get rid at all now. I have learned to write *against* it—that's all." Such sentences play like a threnody through Conrad's lengthy correspondence. They make one feel sorry for him. But they also make his achievement seem all the greater.

At the same time, they endanger this achievement by suggesting that the dark vision at the heart of Conrad's fiction is the result of something akin to mental illness. His art could be easily written off as so much solipsism—the egocentric projections of an all but certified depressive. Conrad himself despised such easy biographical criticism, especially of a psychologizing kind. When Edward Garnett, a Russophile and a great friend of the Soviet Union, attributed the strong distaste for Russia shown in *The Secret Agent* to Conrad's being a Pole, Conrad retorted by asking, "Is my earnestness of no account? Is that a Slavonic trait?"

Conrad reserved to himself the right granted the most serious of artists to announce a plague on both your houses when he felt that neither side in a political conflict was the right side—and the right side was that of human solidarity. Thus, in his Author's Note to *Under Western Eyes* (1911), a book which anticipates the Russian Revolution of 1917, Conrad wrote:

> The ferocity and imbecility of an autocratic rule rejecting all
> legality and in fact basing itself upon complete moral anar-

chism provokes the no less imbecile and atrocious answer of a purely Utopian revolutionism encompassing destruction by the first means to hand, in the strange conviction that a fundamental change of hearts must follow the downfall of any given human institutions. These people are unable to see that all they can effect is merely a change of names.

In a contemporary spirit of proving that the great writers of the past were less great-souled than academic critics of the present, Conrad has in recent years been taken as a racist who was on the side of imperialism for "Heart of Darkness" and as a reactionary for *The Secret Agent* and *Under Western Eyes.* Conrad in fact detested Belgian imperialism in central Africa for its selfishness, its brutishness, its extracting everything and leaving nothing behind but destruction and bloodshed. (As *Nostromo* demonstrates, he was no happier with American business intervention in Latin America.) He was, moreover, fully cognizant of and always made plain in his writings the foolish role that unwarranted white superiority played in distant native cultures. Kurtz's final utterance, "the horror, the horror," is precisely about how little separates supposedly civilized man from savagery when the bounds of civilization are transgressed.

For maintaining his views Conrad has been taken, variously, as a pessimist, a moral nihilist, an inept artist, a right-wing reactionary. What he was, as all great writers are, was on the side of civilization. Having lived as he did—practically born into exile, orphaned by politics, exposed to danger at sea and viciousness in strange lands, under siege his lifelong by an unrelenting depression—Conrad had a clearer view than most of the tenuousness of civilization. And yet, he felt, "some kind of belief is very necessary." His own kind of belief was complex, qualified, but nonetheless genuine. "To be hopeful in an artistic sense," Conrad wrote, "it is not necessary to think that the world is good. It is enough to believe that there is no impossibility of its being made so."

But this doesn't mean that the artist has for a moment to believe we are close to realizing the possibility. Despite his own need for belief, his own deeply reserved but quite real hope for a different and better world, Conrad took it as his task as a novelist to show the many ways in which men and women, through their moral blindness—through conceit and vanity, selfishness and false ambition—make life harder for themselves and even for those they all too ineptly love. Yet he must have harbored a clear view of human goodness, for how else could he have so intricately known, and so potently portrayed, the manifold ways it could be betrayed? Joseph Conrad's own career is itself a stellar example of fidelity: to our moral heritage, to the perhaps impossible but nonetheless necessary ideal of civilization, to the fundamental truths we all know and choose to forget and about which he, as a great artist, determined against staggering odds to spend his life reminding us.

The Man Who Wrote Too Much

Milan Kundera, the Czech novelist, has spoken of fiction as a great European invention for the discovery of truth. But what kinds of truth can fiction be said to discover? And how does it go about making such discoveries? These large, not to say bulky, questions are at the heart of Robert Musil's *The Man Without Qualities,* a vast work whose first sections began to appear in Germany in the early 1930's and which has now been newly translated into English in a handsome edition that includes many of the author's notes.

The Man Without Qualities has frequently been linked with *Ulysses* and *Remembrance of Things Past* as one of the great masterworks of modern literature. But, despite its monumentality—it is nearly 1,800 pages long—and its large cast of characters, it does not otherwise much resemble the novels of either James Joyce or Marcel Proust. Musil's assumptions, psychology, style, aesthetic goals are each distinctly and significantly different—and not only from Joyce and Proust, but from just about every other modern master one is likely to encounter.

"Yop, I botched it," Ezra Pound is reported to have said of his own vastly ambitious poetic work, *The Cantos,* and one may wonder if Robert Musil, who worked on his book for more than twenty years, did not go to his grave feeling similarly. The literary historian Henry Hatfield has called *The Man Without Qualities* "a great book but not a successful work of art." The critic J. P. Stern puts a slightly different spin on the same paradoxical judgment: "To the question whether what [Musil] has written is a great novel there is, I think, only one answer: it is great, but it is not a novel." I myself would say that Musil wrote neither a great work of art nor a great book but is the author of modern literature's most impressive failure, which is itself no small achievement.

The first bald, brutal fact about *The Man Without Qualities* is that it is unfinished. The novel is unfinished not in the way of Schubert's great symphony or of works that require another draft or a final polish, but so substantially unfinished, despite its immense length, that one cannot claim to be certain what its major drift, or direction, or even denouement (if Musil had one in mind) was finally meant to have been.

Some critics have attempted to make a virtue of this deficiency. The novelist and memoirist Elias Canetti once claimed that Musil's novel is endless in two senses: "immortal as well as unfinished." In a review of the new translation in *The New Yorker,* George Steiner has taken this a step further by remarking that "there is something strangely right about the 'interminability' of *The Man Without Qualities*."

Is that so—or did Musil, Pound-like, botch it? Why was he unable to complete his novel? Is it possible that *The Man Without Qualities* is a book that, in a fundamental way, badly misunderstands, and hence sadly misuses, the art of fiction itself?

Born in Austria in 1880, Robert Musil was of that remarkable generation of German-language writers—often referred to as the "Generation of 1905"—who came into their literary maturity in the decade before World War I. Franz Kafka, Hermann Hesse, Thomas Mann, and Hermann Broch were the leading figures in this generation.

Musil's family was, in terms we would recognize today, upper-middle-class academic, of Austrian and part-Czech descent. His father was a professor of mechanical engineering at the Technical Institute at Brno. Of this man, Musil would say that "he believed nothing and offered nothing as a surrogate" for belief. But if, in his father, intellection predominated over feeling, in Musil's mother nearly the reverse obtained: she was a woman of unruly emotions, whom her son once likened to a pretty woman with messy hair. One of her male admirers actually moved into the household when Musil was a boy and remained there for years.

Musil grew up, as David S. Luft, one of his best critics, writes, "in an entirely secular atmosphere, virtually untouched by religion." One of the results of this upbringing was to leave him with a spiritual hunger that neither philosophy nor finally, it appears, literature could satisfy. At eleven, he was sent off to military school, first in Burgenland in eastern Austria, and then in Moravia—the latter school was also attended, and detested, by Rilke—and for a time he planned a career as a professional soldier. At seventeen he dropped this notion to study engineering. From there he went on to philosophy, logic, and experimental psychology.

Although Musil is identified with Vienna—the scene of *The Man Without Qualities*—he came into his intellectual maturity in Berlin. There he cut a minor figure in the salon of Paul Cassirer, the brother of the philosopher Ernst Cassirer. He wrote his dissertation, at the University of Berlin, on the physicist and philosopher Ernst Mach, published scientific papers, and had to his credit the invention of a chromameter (a color wheel for use in optical experiments). He remained dependent on his parents until 1911, when he was past thirty and already married to Martha Macovaldi, a partly Jewish woman, seven years his elder, who had been married twice before and had young children.

Engineering, science, and philosophy all having proved in-adequate, Musil at last settled on literature as a career. There is no evidence that he read widely in fiction, though he is said to have admired Stendhal, no doubt for his coolness and lucidity, and to have disliked Joyce. As a literary intellectual (Luft reports), he much preferred Nietzsche to Wagner, favoring the clarity of the former over the darkness of the latter. In his student years in Berlin, Musil had been swept up by artistic modernism and its ideals, and so he would remain. "Since my youth," he wrote in his diary, "I have looked upon the aesthetic as the ethical."

Although Musil would die broke, thinking himself a neglected writer, his first novel, *Young Törless* (1906), received a generous response. In Berlin, Alfred Kerr, one of the leading critics of the day, called it "a book that will last." Other reviewers lined up to praise it, some as an important generational work. Much later, Erich Kahler would cite the book as one of the first existential texts in modern German literature.

Like a good deal that Musil wrote, *Young Törless* has a strong if not a direct basis in autobiography. The novel is set in a military school, not so different from the one Musil himself attended in Moravia. In it Törless, taken up by two older, aristocratic youths, is maneuvered into helping them bully a younger boy who has been caught stealing from his fellow students. This boy, Basini, is put through hell by the two older boys; in Törless, he arouses both disgust and sexual excitement.

Less an indictment of the cruelty of military schools than a novel about the psychology of adolescence, *Young Törless* is even more a portrait of a rather peculiar artist as a young man. Törless is a premature artist, groping his way: "It's as if I had one extra sense, one more than the others have, but not completely developed, a sense that's there and makes itself noticed, but doesn't function." In the book, Törless attempts to understand his own irrational desires and the no less irrational arrangements that pass for adult behavior. As so often in Musil—as so often in so many writers who worked in the atmosphere of turn-of-the-century Austria-Hungary—sexual excitement jump-starts elaborate mental activity. In this instance, the activity being recorded has to do with how people think, with the bridges between thought and experience, with the intuition of artists, and with the link between the sexual and the artistic impulse.

That is a lot for a slender novel, written by a man of twenty-five, to bear, and one tends to admire the book's intellectual earnestness rather more than one takes pleasure in reading it. Though it shows every sign of an emerging talent, *Young Törless* is also pervaded by an airlessness and the less than enticing feeling of ambiguity that comes from irresolution in art.

As might be expected of one trained in science and philosophy, Musil's fiction was generally set into motion by ideas. Yet there was one distinct body of ideas in the air that he never took at all seriously: psychoanalytic theory. Vladimir Nabokov's characterization of Freudian psychoanalysis as the application of Greek myths to private parts was something with which Musil would have agreed. Psychoanalysis, he wrote, took the individual, confused and stunted, and instructed him that "all he needs is courage and healthy gonads." This was very far indeed from Musil's own notion of either the problem or the solution to the complexities of life in the modern world.

The central problem of modernity was, for Musil, the state of fragmentation in which men and women found themselves. As for the solution, it had to do with somehow bringing the intellect, with its capacity for concentration and precision, into alignment with the soul. "Everything which is currently expressed by the word soul one does not understand with the intellect," Musil lamented, "in the way in which one always understands scientific philosophy with the necessary concentration." In *The Man Without Qualities,* Musil has his hero propose that the Austrian government set up a World Secretariat for Precision and Soul, and *Precision and Soul* is the English title of a volume of Musil's essays.

The word "soul" seems to mean many things in Musil, ranging from one's animal energies and appetites, to one's unconscious, to that which cannot be understood by anyone else, to one's religious essence. Inexact, even irritating, though this may be, what Musil essentially argued is that intellect and soul, mind and spirit, would have to be brought into conjunction if the fragmentation of modern life was ever to be healed, and later he would claim just this as his own artistic program. In an essay entitled "Mind and Experience," Musil noted that "those who wanted to introduce intellect into literature could not think. They couldn't because they thought in airy words whose content lacked any empirical restraint." By finding a way to join art and intellect, he planned to cut through what he saw as the impotence of each.

It would be a hard slog. In the years between the publication of *Young Törless* and World War I, during which he served four years as an officer in the Austrian army, Musil produced two plays and five stories, along with a quantity of drama criticism, essays, and literary criticism. None would give anything like a hint of the vastness of his artistic ambitions, though evidence of his subtlety and depth is unarguably on display in the stories. One of them, "The Lady from Portugal," is a mythic tale about a family of Teutonic barons who select brides from far-off lands. In it, Musil demonstrates his ability to deploy a beautifully paced narrative that enraptures the reader in the customary and timeworn way of fiction. He can do death scenes, he displays descriptive power, he can strike the persuasive philosophical note.

Yet, though it was available to him, Musil seems to have rejected this sort of traditional writing. "What I value in art," says a character in his story, "The Perfecting of a Love," "is the subtlety of the right ending, which consoles us for the humdrum of everyday life." But we are not supposed much to value the views of this character, and Musil himself did not purvey such consolation. With the exception of "Tonka," which retells Musil's own difficult and ultimately hopeless love affair with a woman below his own social class—"How little one knows what one knows," says the narrator, "or wants what one wants"—Musil's stories are chiefly investigations of psychological states. They also foreshadow the core concerns of *The Man Without Qualities:* the loneliness of the solitary mind ("all she knew was that at some point in time something had come between her and life, leaving a barrier"); the paradoxical conditions of emotion ("she knew the wonderful, dangerous intensification of feeling that came with lying and cheating in love"); and what can only be called flirting with God ("She said: 'I have a vague notion of what people might be to each other. . . . What you sometimes call God is like the thing I mean' ").

Musil himself must have grown impatient with the extent of his progress. After World War I, he worked for the Austrian Foreign Ministry as a press secretary of sorts, and following this he was employed as a scientific adviser to the Austrian War Ministry. From 1922 on, he wrote as a free-lance. He apparently traveled nowhere without his wife, who is said to have taken over all the financial and other practical details of their lives. As with just about every Viennese intellectual or artist one has ever heard or read about, Musil suffered no shortage of neuroses (something in the water, or in the ideas, no doubt). He did not handle money; he preferred not to shake hands. He was a heavy smoker who practiced a regular physical workout regimen.

Elias Canetti reports that Musil had no small talk: in the best scientific manner, he felt that a conversation "should start from something precise and aim at something precise." Canetti adds:

For devious ways he felt contempt and hatred. But he did not aim at simplicity; he had an unerring instinct for the inadequacy of the simple and was capable of shattering it with a detailed portrait. His mind was too richly endowed, too active and acute to content itself with simplicity.

Such a man, such a mind, found what might have seemed its perfect project, its ideal objective correlative, in the vast novel that was to be *The Man Without Qualities*. A study of Viennese society, an analysis of the malaise of modern man, an attempt to penetrate the wellsprings of human nature—it was as if Musil had been in training all his early life for writing this novel. He set to work on it not long after the end of the war, and essentially labored on it for the remainder of his days. In the end, the novel defeated him, not only aesthetically but in other ways as well.

In a foreword to an earlier English edition of the first volume of *The Man Without Qualities* (1952), Eithne Wilkins and Ernst Kaiser, its translators, recount the sad publishing history of Musil's would-be masterwork. In Europe the first volume appeared in 1931, during the Depression; still, it sold 8,000 copies and was a *succès d'estime*. Publication of the second volume was badly timed, coinciding with the rise to power of the Nazis. Musil did not permit the third volume to come out, withdrawing the first twenty chapters when they were already in galley proof. Whenever and wherever he traveled, three suitcases went with him, containing the manuscript and notes for later chapters. Talk about a stone around one's neck.

With no money coming in, Musil was forced to rely on the patronage of friends of literature who formed a Musil Society; its members, chiefly professionals and businessmen, made quarterly payments to help support him, though not in very grand style. As most members of the society were Jews, Hitler's racial policies had the additional effect of putting an end to Musil's financial backing. In 1938, he emigrated to Switzerland, where he continued to add to his out-of-control book until the very morning in 1942 when, after a good session at the writing table in his garden in Geneva, he died. The expression on his face is said to have been a mixture of mockery and astonishment—in some ways the perfect death mask for a novelist. Eight people, reportedly, attended his funeral.

Always treat a work of art like a prince, an old proverb has it—that is, let it speak to you first. I take this to mean that it is best to confront a work of art directly, without any introductions, critical aids, or the rest of the contemporary apparatus of literary understanding. But in the case of *The Man Without Qualities* the trouble is that the work's reputation as a modern classic precedes it, and this reputation has only been further burnished by the enthusiastic critical reception accorded the new English version. So impressive have been some of the essays occasioned by its appearance that one wonders, in fact, whether Robert Musil may not be one of those writers—Walter Benjamin, Roland Barthes, Elias Canetti—who are rather more interesting to read about than actually to read.

Of the two possible ways of reading *The Man Without Qualities,* the first and perhaps more sympathetic is to recognize its brilliance, be grateful that we have what we do of it, explain away its weaknesses where possible, and let it go at that. The second, which I propose, is to attempt to fathom why Musil could not finish this, his life's work, the book he seems to have been born to write yet did not come anywhere near close to completing. What is even sadder, there is good reason to believe that had he lived another twenty years, he still would not have been able to finish the monster to which he had given birth.

The Man Without Qualities begins in August 1913, one year before Europe will be drawn into war. Its protagonist, Ulrich (his last name is never given), a man of thirty-two, a former military officer, a mathematician of some power, a man attractive to women, and, most pertinently, the possessor of a philosophical temperament matched perhaps only by his detachment, has decided to take a year off, in effect a "vacation from life," to get his bearings. But the city he chooses for this purpose, Vienna, is not the perfect place, for of all cities in Europe at the time it might well be the most uncentered, unhinged, unreal. (The satirist Kark Kraus was able to keep his magazine, *Die Fackel,* afloat chiefly by attacking the madhouse quality of Viennese intellectual life, and he never ran out of material.)

The ostensible premise of *The Man Without Qualities* is built on a socio-political swamp. The swamp is the notion, held by many of the novel's chief characters, that life in Austria, with its empire and emperor, will go on, pretty much business-as-usual. We know, of course, that only a year later in historical time, in August 1914, Franz Ferdinand, the Archduke and presumptive heir to the throne of Franz Joseph, will be assassinated, an event that will set off World War I, and by that war's end the Austro-Hungarian empire will be finished, the monarchy replaced by a republic, the class system and intricate European balance of power done for. But in 1913, the scene and setting of Musil's novel, everyone, though perhaps a little nervous in the service, is still playing let's pretend, assuming the best, *mit schlag.*

In this atmosphere, a rich muddle characterized by only a slight apprehension of decline but no genuine belief in a fall, the intellectually ruthless Ulrich attempts to find a way. But a way toward what? Early in the first volume, Ulrich is mugged on the streets of Vienna, and the next morning his mind turns to the complexities of a society in which the violent and the civilized live side by side. "It is the old story of the contradictions, the inconsistency, and the imperfections of life," writes Musil. But Ulrich himself has no tolerance for contradictions and inconsistencies; instead, he feels the need to work through them to discover explanations, solutions, answers.

As we soon learn, however, that is almost the only need

he does feel. For along with his desire to get to the bottom of everything, Ulrich coolly distances himself from what the rest of the world is pleased to call reality. He cannot, Musil tells us, summon up "a sense of reality even in relation to himself." From this it follows that nothing is understood by him as stable, everything is open to question, standard motives for human conduct are viewed comically, and the world is seen as through a series of funhouse mirrors. Ulrich, in short, is of the type of the intellectual, but the intellectual taken to the highest power: unaffiliated, utterly skeptical, without any loyalties except to those ideas that hold up under the deepest scrutiny—of which, one must immediately add, none does.

From Dostoevsky's *Notes from the Underground* through Kundera's *The Unbearable Lightness of Being,* the socially detached, spiritually deracinated intellectual has been a recurring type in literature and in life. As a secondary character in Musil's novel says of Ulrich: "There are millions of them nowadays. It's the human type produced by our time." This chapter also nicely nails the instability of vision of our man without qualities:

> When he is angry, something in him laughs. When he is sad, he is up to something. When something moves him, he turns against it. He'll always see a good side to every bad action. What he thinks of anything will always depend on some possible context—nothing is, to him, what it is; everything is subject to change, in flux, part of a whole, of an infinite number of wholes presumably adding up to a super-whole that, however, he knows nothing about.

This man without qualities, this pure type of the intellectual, would be really quite hopeless if he were not so clever and entertaining. And Musil, speaking through Ulrich, can be spectacularly clever and delightfully entertaining. On such subjects as the democratization of genius—so that one speaks, these days, of an advertising or a basketball genius, or even the genius of a racehorse; or the strange way in which presumably new cultural eras arrive (so that "finally one has no way of knowing whether the world has really grown worse, or oneself merely older"); or the phenomenon of those who practice "the profession of being the next generation," Ulrich/Musil is dazzling. Reading the first hundred or so pages of *The Man Without Qualities,* watching Musil set up the furniture for all that is to follow, one cannot mistake that one is in the presence of a superior mind and a major talent. One also senses that Musil himself is writing more expansively than ever before. Wit, till now not in strong evidence in his fiction, gets free play. His lens has widened; windows have been opened. The only question, again, is to what end it will all conduce.

Initially, one is led to believe that the end is satire—lovely, devastating, utterly destructive satire. Clearly, satire seems intended when Ulrich meets a cousin, a woman of whom he is enamored and to whom he gives the classical name Diotima. It is she who arranges for him to become secretary to something called the Committee for the Parallel Campaign. This has been organized for the purpose of celebrating, five years hence, the seventieth anniversary of the rule of Franz Joseph, and the reason the committee's project is "parallel" is that it is in a natural rivalry with the German campaign to celebrate the thirtieth anniversary of the rule of Kaiser Wilhelm II.

The Parallel Campaign is itself sheer PR, but the people organizing it have not yet reached the stage of cynicism that successful public relations requires; in other words, they half-believe their own nonsense. The campaign thus functions as a brilliant device, allowing Musil (by way of Ulrich) to view Viennese society through the complex prism of its various social classes, institutions, and characteristic types, the list of which includes aristocrats, young radicals, businessmen, Jews, false poets, military men, social climbers, and the rest.

And not Viennese society alone. Our man without qualities views, with proper ironic detachment, the last days of the Austro-Hungarian empire, the *state* without qualities. This was a state, as the historian Lewis Namier once put it, that "did not exist except in reminiscences of the past and pious hopes for the future," and that "displayed more frontier and less coherence than any other state in Europe." With its smug aristocrats, its middle classes encased in a "corset of culture," its pretensions to military power, it has, in the pages of this novel, doom written all over it. Glut and confusion rule the day; integrity in such circumstances is not so much impossible as beside the point. "There's no longer a whole man confronting a whole world," says Ulrich, "only a human something moving about in a general culture-medium."

In this "general culture-medium," the hardest question is the question of reality: what is it, where is it, who claims to have grasped it, does it truly exist? As it turns out, anyone who feels he has the answers to these questions is in for the greatest mockery of all. The true fools are those who think they know something.

Perhaps the greatest fool of all is one of the novel's most interesting characters: Paul Arnheim, a German-Jewish industrialist of philosophical bent whom Musil is said to have modeled on Walter Rathenau, the Foreign Minister in the Weimar Republic who was assassinated in Berlin in 1922. In the novel, Arnheim joins the Parallel Campaign to give it a more international flavor, and also becomes a competitor of sorts with Ulrich for Diotima's affections. Apart from sexual rivalrousness, what Ulrich despises about Arnheim is his certainty about how the world is not only meant to be but actually works. Arnheim is a global explainer who always finds time to look after his own business first.

Alas, because of the unfinished state of *The Man Without Qualities,* Arnheim, a delicious character, drops out, as do many other characters, subplots, and promising threads. Most frustrating in its inconclusiveness is the story of another central character, a mad sex murderer named Christian Moosbrugger. Ulrich and others are obsessed with the case of Moosbrugger, who figures alternately for them as a martyr, a monster, and someone in whom the civilized and the rational can indulge their fascination with the barbaric and the irrational. One character—herself quite mad—describes Moosbrugger as "Nietzsche in the shape of a sinner." But as to what, precisely, Musil himself meant Moosbrugger to signify, this remains a mystery. As Burton Pike, the editorial consultant to the new English version, puts it, he "is so ambiguously presented that any clearly symbolic interpretation of his character is impossible."

This, unfortunately, could be said of numerous aspects of *The Man Without Qualities.* Many promises, in the literary sense which Chekhov intended when he said that a shotgun placed over the mantel in the first act of a play ought to be fired by the third, are made yet not really kept in this sprawling work. *The Man Without Qualities* is a novel filled with brilliant scenes, patches, observations, and aphorisms, usually bitter: "That one is not loved as one deserves is the sorrow of all old maids of both sexes." "When the father is poor the sons love money; when Papa has money, the sons love mankind." "Isn't it strange that almost every single person knows himself least of all and loves himself most of all?" And, a thought to prevent one from falling asleep at night: "This freedom of will is man's ability to do voluntarily what he wishes involuntarily."

Musil's penchant for the aphorism is related to his admiration for the essay. Time and again he stops his novel for diverse reflections of a kind more natural to that form, though generally without its successful sense of a safe landing. The novel even contains a brief essay *on* the essay, where the reader is told that it is "the unique and unalterable form assumed by a man's inner life in decisive thought." Of Musil's essayism, Pike rightly notes: "I would say that it generally arises from a feeling on the part of the author . . . that a fictional vehicle is an inadequate means of presenting all that he is trying to say."

The English critic V. S. Pritchett has defended *The Man Without Qualities* by saying that in it "the habit of intellectual analysis is not stultifying to drama, movement, or invention, but enhances them"—but Pritchett was writing before the publication of this, the more complete edition. It is true that early in the novel, the essayistic element is fairly well integrated with the story. In the new material, however, essayism looms larger, all but takes over, so that at the close of yet another discourse on, say, the precise definition of emotion, one feels almost as if the story were an interruption and that one ought really to be getting back to yet another longueur.

The reason the essayistic element begins to take over is that Musil has begun to lose control of his novel and to steer it in an entirely new direction—on "a journey of no return," as J. P. Stern has observed. In the third part, he in fact all but abandons his account of the Parallel Campaign, with its many interesting characters and possibilities, and begins to tell a love story, although one which also never comes to anything like true fruition. It is a story of incest, of Ulrich and his sister Agathe's love for each other; it is, if one has a taste for the mythical, also the story of Isis, the deity of ancient Egypt, and her husband Osiris; it is a story of hermaphroditic completeness; and it is, in a sense no novelist would wish to hear pronounced about his work, quite incredible.

When Musil takes up this story line, he shifts from analysis of reality to the search, through mysticism, for a higher plane of morality, a second state of being, a new union between the world and the self. This search ends in muddle, boredom, and emptiness. Very late in the novel, Musil writes:

> The blows of confused and anarchic ideas that Ulrich received every day, and the movement of these thoughts in an imprudent but clearly palpable direction, had in fact gradually swept him up, and the only thing that still differentiated his life from that of the insane was a consciousness of his situation, which he could interrupt by an effort.

As so often, Musil appears to be speaking here quite as much about himself and his intractable novel as about his protagonist. Poor Musil, he must have sensed that his readers would not be similarly "swept up" by the ideas he had given to Ulrich to discover; nor would they, even by an effort, be able to sustain interest in a by now all but interminable novel, if novel it could any longer be called.

Musil's own dubiety about his project seems to have grown greater with time. A note printed toward the end of this edition reads: "Does greatness never lie in content? In a way of ordering things?" Another, a self-invocation, reads: "Dramatize! Make all this present!" Endlessly revising, turning out countless drafts, withdrawing sections at the last moment before print, rethinking, reworking, devising divergences in plot, coming up with different endings—all that brilliance, all that literary talent, all for nearly nothing.

In a very sensible chapter on Musil in *The Dear Purchase,* his study of modern German literature, J. P. Stern writes: "With Musil, the tug-of-war between philosophical ambition and literary gifts is never resolved; on the contrary, it is exacerbated by his passionate conviction that 'the only function of a writer is to produce a masterpiece.' " Thomas Mann and Marcel Proust, among modern novelists, were able to get the literary and the philosophical in the right balance. But Musil, more the trained philosopher than either, could not.

The literary problem that is at the center of *The Man Without Qualities* was touched upon by Musil himself—before he began writing his novel—in an essay entitled "Sketch of What the Writer Knows" (1918). There, he set up two realms—they are not quite methods—of thinking, which he gave the inelegant names of "ratoid" and "nonratoid." The former mode works from cause to effect, with proven facts, toward the creation of rules, laws, and concepts. The thinking of the scientist, psychologist, philosopher is ratoid. By contrast, Musil goes on, "if the ratoid is the domination of the 'rule with exceptions,' the nonratoid area is that of the dominance of the exceptions over the rule."

The imaginative writer is the nonratoid thinker *par excellence,* concerned with values and valuations, ethics and aesthetic relationships. He steps in where "facts do not submit, laws are sieves, events do not repeat themselves but are infinitely variable and individual." Writers do not build systems, create concepts, shore up laws; when they are at their best they demonstrate how, in some of the most interesting cases, none of these quite applies. "Create a concept," said Ortega y Gasset, "and reality leaves the room." The job of the imaginative writer is sometimes to smash the concept and bring reality back into the room.

Musil knew all this, of course. He must have sensed, in writing the first two parts of his novel, that the philosophical skepticism behind his satire could only take him so far. So in the second half of his novel he decided to go farther—as it turned out, however, much too far. Attempting to reinstate a myth, to found a morality, to build a utopia, if only for two people caught up in an incestuous love, Musil worked at everything but telling his story, whose thread he had irrevocably lost.

In the end, perhaps, it was his hunger for precision, for the kind of truth which philosophy but not fiction can provide, that snuffed the literary flame in Robert Musil. He remained too much the true writer not to know that he had failed—failed grandly, failed heroically, but in the end failed indubitably. Fiction cannot create morality; it can only show what morality is about. Nor is it properly in the business of limning utopias, or endorsing myths. This, to his sorrow, the author of *The Man Without Qualities* came to learn. "The story of this novel," Musil wrote in a note, "amounts to this, that the story that ought to be told is not told." Case, sadly, closed.

Bye-Bye, Bunny

Although I never met Edmund Wilson, he was the literary equivalent of my Father Flanagan, a role he performed, I long ago discovered, for a number of other literary young men who felt orphaned from literature by the study of it in universities. Such at any rate was my experience at the University of Chicago in the middle fifties, where literature was put through the grinder of Aristotle, which did not seem to me to grind exceedingly fine, and where in a bookshop on 57th Street I one day found an Anchor paperback by Edmund Wilson carrying the title, I believe, of *The All-Star Literary Vaudeville*. This was an anthology of Wilson's pieces taken from his literary chronicles published up to that time. I read it and was, instanter, swept away. This, I felt, was how a literary man ought to write: with solid style, a commanding tone, a virile professionalism. (That Wilson was F. Scott Fitzgerald's friend at Princeton, earlier his literary conscience and later his literary executor, added to his allure.) Metropolitan and worldly, there was nothing academic about Wilson, nothing pedantic or precious.

Nothing, truth to tell, very chummy, either. Quite the reverse of the writer Salinger mentions in *The Catcher in the Rye* whom one wants to call up on the telephone after reading him,

Edmund Wilson, on the page, gave off a shudder of formality. A cold number, Wilson, nothing light or breezy about him, or so his writing led one to believe. "If I now play at being old," he wrote in *The Sixties,* the last of the six volumes of his published journals, "I never played at being young." Wilson is one of those writers who seemed to come into the world fully formed—he was very smart very young, which is an immense advantage—but who, owing to this, show little in the way of development.

Physically, Edmund Wilson was no great beauty. In his young manhood he looked rather like a disagreeable Herbert Hoover pictured in a squattening fun-house mirror; in middle-age, like a redneck Southern sheriff; and ended like a pretty fair stand-in for Sydney Greenstreet. He looked, certainly, not at all like the nickname Bunny, given to him in childhood and for which he never cared. Karl Shapiro used to refer to Wilson as "the Bunny," adding a definite article that comically points up the utter inappropriateness of this cuddly nickname for this most formidable and uncuddly of men.

Long before his death in 1972 at the age of seventy-seven, Edmund Wilson was everywhere referred to as America's last great man of letters. Reviewers would cite his having written criticism, history, journalism, fiction, poetry, plays, and much else; they would blather on about his being in the tradition of Sainte-Beuve, Taine, and Saintsbury. All true enough, if a trifle stale. (Wilson himself complained about a man named Chanler Chapman always comparing him to Dr. Johnson.) Honorific though it may be, the label of man of letters is also one that brings with it a strong aroma of the old-fashioned, even the distinctly out of it. Wilson may have been old-fashioned, but, as his journals show, he struggled manfully right up to the end not to be out of it.

As a writer, Wilson was known less for any discrete work than for an impressive body of work. He produced more than thirty books. A man with sufficient reputation and force of character to dictate to his publisher the size and shape of his books, Wilson was able to have almost all his books made on the model of the *Pléiade* editions, short and stout, rather like himself. People differ about which are the best of Wilson's books, agreeing only that his fiction was stillborn. Of all Wilson's books, the ones I most admire are his chronicles of criticism, *Shores of Light, Classics and Commercials, The Bit Between My Teeth,* and those others in which he gathered together his magazine pieces, and *Patriotic Gore,* his really quite majestic book on the literature of the American Civil War. But there were few books—even essays—of his from which I, for one, didn't feel I had learned something I did not know before. As a critic, Wilson was the great maitre d' of literature in the twentieth century, always showing one to a good table on which rich literary provender was piled.

Wilson had his famous blind spots: he was a Hispanophobe, he had no taste for German literature, he failed to grasp the profundity in Conrad, and the excitement about Kafka was a mystery to him. Still, he wrote well about a vast number of wide-ranging subjects, and ended with a large and cohering body of work, a genuine *oeuvre,* one of the few American writers about whom this could be said. One of the rare entries in *The Sixties* that expresses contentment comes in Wilson's seventies, when he writes: "I might as well settle down to the kind of satisfaction I can have: little worry about money, comfort in sitting around reading and playing the phonograph, having books and letters sent to me, enjoying a reputation and no great pressure to produce." Yet this turns out to be cold comfort, for in the very next entry we find our last great American man of letters, trousers round his ankles, on the can, where "I read the folders of old reviews of my books, in order to support my morale—though this only makes me realize again how slipshod most reviewing is." Nothing quite takes the joy out of life like having standards.

As a young man, Wilson was told by Christian Gauss, his teacher at Princeton, that he ought to write a *confession d'un en-*

fant du siècle. Wilson responded by saying that "that kind of thing is really repugnant to me, and I expect to become more and more objective instead of more and more personal." Aspiring to the objective is certainly how Wilson began his career. Authority, that indispensable and yet unteachable quality of the critic, seemed to come easily to Wilson, who put the case plainly enough: "The implied position of the people who know about literature (as is also the case in every other art) is simply that they know what they know, and that they are determined to impose their opinions by main force of eloquence or assertion on the people who do not know."

"The shy little scholar of Holden Court," as Fitzgerald described Wilson at Princeton, soon became the critical equivalent of a traffic cop, as Maxwell Bodenheim once called him, directing the flow of literary reputations in the 1920's from his perch as literary editor of *The New Republic*. In his autobiography, T. S. Matthews has described how Wilson aimed him, Matthews, then his underling on the magazine, by instructing him about whose reputations deserved inflation and whose deflation through reviews Wilson assigned him. Less interested in making friends than in influencing people, Wilson early acquired a full share of enemies. Hart Crane disliked Wilson's propensity to "hatch little squibs of advice to poets not to be so professional." One of those poets, E. E. Cummings, whom Wilson lectured to in print and in a letter cited as "that young man [who] is very half-baked and needs correction rather than encouragement," struck back by calling Wilson "the man in the iron necktie."

"The man in the iron necktie" once seemed a bang-on perfect description of Edmund Wilson, but no longer. The publication of Wilson's journals has changed that. Changed it for better or worse is unclear, but that it is changed is beyond dispute. The same young Wilson who despised the personal has been laid out for the public gaze in a way that one might think he would have hated, except that it has been done through his own choosing. Wilson not only chose to publish his journals, which he had begun to do in his lifetime, but left instructions to continue their publication after his death.

Upstate, the first of the Wilson journal volumes to be published, gave only an inkling of what was to follow. That book showed Wilson camping out during steaming summers in the large stone house in Talcottville, New York, that was left him by his mother. Chiefly a chronicle of complaint, it puts on display an Edmund Wilson rolling round the old stone house, both structure and occupant in considerable disrepair. From this volume, one learned about Wilson's loneliness, his many illnesses, something of his serious drinking, his strong feeling of being thoroughly out of sympathy with the new and (to him) displeasing era in which he found himself. Working away on his various literary projects in the morning, sitting on the porch of the Talcottville house with a shotgun on his lap while juvenile delinquents roared past on motorcycles, drunk and with broken bridgework, such were among the tableaux Wilson left of the man of letters in old age.

From the evidence of *Upstate* one could perhaps understand the dark views set out in Wilson's introduction to *Patriotic Gore,* where the conduct of men and nations is likened to schools of fish, clouds of grasshoppers, voracious sea slugs, and compared unfavorably to the anthropoid gorilla. Wilson was during these years a man in trouble with the Internal Revenue Service and in wretched health, to whom the world seemed to conspire to displease him. In *Upstate,* Wilson seemed to be recapitulating the life of a less refined Henry Adams, ending his days in petulance and literary crankishness.

The publication of the subsequent volumes of journals altered the picture dramatically. We learn in *Upstate,* for example, that Wilson needs dental help. In *The Sixties,* we learn that he is also eager to bed down his dentist's wife—and is only slightly though not finally restrained from doing so by the prospect of losing the services of a good dentist. What the publication of the journals has done, certainly in this final volume, is exhibit Edmund Wilson as a sex-crazed old coot. All the Wilson journal volumes have been sex-ridden, but *The Sixties* demonstrates the sad if rather obvious truth that the last stage of sex, for those who do not know when to leave the field, is degradation. In this book Wilson becomes the least dignified of sexual clowns—the old goat.

Philip Larkin, another journal-keeper, left an order for one of his literary executors, his long-time friend and lover Monica Jones, to shred his thirty volumes of journals, which Miss Jones—luckily for Larkin, no Max Brod she—did straight-away after his death. Larkin's biographer, Andrew Motion, con-jectures that, among other things, these volumes may have contained "a sexual log book full of masturbatory fantasies." If so, much better not to know about them, I say, so, Emily, please send a dozen long-stem roses and a note of appreciation to the faithful Miss Jones.

No such luck for Wilson, the sexual material in whose journals has nothing to do with fantasy but is, alas, entirely fac-tual. In one of the earlier journal volumes Wilson makes ref-erence to his "large pink prong"—one of the few of Wilson's phrases that refuse to depart the mind—and he never hesitates to record that member's escapades, including those with his fourth wife, Elena, who is the dominant female personage in *The Fifties* and *The Sixties*. "When I came back from my walk, Elena had opened her eyes, and we made love in the sand. . . . Divine—I had had (the new and better kind of white wine) just enough to drink—no anesthetising of sensation in the last mo-ments for me, as I felt myself driving the charge home." In one of the earlier journals—*The Twenties,* I believe—Wilson, record-ing himself in action, notes that "I addressed myself to her bloomers." Now, in *The Sixties,* in the sack with his dentist's wife, "I invited her to do fellatio." (Let us hope this was not the best invitation the poor woman had had that week). Anti-aphrodisiacal, sounding in his no-nonsense approach to sex like no one so much as Frank Harris, Wilson's writing on sex could give an alley cat the droops on a warm Saturday night.

Perhaps this is the place to put Elena Wilson's name in posthumous nomination for an award I have long wished Alfred Nobel had left money to institute: the Nobel Prize for Marriage. Along with such figures as Sonya Tolstoy and Anna Dostoyevsky, Leonard Woolf and Lionel Trilling, Elena Wilson qualifies among those husbands and wives of writers who have taken a lot, in sickness and in health, in life and even after death, from troublesome, thoughtless, and often embarrassing mates. Putting up with the Bunny's social antics—one night in a fit he threw an ashtray at Jason Epstein, he never seemed to have any compunction about disparaging people to their faces, he was a man who always demanded his own way—not to mention his amorous Bunny hugs, could not have been what, in the U.S. Army, used to be called light duty. Elena Wilson also edited, with tact and good sense, her husband's letters after his death. Nobel Prize for Marriage material, Mrs. Wilson—no question about it.

In *The Sixties,* Wilson is still bonking away at Elena—and still recording it in his journal. Despite occasional bouts of angina—thoughts of heart attack in the midst of sex can scarcely be encouraging—he keeps at it nonetheless. One salutes him for diligence, but why, one has to ask, does he feel the need to record sex with his wife in his journal? The best conclusion I can come up with is that Edmund Wilson was the true type of the graphomaniac. Some graphomaniacs are defined by their need to be writing always. But to the true, the deep, the incurable graphomaniac nothing has really happened, nothing is quite real—not even, apparently, sex with one's wife—until one has written it out.

Nothing was alive to Wilson, one suspects, except words, which were everything to him. In *The Forties,* he could write of Gogol's "nutritious long paragraphs that flow thickly, like jam poured into a jar, or are stirred round like dough in a bowl."

Writing out his sexual congress with his wife, to use good stiff Wilson-like language, is one thing, publishing it for the world to read quite another. In an age such as ours, high marks can no longer be given for candor; and true nonconformity, nowadays, would seem to reside with reticence. Wilson is, I think, paying the price for his decision by becoming something like a sexual laughingstock. Certainly, the reviews of *The Sixties* tended to concentrate on what one can only describe as Edmund Wilson's sexual low jinks: scoring in the Princeton Club in his seventies, mounting the old bed in his Talcottville house in BVD's and his "uncomfortably bristling double garters" with his dentist's wife.

A shame, really, for there is much in this, Wilson's final journal, that makes him immensely attractive—more attractive than he had hitherto seemed. In *The Forties,* Wilson records, apropos of his visit to Santayana in the Hospital of the Blue Nuns in Rome, that "the writer, when he ages, is in a better situation than the practitioner of some kind of work which requires more physical exertion: he only has to sit and write, and he finds that he now knows his business better and is in full command of his forces. I have been feeling something of this as I have been coming closer to fifty." Much to this, I suppose, but within fairly severe limits. One of these limits is health, and the breakdown thereof, of which *The Sixties* is sadly replete with details. In the last decade of his life Wilson suffered from heart trouble, gout (developing into rheumatoid arthritis), auditory hallucinations, dental difficulties, shingles, an enlarged liver, and deafness; add to this his impressive drinking, his worries about his children, his problems with the IRS (he had failed to pay his taxes for years)—and put them all together they do not spell golden pond.

"Growing old," wrote Anthony Powell in *Temporary Kings,* "is like being increasingly penalized for a crime you haven't committed." In *The Sixties,* Wilson teeters toward and then away from this view. He writes that "I no longer have my old curiosity, sympathetic or antipathetic emotions. Since I'll soon be fading out of it, why bother to read books, meet people, travel to foreign countries. . . . All of my delightful adventures are now in the past. I sometimes enjoy remembering them, but even that is losing its attraction." Yet when his friend the Harvard classicist Arthur Nock dies, after lamenting the transitoriness even of true scholarship, and that all that his friend Nock had stored in his mind is now gone, Wilson takes courage, noting that "though I suffer from various ailments, I am not yet so badly off as he was and may yet accomplish something." One of the advantages of being an atheist, as Wilson was, is that one is never without hope for personal if not for ultimate salvation.

A feeling of loneliness broods over these journals. Although Wilson had a regular social round—in Manhattan, in Wellfleet, in Talcottville—he nonetheless seems oddly friendless. Perhaps this had much to do with his having among his friends no true equals. He had long ago given up the friendship of John Dos Passos, his contemporary and another man of the twenties, over political disagreement. Leon Edel, Alfred Kazin, Jason Epstein were often in his company, but none existed on a plane of intellectual equality with him. Those who did— Isaiah Berlin, André Malraux—were, like Wilson himself, essentially intellectual monologists. Equality implies the possibility of intimacy, and it may well be that that quality was long before killed off in Wilson by a formidable father with a delicate nervous organization and an unyielding mother who was hard of hearing. Like many a small boy who sought succour in books, he grew into a solitary and rather sad man.

The day-by-day grind of life for the aging Edmund Wilson was no *déjeuner sur l' herbe*. Under the rubric of *"Monotony of my life and its limitations,"* writing about his life in his early seventies, he describes his standard day:

> I wake up first about 4 and read for a couple of hours. . . . Then I go to sleep again and have an unpleasant dream, from which I wake feeling rather worse than I had at

four o'clock. I sit on the edge of the bed for a while and stare at my bare feet. . . . I then go to my bathroom and sit on the toilet, reading Jules Renard's journal or something, which helps me to face the rest: getting the yellow goo off my tongue with a washcloth or a towel, hawking up blood-phlegm, perfunctorily brushing my largely artificial teeth. I then sit down in the middle room, and Elena brings me breakfast, at the end of which I take a digitalis. Before breakfast, I do serious reading, which I continue for a time after, but during breakfast I read papers and magazines, which are easier to skim through and handle. I don't get to work as a rule till eleven or twelve o'clock. . . . About 3, we go to town for the mail, the papers and a pint of whisky. If it is fine and I feel up to it, E. takes me for a little walk like a dog, or a short drive. In the late afternoon I get a drink and shave, playing the phonograph. . . . Then I go into the middle room and play solitaire, slowly nursing my drink. Elena gets us a modest supper, after which I read or play more solitaire or am so muggy and sleepy that I go to bed and take a Nembutal or a whisky and go right to sleep. I now try to resist the temptation to finish my unfinished drink in the early morning or to supplement it from downstairs. If I do, I lie in bed, my mind very active with attractive ideas, which, however, when I come to rather later, I know that I am in no shape to realize and can only crawl to my bathroom and mechanically get a new day under way.

So, for the poor Bunny, it went—another day, another dolor.

And yet it must be said that, greatly to his credit, Wilson hung in, trying to the end to get the most out of life. *The Sixties* reveals facets of Wilson one had not known before, some surprisingly charming. He was, for example, an ardent reader of *Dick Tracy* and other comic strips. He cared more about music than I had realized. He remains interested in magic, "a childish recreation that I have carried all through my life," and exults at finding a new magic shop on 42nd Street in Manhattan. He continues to go to the theater and the movies. He retains a strong interest in gossip, recording John F. Kennedy's sex adventures or the late president telling the too obsequious Arthur Schlesinger, Jr.——"he is naive in so many ways," Wilson notes—— "go to your kennel."

Boozing is part of his regular hygiene. A man of the twenties, Wilson was, like many who came of age in that decade of Prohibition, an industrious boozer. On a not untypical night at home in Wellfleet, on Cape Cod, where he lived with his wife when not at Talcottville, along with a night of listening to phonograph records and playing solitaire, he records: "I drink a pint of scotch and sometimes half a bottle of wine. This puts me to sleep." In *Near the Magician,* his daughter Rosalind's memoir of her father, she recalls him going to bed in Talcottville with a full tumbler of whiskey, hearing him ramble round the house late at night, then wake in a room other than the one in which he had first gone to bed. In an entry from 1966, Wilson talks about a dinner at his younger friends Jason and Barbara Epstein's with Erich Heller in attendance at which he, Wilson, grew so tired "that I decided I'd better leave and dragged Elena away—— she said at 9 and before we'd had dessert. This is rude. I am handling this badly." I recall Erich Heller recounting that same evening to me somewhat differently; in his account, Wilson was so drunk he passed out in his chair at table.

Still, through his illnesses, despite the heavy boozing, Wilson nonetheless functioned impressively well. He relied on reading as other people do on breathing. He once remarked that the Marquis de Sade was the only writer he couldn't bear to read at breakfast. He claims that only "the *Koran* is unreadable" and that he can never finish a book by Henry Miller. In *The Sixties,* he lists all the Elizabethan, Jacobean, and other English plays he read in 1965–66——they were thirty-four in number, thirty-five if you add Racine's *Britannicus*——all of which he read in preparation for a "farce-melodrama" of academic life he was planning. He notes: "I find myself more and more addicted to reading Victorian and Edwardian and later English memoirs." He decides that the best thing to travel with is a volume of Balzac. He finds dull stretches in Francis Parkman's histories, yet admires them for "the avoidance of generalization, the description of events always in concrete detail. The larger tendencies are shown by a chronicle of individualized persons and actions. It is what I try to do myself." When he doesn't have an intellectual project going, he allows that he falls into a state of nervous collapse. When he isn't working hard on one or another of his projects, he feels "rather guilty about frittering my time away: . . . writing nothing but letters and drooling along in this diary."

One of the items about Wilson's career that *The Sixties* clarifies is the quality of his famous talent as a polyglot, which, it seems, has been greatly overrated. Apparently he spoke no foreign languages well. He remarks on his lack of fluency in French; reading *Faust* with his cosmopolitan wife, he allows that "the weakness of my knowledge of German undoubtedly largely prevents me from appreciating Goethe as a poet." In the years covered by this volume of the journals, he is taking tutoring in Hungarian, most difficult of European languages, though one gathers without much progress. All this makes it even more astonishing that Wilson would take on Vladimir Nabokov in a dispute over the latter's translation of Pushkin from what was, after all, Nabokov's native language—a dispute that caused a final falling out between the two friends.

The publication of journals, diaries, and letters of recent vintage are often hard on the living, whose names come in for mention. Lewis M. Dabney, who is at work on Wilson's authorized biography, writes in his editor's foreword to *The Sixties* that "almost without exception his [Wilson's] friends have graciously accepted being subjects of his scrutiny." Genuine graciousness is required. It cannot be pleasant to be Daniel Aaron and discover, in *The Sixties,* that Wilson thought you a man with "no imaginative grasp or intellectual penetration"; or Harry Levin, who is written off as "the perfect type of the envious literary man *manqué*"; or Paul Horgan, from whose mouth "the dropping of names was like the rattle of rain on the roof";

or V. S. Pritchett, who "laughs too much, and you have to laugh with him"; or Isaiah Berlin, who is cited for conversational overkill of a kind such that "an evening with him is quite fatiguing"; or Susan Sontag, whose "usual pretentious and esoteric way" fails to impress him; or Brendan Gill, who is memorialized in these pages for his partiality for porno, specifically "flesh flicks." No, the Bunny is even more emphatically not Salinger's writer that one wants to call on the telephone after reading him. Had he called you, perhaps you would have done better to have hung up.

The other danger inherent in publishing private thoughts of near contemporary writers is that they fail one or another of the current political correctness tests. Mencken has taken his lumps for this; more recently and quite as thumpingly, so has Philip Larkin. Wilson, in this volume, looks to be in danger in two realms—Jews and homosexuals—but turns out to be so only in one. One is ready to dial up the Anti-Defamation League when, early in *The Sixties,* Wilson, in 1963, writes that "one does get the impression that the Jews regard themselves as having a monopoly on suffering, and do not want the Negroes to muscle in." In fact, Wilson turns out to be rather philo-Semitic. Jason Epstein tells Wilson that he "overrated the Jews, on account of the New England identification with them; they were really awful people." (What's that ADL number again?) Early at a dinner party, after a few volleys against the Boston Irish and a woman from Scotland, he remarks that "Jews are rarely silly or sloppy." And at a party for the English historian Cecil Roth, he, Wilson, notes that "I seem to be the only goy." Whew, a near thing, but the Bunny earns a pass on the Jews.

Arranging a pass on homosexuals is not so easily effected. Wilson was of the generation that did not view homosexuality as a negligible fact in human character and his own views on the subject are harsh and without subtlety. He thinks W. H. Auden does not have "much understanding of people"; that, owing to his homosexuality, he "is likely to be put off by poets who are lyrical about women"; and that his "appetite for Tolkien" is evidence that homosexuals "don't seem to have fully matured." In London, he is at a dinner where Geoffrey Gorer kissed Auden, "and I found myself in the gelatinous medium of the London homosexual-literary world"—a world in which he does not find himself at all comfortable. After reading Michael Holroyd's biography of Lytton Strachey, he notes: "To imagine those whiskered Cambridge men such as Strachey and Maynard Keynes kissing and rolling around together!" Of a book by Parker Tyler on Tchetilchew, he writes that it is "a book about a pansy written by a pansy for pansies."

Publication of such remarks nowadays would easily have deprived Edmund Wilson of the many awards that began to come his way in the last years of his life. Wilson lived just long enough to reap such rewards, though there is not much evidence that they gave him pleasure nor quietened the dubiety about his own literary quality that resides in every good writer. In 1963, he was awarded the Presidential Medal of Freedom, despite his troubles with the IRS. In 1965, he was made a fellow at the Wesleyan Center for Advanced Study. The following year he won an award from the the American Academy of Arts and the National Medal for Literature. In 1966, he won the $30,000 prize of the Aspen Institute for Humanistic Studies. When asked why he accepted such awards, he answered, "For the money of course." At the dinner at which he received the Aspen prize, the wife of the director of the Aspen Institute, confusing his authorship of *To the Finland Station,* asked him if he wrote *Finlandia,* to which he replied, grumpily, "No, that was written by a Finn." In his journal he wrote that "these awards I am getting make me rather nervous. They mean I am an O.K. character like Thornton Wilder."

But the true interior drama in this last of Edmund Wilson's journal volumes has to do with Wilson's final verdict on the meaning of life. "I find that I more and more feel a boredom with and a scorn for the human race," is, in its tone, a fairly standard entry in this book. He remains utterly distant from any religious feeling or even interest, and allows that he can't even "enter into the point of view of someone who talks about this love between God and the human race." This utter want of the spiritual element in Wilson, his deep incuriosity about the metaphysical, was at once his greatest weakness and his greatest strength: it left him baffled before those writers who sought or sorely felt the loss of religion; and it caused him to concentrate always on the concrete, the rational, the explainable.

In the last year of his life, Wilson had his beds moved into his studies in his houses at Talcottville and at Wellfleet. In the midst of his own dark views and physical ruin, he reads Macaulay and "somewhat regained my equanimity and inspiration to live." He doubts that he will live to see eighty, and aids his own prediction by refusing a pacemaker for his weakened heart. When in hospitals, he corrects the grammar of a hospital attendant who instructs him to "lay" on the table and gives other hospital workers a hard time over their ending every sentence with "O.K." He up and walks out of hospitals when he damn well pleases. Nobody, not even his physicians, orders the Bunny about.

In the end, Edmund Wilson is a man whom it may be difficult to like but whom it is impossible not to admire. He had the courage of his lack of religious convictions: no whining about death occurs in these journals, no terror about the prospect of oblivion is expressed. With lust guttering out, curiosity narrowing, even his need for intellectual domination waning, he regrets only that he has reached the point when "one cannot even imagine any more the time when one had once participated [in life]" and avers that "one ought perhaps to have died before reaching this point, when one still had the illusion of participating. One looks down on an empty arena."

Did Wilson know that, through the long years of hard work and relentless literary production, he had become part of the chain of writers whom, forty-five years before his own death in 1972, he had cited in his essay "A Preface to Persius"? In the penultimate paragraph of that essay Wilson wrote: "In the meantime, there was nothing to do save to work with the dead for allies, and at odds with the ignorance of most of the living, that the edifice [of serious culture], so many times begun, so discouragingly reduced to ruins, might yet stand as the head-quarters of humanity!" He is one of those dead allies now, an ancestor to the small, self-formed family that still cares about that edifice, and his career an inspiration. Edmund Wilson, so much of whose work entailed searching out greatness in others, in the end, even with all his flaws, was himself a great man.

La Rochefoucauld:
Maximum Maximist

<hr />

François VI, Duc de La Rochefoucauld (1613–1680), did not invent the form known as the maxim, but instead, fairly early in its history, merely perfected it. Defying any notion of progress in the arts, nobody has come along in more than three centuries who has done it better; he remains unsurpassed. "We all have strength enough to endure the misfortunes of others," he wrote, and later, not gilding but crushing the lily, he added: "We are easily consoled for the misfortunes of our friends, if they afford us an opportunity of displaying our affection." He also wrote that "hypocrisy is the homage that vice pays to virtue" and that "however much good we hear of ourselves, we never learn anything new." Bull's-eyes, all of them, but then La Rochefoucauld hits the target more than any other writer of maxims in the history of the form, making him, beyond all argument, the maximum maximist.

The taste for maxims is rather like that for oysters: a taste for something sharp, faintly metallic, a pleasure brief but memorable, leaving an aftertaste (afterthought) and causing a felicitous ping to go off at the back of the throat (head). Epigrams, aphorisms, apothegms, maxims, there is a small problem of nomenclature here, but scarcely an intolerable one. The element common to all is economy of thought, the objective to say more by saying less. The point is to place a few well-chosen words in a perfect order, giving it at once an elegant shape, with sound and sense nicely meshed, paradox highlighted, truthfulness (not quite the same as the truth) reigning, and, with luck, a piquant touch of wisdom emerging.

Maxims are condensed essays, or at any rate each might stand as the last sentence of an excellent essay. They are written in the same grammatical tense in which paintings are painted, in what Richard G. Hodgson, in *Falsehood Disguised,* his excellent study of La Rochefoucauld, calls "the eternal present." In the composition of maxims, economy is of the essence; behind each is, or ought to be, the spirit of Hazlitt's saying that "a thought must tell quickly or not at all." Meant to give form to the most elusive and often paradoxical of truths, maxims are also meant to endure, which means that they must be pitched at a high level of generality and not be lashed to the time and place of their composition.

Nietzsche, who himself favored the maxim in *Human, All Too Human* and other works, held La Rochefoucauld's writing in the highest regard; so, too, did Voltaire, who claimed that no other book did more to form the literary taste of the French than La Rochefoucauld's *Maximes.* Schopenhauer, who also wrote maxims, almost always quotes La Rochefoucauld approvingly. Gide thought that he had carried the form to *perfection* (his italics). Rousseau, it will perhaps surprise no one to learn, felt that La Rochefoucauld was working the wrong vein, with *"son triste livre."* But then La Rochefoucauld would have thought Rousseau's ideas, not least the social contract, overly, if not comically, simplified. The only contract every man has is with himself, as La Rochefoucauld frequently pointed out, and he can usually be relied upon not to keep even that.

The great writers of maxims labor under the reputation of pessimism, if not cynicism. Some have been pessimists and cynics both. The best, as always, evade labels of any kind. Yet there is little doubt that a certain world-weariness attracts people to the writing of maxims. It is an older man's form—few women have published maxims—probably best not written much before fifty and not read much until after forty, when one has had the chance to test the waters (tepid, salty) of life.

In defense of the dourness of most successful maxims, it could be said that cheerfulness in literature, if not in life, does not travel well. The quickest way for a maxim to become a platitude is for it to attempt to glorify men or women or even hold out some hope for the human race. Consider "Love conquers all," which began life as a maxim and ended, where it resides today, in the nursing home of clichés. More in the spirit of maxim writing, on the same subject, is E. M. Cioran's "Love is an agreement on the part of two people to over-estimate each other."

The Cioran maxim can no more be proved than a statement expressing the opposite sentiment, but it does tantalize in the way maxims, when they succeed, tend to do. Cioran's maxim may not be the truth, but it contains sufficient truth to provoke further thought on the subject. A successful maxim tells the truth, and nothing but the truth, but it does not, it really cannot, tell the whole truth. The implications of such truth—perhaps revelation is the better word here—as a maxim delivers must be weighed and worked out by the person reading it. Does the maxim fit one's own case? Have the women who have loved me had to over-estimate me in order to do so, and in precisely what ways? Anyone else here beginning to feel the room getting a bit warm?

Maximists are psychologists not philosophers, anatomists not biologists. They describe rather than prescribe, dissect rather than connect. The word "moralist" best captures what they are, though not all moralists wrote maxims. No moralizer, the moralist propounds neither an ethics nor a morality, at least not directly. His claims are limited to telling his readers why men and women—and the moralists almost all delighted in the attempt to fathom women—behave as they do. In so doing, he rarely invokes the religious or the metaphysical; instead he is content to peel back false assumptions and asseverations in the hope of revealing true feelings and motives. "Mankind," wrote La Rochefoucauld, "may be said to be a mere mass of poses." The moralist's task is to discover what lies behind them.

Idealism, it all but goes without saying, is no part of the equipment of the moralist. Any impulse toward the romantic in him must be strangled. All illusions must be rooted out, including—here's the rub—the illusion that we can live without illusions. Illusion is for the human race the *spécialité de la maison*. Perhaps the greatest of these illusions is that we can steer a steady course of virtue through our lives, with victorious recognition of our goodness arriving at the end. On this illusion alone any moralist worth his vinegar could make a career. If I may be permitted a maxim of my own devising: Most of us think our lives a tragedy for which life will supply a happy ending rather than, what for most of us is much more likely the case, a farce with a tragic ending.

A farce with a tragic ending comes close, I suspect, to the way La Rochefoucauld viewed his own life. From his brilliant beginning there was no clue that it would turn out that way. His gifts, both natural and acquired, were prodigious. He was handsome, gracious, witty. He was a firstborn son, and hence first in line for his father's title and estates. (Until the death of his father, in 1650, he was the Prince de Marsillac.) Like other young aristocrats under the reign of Louis XIII, La Rochefoucauld, though married (as was not uncommon then) at fourteen, observed the breathtaking complexity of status and its ritual at court and, joining in the general skirt chase of the day, attempted, with some success, to sleep above himself. Women were always at the center of his life, except, it seems, for his wife, who bore him seven children and was apparently content to be one of those persons lost in the mists of history.

If there is a pattern in La Rochefoucauld's early life, it is perhaps to be found in his penchant for beautiful women who themselves had a stronger penchant for intrigue than for him. At the courts of Louis XIII and Louis XIV, intrigue was more thickly in the air than sexual innuendo at a conference of psychoanalysts. A foreign queen, Anne of Austria, unloved by her frivolous husband, Louis XIII, caused the royal court to be divided between her and Cardinal Richelieu, whom the King was all too ready to let rule France while he played games, made jams, and mimicked the grimaces of men on their deathbeds. La Rochefoucauld sided with Queen Anne, which was the wrong, because the losing, side. (And only winning and losing, nothing in the way of principles, seemed really at stake.) He himself took up the Queen's part chiefly because of his attraction to the Duchesse de Chevreuse, who was one of the Queen's confidants. In time, of course, the Duchesse de Chevreuse and the Queen would argue, leaving La Rochefoucauld in his accustomed position of odd man out.

Easily the most elegant book written about La Rochefoucauld is Morris Bishop's *The Life and Adventures of La Rochefoucauld* (1951). In 273 pages, Bishop provides an account of his subject's life, while recounting the intricacies of the two French civil wars that went by the name of the Frondes along with other, manifold conspiracies and gracefully interweaving no fewer than 242 of La Rochefoucauld's maxims into the work. A book in the best scholarly-belletristic tradition, it is immensely useful in taking its readers gently through the maze of French court life and the super-subtle machinations of some of the most delicate operators the world has ever known. Princes ride off to war, their servants carrying gold dishes and hampers filled with exquisite wines and poultry—a man has to eat, after all, and why not elegantly? Men fight and die, but court conspiracies turn out to be of greater consequence than campaigns afield. Three of the shrewdest Cardinals the world has ever known—Richelieu, Mazarin, Retz—take a hand in geopolitical poker, playing with countries for chips. Advancement, self-aggrandizement, acquisition of personal power, these seemed to be the chief points in a dangerous but otherwise pointless game.

His mind muddled by his youthful romanticism, La Rochefoucauld had not the subtlety or perhaps the strength of character to play with these men, though take a hand he did. Cardinal de Retz, with whom at various times he was variously aligned and at loggerheads, wrote in his memoirs of La Rochefoucauld that he could have been "the most polished courtier of his time and the man of the highest principle in regard to public affairs," but instead he was "ambitious to be mixed up in political intrigues" when he had "no knowledge of affairs of state." He had, according to Retz, an abundance of common sense, though "he did not display this quality in practical affairs"; and he was irresolute. "A fine soldier, he made no reputation in war. He never succeeded by his own efforts as a courtier. . . . He was never a successful politician, though he engaged in politics throughout his life." In short, La Rochefoucauld was a bust-out, a brilliant bust-out to be sure, but still a bust-out. La Rochefoucauld himself, one suspects, would not greatly have disagreed.

No need to rehearse all the endlessly intricate conspiracies through which La Rochefoucauld put himself over a more than twenty-year life of political intriguing. Sufficient, I think, to say that he came out a loser: without the love of the Duchesse de Longueville, sister of the Prince de Condé and the Prince de Conti, the woman he ardently pursued and with whom he shared an illegitimate son, whom he is said to have loved more than his sons by marriage; without his health, which he lost when he took a musket ball full in the face at the age of forty at the battle of Faubourg Saint-Antoine that cost him the loss of one eye and permanent disfigurement; without his estates intact (they were saved only by the perspicacity of a former servant, one M. Gourville, a sensible Sancho Panza to his rather hare-brained Don Quixote, who made wise investments for him); and without, finally, ever satisfying that vast romantic ambition that ended in destroying his body and cankering his soul.

The excellent Professor Bishop describes La Rochefoucauld at the end of the second Fronde, in 1653: "La Rochefoucauld, just turned forty, recognized by his dimmed eyesight, by the gouty pains of his body, that his active life was over." Ah, but his literary life, which would bring him much greater fame than his political activism at its most successful could ever have done, was just about to begin. He was not a man to take succor in religion, to shore up his ruins in piety. Morris Bishop again: "He was essentially a faithless man, unmystical, unbending to God. The zeal of the pious seemed to him vulgar, even disgusting." Instead he took to wisdom literature—Seneca & Co.—first to reading it, then to writing it. La Rochefoucauld the dreamer and La Rochefoucauld the intriguer were now done for. "The third La Rochefoucauld," as Bishop writes, "will be only the spectator, looking at the world with dimmed, wounded eyes."

It was in writing his memoirs, self-justifying and therefore not very distinguished memoirs, that La Rochefoucauld discovered his pleasure in prose. In a self-portrait, he wrote that, though he possessed "language fairly well, though I have a good memory and can think without confusion, I am still so bound to my sulky humor that I often express badly what I mean." He added that "the conversation of cultivated people is one of the pleasures I enjoy most." He might have qualified that by adding that he enjoyed the conversation of intelligent women most of all—"it seems to me that they explain themselves with more acuteness, and they give a more agreeable turn to their words"—and that he was fortunate in finding it in the salons first of Mme de Rambouillet and then, more decisively, in that of Mme de Sablé, the latter a confidante of Pascal.

Much has been written about the language games played at these salons, where extreme politesse was professed and no less extreme gossip practiced. At Mme de Sablé's what was known as the proverb game was frequently played. In this game, one of the guests set out an observation on human behavior, usually in epigrammatic form, which all the guests then fell to criticizing, honing, and polishing, usually in the direction of ever more concise formulation. Many of these exercises were on La Rochefoucauld's *maximes,* as he called them, some of which he himself is said to have rewritten as many as thirty times.

La Rochefoucauld's maxims were pirated by a Dutch publisher, who in 1665 bound together 316 of them, without putting their author's name on the title page, though most people who read the slender volume seemed to know his identity. At its first appearance, the book scandalized many. Mme de La Fayette, who was later to become La Rochefoucauld's great good friend, upon first reading his maxims reported to Mme de Sévigné: "Ah, Madame! quelle corruption il faut avoir dans l'esprit et dans le coeur pour être capable d'imaginer tout cela." It was as if the Misanthrope himself had written *Tartuffe,* and in fact Sainte-Beuve says that La Rochefoucauld's *Réflexions ou sentences et maximes morales,* as the book was titled, "delightfully prepared the way for that other Misanthrope," of Molière, which was first mounted the following year (1666).

Its readers might have argued about the truth quotient in La Rochefoucauld's book, but no one disputed its high style. "People read the little volume eagerly," Voltaire wrote; "it accustomed them to think, and to enclose their thoughts in a lively, precise and delicate form. This was a merit no one had had before him in Europe since the renascence of letters." Sainte-Beuve adds that La Rochefoucauld "has the clearness and conciseness of phrase that Pascal alone, in that century, had before him."

The first temptation is to conclude that it is chiefly because of what life had dealt out to him that La Rochefoucauld became the kind of writer he did. "The maxims were the revenge of the Romance," writes Sainte-Beuve. He takes this a step further, writing that his maxims "please whoever has had his

Fronde and a musket-shot between the eyes." Taken together the two remarks imply that not only does one have to have suffered to have written so darkly as La Rochefoucauld but one has to have suffered one's share even to enjoy reading him. Suffering perhaps helps, but having kept one's eyes open helps even more.

Doubtless La Rochefoucauld would not have written as he had if life had turned out other than it did for him. Life dealt him a fine hand, which he overplayed. Still, he earned his worldly wisdom, as he watched all of his illusions sour in the brine of disappointment. But to say that the *Maximes* are the work of a disappointed man in order to disqualify them is, I think, a great mistake. Quite as great a mistake is it to claim that one has to be disappointed oneself to be enamored of them, though if La Rochefoucauld could be guaranteed a readership of only one percent of those disappointed in life, the *Maximes,* I think it safe to say, would vastly outsell the Bible.

The test of the worth of La Rochefoucauld is not to be found in his biography, but in ours—in the discovery of just how self-revealing to us his revelations are. A peek here—just a small one—into my own heart, where, perhaps shocking to report, the skies are not sunny all day. A month or so ago, I learned that a man I have not seen for more than thirty years died, of cancer. He was not yet sixty. I scarcely knew him; I dare say, had we met on the street, he would not have recognized me. I might have recognized him, for as a young man he was very handsome, devastatingly so. I was once at a party with him with a woman I loved; she, it was very clear, was attracted to him, as was perhaps every other woman in the room. So far as I know, she did nothing about it; nor did he. I have not seen this woman for nearly thirty years either. Still, when I learned of this man's death, my first feeling—a fleeting feeling, but, let me assure you, a very real one—was the feeling of pleasure. Why? La Rochefoucauld covers the case. "Jealousy," he writes, "is born with love, but does not always die with it."

Let me delve just a bit further here, with La Rochefoucauld as my guide. Why did I take instant pleasure in this man's death, a man who had caused me no harm, if he even ever thought of me at all. The great moralist would have no difficulty in supplying the answer. *Amour-propre* was entailed, he would say; *amour-propre* was behind my jealousy, even over a love about which I no longer cared in the least. This handsome man represented a threat to my *amour-propre;* in his good looks he held the potential power to humiliate me, or at any rate once held such power. Better, my *amour-propre* tells me, that this man should be dead. Stupid, horrible, vile, but, alas, there it is.

The notion (idea? discovery?) of *amour-propre* is central to La Rochefoucauld's thought. In the richness of its possibilities, *amour-propre* makes our old buddy the ego seem a piker indeed. To define *amour-propre* is only to describe it, but not truly to account for the insidiousness and grandeur of its powers. *Amour-propre* has been variously defined as self-regard, self-love, self-interest, self-respect. In the first of his supplementary maxims, La Rochefoucauld describes it, in part, thus:

> *Amour-propre* is the love of oneself and of all other things for one's own sake; it makes men idolize themselves and would cause them to tyrannize over their neighbors had they the opportunity. . . . Nothing equals the impetuosity of its desires, the depths of its schemes, or the ingenuity of its methods. . . . It is impossible to fathom the depths or pierce the gloom of the abyss in which it dwells. . . . There it conceives, breeds, and rears, unknowingly, a vast number of appetites and dislikes—some of so monstrous a shape that it fails to recognize them when exposed to the light of day, or cannot bring itself to own them. Out of the night that covers it are born the absurd ideas it entertains of itself; thence come its errors, its ignorance, its clumsiness, and its fatuous beliefs about itself—its notion that its feelings are dead when they are but asleep, that it has lost its activity when once it is at rest, and that it has got rid of the appetites it has for the moment appeased.

For La Rochefoucauld, *amour-propre* was not some intellectual construct, as the ego is for Freud, but a psycho-biological fact. To be human is to have *amour-propre;* to have *amour-propre* is to be imprisoned by it; yet to understand that one is in fact imprisoned does not ever quite set one free. In one of his maxims, La Rochefoucauld wrote: "*Amour-propre* is responsible for more cruelty than natural ferocity." Yet, he also suggested that *amour-propre,* in its devious way, was responsible for much of the good men accomplish.

In its subtlety, *amour-propre* makes Freudianism and Marxism seem the intellectual equivalent of small change. With his emphasis on sex, Freud makes the world seem so much chasing after the brief spasm at the end of sexual conquest, though who exactly has conquered whom in this scheme is in actual practice never all that clear; with his emphasis on economics, Marx makes the world seem so much chasing after gold, which doesn't make for much of a story, especially after one has piled up a vast quantity of it and finds one is still unhappy. But what is behind both pursuits, and many others into the bargain, La Rochefoucauld would say, is that strange, restless, perverse imp-villain-hero, *amour-propre.*

Straight out of the gate, in Maxim I, La Rochefoucauld reports that, in the ethical realm, appearances and realities generally are not what they seem: "What we take for virtues are often merely a collection of different acts and personal interests pieced together by chance or our own ingenuity and it is not always because of valor or chastity that men are valiant or women chaste." Nothing is pure; most acts are a mélange of motives in which virtue and vice mix, so that "vices are ingredients of virtue, just as poisons are ingredients of medicine." What is more: "We should often blush for our noblest deeds if the world could see all the motives which underlay them." Selflessness and disinterest dissolve before the elusive genius of *amour-propre.* "Self-interest speaks all manner of tongues and plays all manner of parts, even that of disinterest." *Amour-propre,* as La Rochefoucauld notes, is like "the eye that can see everything but itself."

La Rochefoucauld would not have been much of a hit at the Hallmark Cards company in Kansas City, Missouri. "All human life is sunk deep in untruth," said Nietzsche in *Human, All Too Human,* and La Rochefoucauld took it as his job to show just how deep the untruth goes. In his study, Professor Hodgson writes: "The task of the moralist, as La Rochefoucauld conceived and practiced it, is to look behind the veil of appearances, to unmask the passions and prejudices being disguised as positive moral values. A whole range of attitudes and qualities traditionally associated with a strong sense of morality . . . are revealed in the *Maximes* as mere cover or camouflage for much baser instincts."

La Rochefoucauld's tendency is to find those infected spots in our moral constitution—vanity, pride, cowardice, envy, self-congratulation—and, with the sharp prick of a maxim, let the pus out of them. Whatever one prides oneself upon—loyalty, humility, courage, magnanimity—La Rochefoucauld can show that not very far beneath the surface of these professions lies self-love and personal ambition. Even civility—"Civility to others arises from a desire to receive it in return, and be accounted well-bred"—is suspect. Pity is not much better: "Pity is often a sense of personal calamity aroused by the calamities of others. It is a subtle insurance against possible adversity." As for generosity, it is "generally mere pride of giving, which we value more than the thing we give." And of course no profession is more to be distrusted than love: "In none of the passions does selfishness play so great a part as in love; we are always ready to sacrifice the comfort of those we love rather than our own," and "In the pursuit of women nothing plays a smaller part than love."

In Randall Jarrell's novel *Pictures at an Institution,* one of the principal characters is accused of hypocrisy, to which the novel's narrator responds by saying that he cannot be accused of hypocrisy since he hasn't as yet reached the stage of moral development to know right from wrong. Just so in La Rochefoucauld, where most of us sleepwalk through life, with our grand attitudes and high principles, which we like to think we can retain through the knocks life so generously hands out. It is not that we are hypocrites; it is that where we are not blinded by *amour-propre,* our passions and the forceful, often brutal, coercions of fortune kick in. W. G. Moore, who has written perhaps the best book on La Rochefoucauld's thought, remarks that in his pages man is "seen as a creature more impotent than wicked, as impotent to do good rather than intent to do evil." For La Rochefoucauld, inconstancy is perhaps the only constant in human existence.

Moore maintains that La Rochefoucauld's *Maximes* "speak less of false virtue than of mixed virtue," for "as *amour-propre* is insatiable, so is it incalculable." This it is that makes La Rochefoucauld no simple cynic, but something richer, deeper. He is the first writer to have a true respect for the role of chance and timing in human affairs. Nor does he forget the role that simple laziness plays in our fate, especially mental laziness: "The mind is more indolent than the body." His taste for paradox, which runs through the maxims, is very strong: "Nothing makes it so difficult to be natural as the desire to be so." Everywhere he finds the spectacle of people acting against their professions, against their interests, against all logic—yes, finally, even against their sense of what they believe to be their own *amour-propre.* In the end, "Our enemies' opinion of us is nearer the truth than our own."

A Mme de Shomberg, in a letter to Mme de Sablé after reading La Rochefoucauld's *Maximes,* wrote: "In this work there is a great deal of wit, very little goodness, and many truths of which I would have been ignorant all my life had I not been made to see them." But is it so that La Rochefoucauld's book contains "very little goodness"? I don't believe it is, even though the preponderance of his maxims are devoted to unmaskings: of false motives, false feeling, false virtues. Beneath the flash of penetration into human pretension, apart from the portrayal of human absurdity, there is in the *Maximes* an attempt to discover what is authentic, and hence dignified and serious, in human beings. Because of the organization of the book, which sometimes presents maxims back-to-back as if in argument, but more often spreads maxims on the same subject thirty and forty pages apart, the search for the authentic that is at the heart of La Rochefoucauld's book often goes astray.

Authenticity in La Rochefoucauld, Professor Hodgson remarks, is a "combination of lucidity, sincerity, and internal harmony" and "is a rare phenomenon indeed." La Rochefoucauld's views on authenticity are discovered in a handful of maxims and through latching onto the reverse of those qualities he chooses to mock. Professor Hodgson notes that *"l'être vrai* is thus an ideal toward which we must all strive, but one which most of us will never attain, given the illusory nature of the world around us, the unpredictability of human nature, and the elusive character of truth itself." This *être vrai,* or true being or genuine person, is someone who attains as much lucidity about his own motives and those of people he deals with as possible—no easy achievement when everything in society encourages the perpetuation of falsehoods, the exchange of lies, and the proliferation of illusions. Life in society—ours no less than La Rochefoucauld's—is predicated on most people seeming to be what they are not.

As Maxim 62 has it, "Sincerity comes directly from the heart. One finds it in very few people; what one usually finds is but a deft pretense designed to gain the confidence of others." *L'être vrai* combines in La Rochefoucauld with *l'honnête homme,* the true gentleman, who lives without pretension. Such a man has no need for pretension. "It is a sign of true goodness to be willing to live always in the sight of good men"—just as "the truly honest man is without conceit" and "lives in public as he does in private." Still, make no mistake, to live with such lucidity and in such harmony is all but impossible.

What with the maelstrom of self-love and self-interest in which we live, the added force of the passions that addle our minds, the banging about that the winds of fortune subject us to—"The world is ruled by chance and caprice"—nothing is more difficult, in La Rochefoucauld's view, than correct judgment. Our youth is *"une ivresse perpetuelle";* yet we arrive at each successive stage of life *"tout nouveaux."* It was La Rochefoucauld who, in Maxim 444, invented that by now oldest of truisms, which has almost the status of folk wisdom, "There is no fool like an old fool." As for the cool wisdom of old age, it was La Rochefoucauld who wrote that "we do not desert our appetites, it is our appetites that desert us."

Given our talent for self-deception—and self-deception is the true theme of the *Maximes*—what chance has any of us to live less than clownishly? La Rochefoucauld posits two possibilities: the rare hope that one can win one's way through to good judgment and the hope, against all hope, that one can find peace in one's heart. "The greatest of all gifts is the power to estimate things at their true worth," he wrote. Yet here the trap is that one can just as easily be too clever, too subtle: "The chief fault of the penetrative mind is not failure to go deep enough, but going too deep," and "It is of the subtlest wisdom that the subtlest folly is begotten." As for living in peace, "If a man cannot find peace in his heart, it is useless to seek it elsewhere." Leave it to La Rochefoucauld to hold out a slender thread of hope, then withdraw it.

All this might be made simpler if we could just assume the worst about ourselves, and play on through from here. But, alas, even this is not so. Good and evil, like vice and virtue, are mixed and admixed. Even "selfishness, which we blame for all our crimes, often deserves to be praised for our good deeds." Meanwhile, *amour-propre* works its devious way, "joins forces with those who attack it, takes part in their schemes, and, marvelous though it may appear, shares their hatred of itself, conspires for its own defeat, and labors for its own ruin; in a word, it cares only to exist, and, provided it exists, is content to be its own enemy." In short and in sum: "Imagination cannot conceive such a medley of inconsistencies as nature has planted in every heart."

In *The Unquiet Grave,* Cyril Connolly writes: "Those who are consumed with curiosity about other people but who do not love them should write maxims, for no one can become a novelist who does not love his fellow-man." Tell it, one is tempted to say in response to this statement, to Céline. Yet, such is the richness and complexity of La Rochefoucauld's view of mankind, that it is to the great novelists that one most readily compares him. With his requirement for lucidity and judgment as the only, if always slight, hope for mankind, he is reminiscent of no one so much as Henry James with his invocation to try to be someone on "whom nothing is lost." La Rochefoucauld wrote that "it is easier to understand mankind in general than any individual man," to which James, across the centuries, responds in agreement: "Never say you know the last word about any human heart." With his grasp of the contradictions that reside in the human heart, as the brilliant anatomist of love, jealousy, and envy, La Rochefoucauld is the proper predecessor of Proust, whose vast novel often reads like nothing quite so much as La Rochefoucauld's 123 pages fleshed out in more than three thousand.

But especially do the *Maximes* seem to anticipate Joseph Conrad who, in *Lord Jim,* has Marlow remark that "it is my belief no man ever understands quite his own artful dodges to escape from the grim shadow of self-knowledge." It is Conrad who, in a letter to Edward Garnett, wrote that "when once the truth is grasped that one's own personality is only a ridiculous and aimless masquerade of something hopelessly unknown, the attainment of serenity is not very far off." In *Victory,* Conrad has his protagonist Alex Heyst aver that he is finished with the moralists, but of course Heyst, wrong about his hope of living without illusions, is wrong about this, too.

Although the moralist would seem to present his readers with what Roland Barthes, writing about La Rochefoucauld, calls "a nightmare of truth," there is something revivifying about reading him. If the drama of human life is to be found in the struggle between egotism and altruism—and La Rochefoucauld, let it be said, is light on the side of exploring the mysteries of the latter—he is nonetheless impressive in his own search for understanding. A man standing up to speak for truth is always a grand spectacle. And when he does so with consummate style, as La Rochefoucauld unfailingly does, it is all the grander.

"The mark of the maxim is form," as W. G. Moore noted, adding that "by form we mean obvious and pleasing shape, a recurrence of sounds and a harmonious grouping of syllables." Moore also points out that most of La Rochefoucauld's maxims convey neither a fact nor an opinion but a relation and that very few of the maxims make absolute statements. Many are aptly qualified: such words as "sometimes," "often," and "most people" crop up time and again; La Rochefoucauld is master of the *ne . . . que* formulation. His metaphors are few, deft, and never draw attention from the main thought. The artfulness in the *Maximes* is both in their economy and the wide range of meaning their few words provoke. Even his ambiguities—the precise meanings of his use of such words as *honnête, esprit, mérite, coeur,* and others—seem to work in his favor, causing Nietzsche, for example, to admire the combination of precision and suggestiveness in La Rochefoucauld, the two nicely blended by an overlay of paradox.

If one wanted to display a not merely characteristic but perfect La Rochefoucauld maxim, one could do worse than choose Maxim 26: "La soleil ni la mort ne se peuvent regarder fixement." ("Neither the sun nor death can be looked upon steadily.") "This is," as Odette De Mourgues writes in *Two French Moralists* (La Bruyère is the other in this study), "perfect communication." And so it is: it has lovely sound, good sense, a touch of poetry, an air of paradox, and—an additional bonus—truthfulness of a revelatory kind and of a very high quotient.

La Rochefoucauld on death is appealing for its author's utter absence of softening nonsense. In his self-portrait, he tells us that he is "not apprehensive, and has absolutely no fear of death." But in Maxim 504, which is nearly as lengthy as his maxim on *amour-propre*, his tells another, more persuasive story. Here he reports on "the unreality of the contempt for death." Although some meet death bravely, no one, he believes, ever despises death, at least not genuinely so. It is "the greatest of all calamities," and "any man who sees it in its true aspect knows how terrifying it is." If we think our reason will stand us in good stead as death approaches, we do better to think again, for "on the contrary, it is reason which generally betrays us, and instead of inspiring contempt for death, reveals to us all its most terrifying horrors."

Before La Rochefoucauld had to face this most democratic of terrors, he found the greatest peace and pleasure he would ever know in his life in the company of Mme de La Fayette. She was a woman nineteen years younger than he—he was fifty-two, she thirty-three when they joined forces—and described by Boileau as "the woman of the most mind in France and the best writer." She was the author of *Princesse de Clèves,* on which La Rochefoucauld is said to have worked with her. In later years, she remarked of their partnership: "M. de La Rochefoucauld gave me a mind, but I have reformed his heart." Each in his and her poor health fell back upon the other for support—and found it, to the highest degree. "Their ill health," Mme de Sévigné wrote to her daughter, "made them necessary to each other, and . . . gave them leisure to taste their good qualities, which is not the case in other liaisons. . . . I believe that no passion can exceed in strength such an intimacy." The man who would be famous for mocking the purity of love had, it seems, himself found it in its purest form.

It is good to learn that, with his full cognizance of the terror of death, he proved among those who faced it bravely. Mme de Sévigné reports of La Rochefoucauld on his deathbed that "it is not in vain my daughter that he did so much thinking all his life; approaching his last hours on earth in the same manner, they held nothing strange for him." After his death, Mme de Sévigné asked her daughter, "Where will Mme de La Fayette find another such friend, such society, such gentleness, pleasantness, confidence, and consideration for her and her son?"

La Rochefoucauld's Maxim 473 reads: "True love may be rare, but true friendship is rarer still." In the same woman, La Rochefoucauld, fortunate man, found both. He wrote, too, that "the only thing that should astonish us is that we are still capable of being astonished." Yet apart from his work on the *Maximes,* La Rochefoucauld's own life was a pure farce with a relatively happy ending. Life, in its richness, does have its astonishments and seems, it is pleasing to report, to have outwitted him in the end.

Why Solzhenitsyn Will
Not Go Away

———————◆———————

For the least fair, but most penetrating, analysis of Russian character, one can do no better than to consult Joseph Conrad. The great novelist was a Russophobe. Little love is lost between Poles and Russians generally, but in Conrad's case there was added ground for animus: Russia orphaned him. Owing to the efforts of his father, a literary man-of-all-work, in behalf of Polish freedom, his family was exiled to Siberia in 1863. There, Conrad's mother became consumptive and died, and four years later his father died of the same illness; the novelist-to-be was then eleven.

Conrad's grievance was not quite in the class of an obsession, but it was there, ready for service when needed. Russia, he wrote in "Autocracy and War," a 1905 essay ostensibly about the Russo-Japanese War, was "this pitiful state of a country held by an evil spell," a "bottomless abyss that has swallowed up every hope of mercy, every aspiration toward personal dignity, toward freedom, toward knowledge, every ennobling desire of the heart, every whisper of conscience." Not even revolution could save it: "In whatever form of upheaval Autocratic Russia is to find her end, it can never be a revolution fruitful of moral consequences to mankind. It cannot be anything but an uprising of slaves." Of course that is just what the Russian Revolution of 1917 turned out to be—an uprising of slaves that enslaved the rest of the country, and most of Eastern Europe along with it, for more than seventy years.

For Conrad, Russia was another heart of darkness, this one in a cold climate. In *The Secret Agent,* it is the Russian embassy in London that puts the novel's central figure, Verloc, to the job of blowing up the Greenwich Observatory, which results in the killing of his own poor imbecile brother-in-law and sets in motion the book's nightmare logic. And in *Under Western Eyes,* not his most famous or even his most successful novel but among his most brilliant, the astounding human spectacle that is the Russian character became Conrad's true subject. According to the novel's *faux-naïf* narrator, an Englishman teaching English to foreigners in Geneva, Russian simplicity is "a terrible corroding simplicity in which mystic phrases clothe a naive and hopeless cynicism"; in Russia, it is all but impossible to "tell a scoundrel from an exceptionally able man." (One immediately thinks of Mikhail Gorbachev, or of Boris Yeltsin.)

When *Under Western Eyes* was published in 1911, Edward Garnett—husband of Constance Garnett, the great translator from Russian, and a friend and long-time supporter of Conrad—accused him of prejudice. Conrad shot back that Garnett was "so russianized . . . that you don't know the truth when you see it—unless it smells of cabbage soup when it at once secures your profound respect." And indeed there are certain Russian characters in *Under Western Eyes*—as it happens, all are women—whose general views Conrad derides and in one instance despises, but whose seriousness, even heroism, he nonetheless freely grants. These characters are all able to live outside themselves, to give themselves to really quite hopeless causes, like the reduction of suffering in a merciless world or the recounting of truth in an undeserving one. Only Russia, one senses in reading this novel, is able to produce people ready to pit themselves against the world's great gray disregard and dark evil—only Russia, out of the depths of its barbarity, is able to produce moral giants.

Joseph Conrad would not only have understood Aleksandr Solzhenitsyn but would, I believe, have been tempted to insert him into a novel. Solzhenitsyn has the scope, the depth, the moral grandeur that stimulated Conrad's imagination to its highest power. He is Conradian, too, in passing what, for Conrad, is the test of authenticity: the willingness to live one's ideas, to sacrifice for them, to make them indivisible with one's very being.

All the great Conradian heroes are isolates, men who have chosen either an occupation or a philosophy that carries with it the condition of apartness. No one could have felt lonelier than Aleksandr Solzhenitsyn during his more than twenty years as an underground writer in the Soviet Union—unless it was Aleksandr Solzhenitsyn during his eighteen years living in a compound outside Cavendish, Vermont, after being expelled from the USSR. In both places, he worked at his self-imposed task of bringing down the Soviet Union—a task whose successful achievement would, I suspect, be beyond the imagining of Joseph Conrad or any other novelist or poet. Even the word "heroic" does not seem quite adequate to describe this accomplishment.

Born in 1918 near Rostov, Solzhenitsyn was arrested and sentenced in 1945 to eight years in a labor camp, presumably for making disparaging jokes about Stalin. After an early release—thanks to the Khrushchev reforms—he was diagnosed with a supposedly terminal cancer, which he conquered. In 1962, during a rare period of cultural thaw, he was allowed to publish, in the Soviet journal *Novy Mir,* his taboo-shattering account of the slave-labor camps, *One Day in the Life of Ivan Denisovich.* Other works, including the novels *Cancer Ward* (English edition 1968) and *The First Circle* (also 1968), followed—but only in the West. In the West, too, appeared *The Gulag Archipelago,* his monumental three-volume exposé of the Soviet slave-labor system which single-handedly destroyed what remained of Western illusions about the great Communist experiment.

In 1970 Solzhenitsyn was awarded the Nobel Prize, but was refused permission to travel to Stockholm to receive it. Always in a relationship of the greatest strain with Soviet leaders, always a thorn in their sides—"This hooligan Solzhenitsyn is out of control," Leonid Brezhnev once said of him—in 1974 he was finally sent into exile.

Fortunate to have survived the war, the slave-labor camp, cancer, and many skirmishes with the KGB, Solzhenitsyn had come to think of himself as God's vessel. In *Invisible Allies,* a book written in 1975 but only recently published in English, and dedicated to the small army of anonymous Russians who helped him during his years as an underground writer, he has this to say about *The Gulag Archipelago:* "It seemed as if it was no longer I who was writing; rather, I was swept along, my hand was being moved by an outside force, and I was only the firing pin attached to a spring." And in *The Oak and the Calf* (English translation 1980), an account of his battles with the Soviet cultural bureaucracy, he writes: "I had learned in my years of imprisonment to sense that guiding hand, to glimpse that bright meaning beyond and above my self and my wishes."

If God was guiding his hand, the mission on which Solzhenitsyn had embarked, at divine bidding, was to bear witness on behalf of his fellow *zeks,* as he refers to the countless prisoners in the Soviet gulag. In *Invisible Allies* and *The Oak and the Calf* he speaks of carrying "the dying wishes of millions whose last whisper, last moan, had been cut short on some hut floor in some prison camp." And again: "My point of departure [was] that I did not belong to myself alone, that my literary destiny was not just my own, but that of millions who had not lived to scrawl or gasp or croak the truth about their lot as jailbirds."

Having been a *zek* himself, Solzhenitsyn identified completely with his fellow prisoners. One sometimes gets the feeling in reading Solzhenitsyn that, in the terrible morality of Stalinist totalitarianism, to have been a *zek* was a mark of the highest distinction, while not to have been a *zek* was to have been on the one hand wondrously lucky, but on the other hand in some sense spiritually deficient. Nadezhda Vasilyevna Bukharina, a woman who helped Solzhenitsyn in storing, reproducing, and smuggling his manuscripts out of the Soviet Union, once told him: "Before I die I have to make up for the fact that I never saw the inside of the camps."

For Solzhenitsyn, the *zeks* were Russia's saving remnant, and he was their voice. But he also viewed himself as speaking for something else: the entire tradition of Russian literature. Not *Soviet* literature—that was permanently in thrall to ideology, to supporting the state, the party, the full grotesque apparatus of Communism. By contrast, Russian literature, represented by Tolstoy, Dostoevsky, Chekhov, Pasternak, and others, was in thrall to nothing but its own freedom of spirit, hostage only to the truth of human complexity. This was a distinction that Solzhenitsyn insisted upon during his days as an underground writer. Of his falling out with Aleksandr Tvardovsky, the editor of *Novy Mir,* he writes: "The Soviet editor and the Russian prose writer could no longer march side by side because his literature and mine had sharply and irrevocably diverged."

These, then, were the twin poles of Solzhenitsyn's mission—to give voice to the *zeks,* and to reclaim the heritage of Russian literature. In *The Oak and the Calf,* at one of many points when he recalls thinking the game might be up for him, he writes: "Why must this work be brought to nothing? It was not just that it was my work; it was almost the only work that had survived as a monument to the truth." Whether or not it was "just" his work, Solzhenitsyn certainly felt that the fate of the truth, and perhaps even of Russia itself, was all on his shoulders. Anyone coming after him would find it "still harder to dig out the truth, while those who had lived earlier had either not survived or had not preserved what they had written."

Was he correct, or did he overdramatize? On the merely mechanical level, what Solzhenitsyn achieved—the writing of his books under the most difficult of conditions—is astounding. While, in effect, in hiding, he produced before his fiftieth year an entire *oeuvre* of stories, novels, poems, a history, memoirs, and a vast historical novel (later to be completed in the United States). In a minuscule handwriting, leaving no margins lest he waste precious paper, he scribbled away at a fantastic clip. In *Invisible Allies* he describes his daily regimen while working on *The Gular Archipelago:* he would rise at 1:00 A.M. and work through till 9:00 A.M., then start on a second day's portion of work, quitting for dinner at 6:00 P.M., sleeping from 7:00 P.M. till 1:00 A.M., and then begin again.

All this was done while awaiting a knock on the door from the KGB. His manuscripts had to be kept hidden not only from the regime but from his own first wife, whose trustworthiness had been forfeited, and he sometimes slept with a pitchfork beside his bed. Yet he continued, relentlessly, to work, without the aid of editors or publishers and without any assurance that the typed and retyped copies of his books which made their uncertain transmission through the underground railroad of *samizdat* would ever see the light of day.

As for the substance of his achievement, even though all sorts of people have scratched about for reasons to deny it, the plain fact is that "in terms of the effect he has had on history," as the journalist David Remnick put it in *The New Yorker* in 1994, Solzhenitsyn is "the dominant writer of this century." He has been something writers often wish to be but rarely are—what he called in *The First Circle* a "second government." One man alone, without aid of weapons, a party, or even a movement behind him, took on the most systematically brutal regime the modern world has known and, without even benefit of support in the realm of public opinion, brought it to its knees.

Given the astonishing clip at which he worked in his underground years, it is not surprising that Solzhenitsyn, in *The Oak and the Calf,* laments about the cost this exacted from him as a writer: "I never had time to look for the precise, the definitive word." True, living underground, he had absolute freedom, with neither an editor's nor a government's censorship to worry about. Yet in sheer literary terms there was an "inevitable drawback":

> When you have been writing for ten or twelve years in impenetrable solitude, you begin without realizing it to let yourself go, to indulge yourself, or simply to lose your eye for jarring invective, for bombast, for banal conventional joins where you should have found a firm fastening.

Because of the extraordinary conditions under which Solzhenitsyn's books were produced, it is difficult to enter standard literary judgments about them. Norman Podhoretz, for example, has declared that Solzhenitsyn's two major non-fiction works, *The Gulag Archipelago* and *The Oak and the Calf,* are "among the very greatest books of the age." But for him the novels and stories, though some are better than others, are finally stillborn: "Despite everything that is right about them, they always fail to live."

This is a more stringent view of Solzhenitsyn's fiction than the orthodox one, which continues to rank *One Day in the Life of Ivan Denisovich* highly and regards both *The First Circle* and *Cancer Ward* as important works in the realist tradition. What is undeniable about them, however, is that they reflect Solzhenitsyn's own constricted view of what literature is for. He has attempted to write Tolstoyan novels, but to do so under the moralizing code adopted by Tolstoy at a time when the latter's own best fiction was long behind him and he had all but disowned it. "You ought not to approach literature without a moral responsibility for every word you write," Solzhenitsyn told David Remnick, who adds that Solzhenitsyn "cannot abide experimentalism for its own sake, or pure pleasure as a literary end."

Every work of Solzhenitsyn's has a point, and the point is always political, from *Ivan Denisovich,* which set out to expose the brute fact of the slave-labor camps, to his attempt to tell the true history of the Russian Revolution in *August 1914* and the subsequent volumes of *The Red Wheel* (completed but not yet fully available in English translation). These works resist judgment on purely or even on largely aesthetic grounds. One would almost do better to judge them by how well they make their points—which is to say, by the degree to which they have fulfilled Solzhenitsyn's mission.

That mission is even larger than one might have thought. Helping to destroy Communism, it turns out, was only part of it. As Solzhenitsyn writes in *Invisible Allies:*

> Beyond the immediate struggle with the Communist state loomed a greater challenge still: the Russian spirit lay comatose, as if crushed beneath a mighty rock, and this vast tombstone . . . must somehow be raised, overturned, and sent crashing downhill.

Here we enter the complicated—one might say Conradian—terrain of Russian mysticism. By mysticism I mean the notion, held by Solzhenitsyn, that in the Russian spirit lie secrets, and, just possibly, a remedy for the spiritual vacuity of the West. "I put no hopes in the West—indeed no Russian ever should," Solzhenitsyn writes in *Invisible Allies.* "If the 20th century has any lesson for mankind, it is we who will teach the West, not the West us. Excessive ease and prosperity have weakened their will and their reason."

This notion of the West as distinctly not the solution, but as part of the same problem of modernity that brought about the hideous excrescence of Communism, has deep roots in Russia's Slavophile past. But it also has roots in Solzhenitsyn's own intense distrust of Western leftists, who stood by for decades while Russians suffered. Throughout his books, he takes shots at "useful idiots" (Lenin's term)—"the anti-fascists and the existentialists, the pacifists, the hearts that bled for Africa [but] had nothing to say about the destruction of our culture, about the destruction of our nation." When Jean-Paul Sartre wished to meet with him, Solzhenitsyn felt honor-bound to refuse this particularly egregious "useful idiot." At one point in 1972, when the Soviet leaders were making it especially hot for him, Solzhenitsyn thought to stage interviews in the *New York Times* and the *Washington Post;* but their respective Moscow correspondents, Hedrick Smith and Robert Kaiser, appalled him with the triviality of their questions.

Solzhenitsyn has never been a public-relations man's dream. "On one score I was adamant," he writes in *Invisible Allies,* "fame would never win me over." It never came close to doing so. When, an exile from his homeland, he arrived in the United States in 1975, Solzhenitsyn promptly told off Americans for their ignorance, their weakness, and worse. He accused us of collusion with tyranny: in pursuit of profit, American businessmen were selling the latest detection devices to the KGB to help imprison Soviet dissidents. He attacked our foreign policy: Soviet dissidents, he reported, "couldn't understand the flabbiness of the truce concluded in Vietnam," and the entire policy of détente showed nothing but a wholesale misunderstanding of Communism. As for our popular culture, it was beneath contempt. Americans, he declared, live behind a "wall of disastrous unawareness or nonchalant superiority."

"Being an émigré is the most difficult skill to master," remarked the Russian émigré Nikita Struve, head of a Russian-language press in Paris; it was a skill Solzhenitsyn showed no desire to learn. Attacks upon him now came not only from the Kremlin but from the West, including from anti-Communists and from his fellow émigrés. Disagreement soon merged into accusation: it was said of Solzhenitsyn that he wanted Russia to become a new Byzantium, that his favored form of government was theocracy, that he was an anti-Semite, and finally that he was nothing more than an ayatollah.

Solzhenitsyn soon decided that speechifying was not worth the energy and the emotional drain it exacted. In the eighteen years he spent in Vermont with his second wife and four sons, he worked on completing the various "knots" of *The Red Wheel,* and putting much of the rest of his enormous *oeuvre* in order. He predicted his own eventual return to Russia, and awaited the time when it would come about.

When it did, after the fall of the Soviet Union, things did not quite work out as he might have envisioned. Having fulfilled his literary duty, Solzhenitsyn now meant to fulfill his duty to society. His ambition, which had very little to do with power or politics in the normal sense, was to revive the Russian spirit, a task at least as hard to accomplish in post-Communist Russia as under the Communist regime, if not harder.

In *The Russian Question at the End of the Twentieth Century,* (1996), Solzhenitsyn explains why that should be so. With an acidulousness of which Joseph Conrad himself might fundamentally approve, he surveys the many barbarities and betrayals of Russian history. He writes of Three Times of Troubles (the capital letters are his): the seventeenth century, when Russian despotism started in earnest; the year 1917, when the Bolsheviks sent the efforts toward reform that had begun under czarism crashing down; and today, when "we are creating a cruel, beastly, criminal society." If Russian population growth is now falling, and male life expectancy is at roughly the same point as it is in Bangladesh, Indonesia, and certain countries of Africa, all this is owing to the despair of the Russian people, a despair Solzhenitsyn understands better than anyone on earth.

What, to ask the question Chernyshevski asked more than a century ago, is to be done? For Solzhenitsyn, there is altogether too much talk in the new Russia about the economy; what such talk signifies to him is, after all, only a "new explosion of materialism, this time a 'capitalist' one," and another dose of materialism will hardly do anything to save the Russian soul. Characteristically, his point of attack is moral. "We must build a moral Russia, or not at all. . . . We must preserve and nourish all the good seeds which miraculously have not been trampled down." But in what soil are these seeds to take root? The character of the Russian people, "so well known to our forebears, so abundantly depicted by our writers and observed by thoughtful foreigners," has been all but killed off by the Bolsheviks, who "scorched out compassion, the willingness to help others, the feeling of brotherhood."

Solzhenitsyn's reception in his homeland has been decidedly mixed, at best. Although, as David Remnick reports, a large number of Russians have told pollsters they would like Solzhenitsyn to be their president, elsewhere "a more ironical attitude . . . has formed. I found the attitude ranging from indifference to mockery." Lots of people, one imagines, and not just in Russia, would prefer that Solzhenitsyn just go away. Even his American publisher has said that he does not anticipate a large sale for the next installment of *The Red Wheel*. "The interest is just not there anymore."

Aleksandr Isayevich Solzhenitsyn is nearly eighty years old, a prophet without honor in his own country. "I feel sorry for Russia," says a character in *August 1914*. So does Solzhenitsyn, but neither his sorrow nor his patriotism has ever gotten in the way of his extravagant idealism, or stopped him from telling his countrymen precisely what he thinks. He is, in short, a fanatic, but of the kind of which true prophets are made. Only Russia could produce such a man—and only Russians could ignore him. Joseph Conrad would have understood.

Mr. Larkin Gets a Life

> *"Get a life!"*
> —Contemporary saying

> *"Really, one should burn everything."*
> —PHILIP LARKIN, March 15, 1980

In a letter written in 1953, when he was thirty-one years old, Philip Larkin remarked that the three poets who had "altered the face" of English poetry in the twentieth century were T.S. Eliot, W.H. Auden, and Dylan Thomas. He could not have known it then, but he was himself to be the fourth.

In a small number of perfect poems, Larkin (who died in 1985 at the age of sixty-three) has left a permanent impress, creating a distinctive mood—the "Larkinesque"—and a compact world. That world is dark—gray, if a color be wanted. It is a middle-class world, bland and provincial, drab, and (in his own bachelor case) lonely. It is a world in which childhood is likely to have been "a forgotten boredom," life is a game of cards (where we "hold poor hands/when we face each other honestly"), time passes too quickly, and death, far and away the major datum, casts a pall over everything.

If this sounds pretty grim, it is, except that, set out in Larkin's poetry with wit, precision, and an exceptionally high quotient of truthfulness, it leaves one, surprisingly, elated. In an unbardic age, Philip Larkin's poems, lucid, accessible, eliminating all false notes, dedicated to snuffing out arty pomposity, seem more genuine than those of any other poet writing in the past fifty years.

Even the best of poets, when young, tend to be adept ventriloquists, using themselves as their own dummies to force through the sounds of other, older poetic voices. Larkin was no exception. For a good while, he wrote in imitation of W. H. Auden; then he went through his Yeats period. A friend at Oxford characterized another phase of his writing as reminiscent of Dylan Thomas, "but you've a sentimentality that's all your own." Before he was twenty-five Larkin had published three books: a derivative—from Yeats—volume of poems entitled *North Ship* (1945) and two novels, *Jill* (1946) and *Girl in Winter* (1947), both of which showed more in the way of dogged determination than talent.

Yet Larkin was very smart very young, and about literature never less than serious. Developing his own precise laconic style took a while—the discovery of the poetry of Thomas Hardy was decisive—but not all that long. When it happened it came very quickly: suddenly, in his own bare-bones explanation, "thoughts, feelings, language cohered and jumped." By the time he published the poems in the volume entitled *The Less Deceived,* in 1955, when he was thirty-three, he had come into his maturity.

It was around that same time that Larkin wrote to his friend Robert Conquest about those poets (himself, Conquest, John Wain, and Kingsley Amis, among others) then known collectively as the Movement:

> For my part I feel we have got the method right—plain language, absence of posturings, sense of proportion, humor, abandonment of the dithyrambic ideal—and are waiting for the matter: a fuller and more sensitive response to life as it appears from day to day, and not only on Mediterranean holidays financed by the British Council.

If such was the method of the poets in the Movement, the true matter would really come only to Larkin. His work is in many ways the poetic equivalent of the novels of his friend Barbara Pym, whose cause he championed in the 1960's and 70's when she was unable to find a publisher. As Larkin wrote to his own publisher, Charles Monteith, attempting to get him interested in Miss Pym:

> I like to read about people who have done nothing spectacular, who aren't beautiful and lucky, who try to behave well in the limited field of activity they command, but who can see, in little autumnal moments of vision, that the so-called "big" experiences of life are going to miss them; and I like to read about such things presented not with self-pity or despair or romanticism, but with realistic firmness and even humor.

Some might dispute whether Larkin's own poems are free of "self-pity or despair"; an easy enough case could be made that many are not, beginning with his remark that "deprivation is for me what daffodils were to Wordsworth." Still, he was entirely and sincerely of the view (as he put it in a brief essay) that poetry, like all art, "is inextricably bound up with giving pleasure, and if a poet loses his pleasure-seeking audience he has lost the only audience worth having, for which the dutiful mob that signs on every September [that is, students] is no substitute." And he meant pleasure in the most fundamental sense; if a poem did not please, he felt, one ought to chuck it. His own recipe for poetry was to "make readers laugh, make them cry, and bring on the dancing girls."

Through self-mockery, comic derision, a fine firm control of language, a nicely subdued lyricism, and an impressive talent for facing awkward and unpleasant facts, Larkin took poetry away from the academics and brought it back within the grasp of the intelligent ordinary reader who looks to poetry for insight, delight, and even consolation. Consider "Love," a poem that is neither one of Larkin's best nor among his most famous, but is a characteristic performance:

> The difficult part of love
> Is being selfish enough,
> Is having the blind persistence
> To upset an existence
> Just for your own sake.
> What cheek it must take.
>
> And then the unselfish side—
> How can you be satisfied,
> Putting someone else first
> So that you come off worst?
> My life is for me.
> As well ignore gravity.
>
> Still, vicious or virtuous,
> Love suits most of us.
> Only the bleeder found
> Selfish this wrong way round
> Is ever wholly rebuffed,
> And he can get stuffed.

Of all modern writers, poets tend to be the most careful promoters of their careers. Perhaps they have to be, working in a form where supply hugely exceeds demand, if one can speak of demand at all. Even the magisterial T. S. Eliot, as the first published volume of his letters shows, was something of a main-chance man. In 1919, Eliot wrote to J. H. Woods, his teacher at Harvard, that "there are only two ways in which a writer can become important—to write a great deal, and have his writings appear everywhere, or to write very little." Eliot goes on to report that he has taken the latter course, having published only one volume of verse and printing only two or three poems each year. "The only thing that matters," he adds, "is that these should be perfect in their kind, so that each should be an event."

To publish infrequently but always to dazzle—this was the way Eliot chose and so did Philip Larkin, though, in Larkin's case, it is perhaps more precise to say that this was the way that chose him. A steady but very slow worker till the last decade or so of his life, when he fell into a nearly complete writer's block, Larkin was painfully perfectionist. After *The Less Deceived* he published only two further slender volumes of verse—*The Whitsun Wedding* (1964) and *High Windows* (1974)—at roughly ten-year intervals. *All What Jazz,* a collection of the record reviews he wrote for the *Daily Telegraph,* appeared in 1970, and *Required Writing,* his collected journalism and interviews, in 1982, three years before his death.

Larkin could not have hoped to live off such limited literary production, and in fact his principal income came from his job as the head librarian at the University of Hull. He had drifted into librarianship after failing, not long after graduating with a First from Oxford, to find a position in either the civil service or the Foreign Office. "At interviews," he wrote to a friend, "I must obviously show that I don't give a zebra's turd for any kind of job."

Larkin became a librarian largely because he felt himself unfit to do much else. A poet, the Russian proverb has it, always cheats his boss: usually by thinking about, if not actually writing, poems on the job. Not so Larkin, who was a highly competent librarian, managing a staff of more than 100 employees at Hull, where he oversaw a vast rebuilding of the university's library and, from all accounts, kept things generally humming along smoothly.

Small though Larkin's literary production was, he was handsomely rewarded for it. He won every major poetry prize offered in England, including the Queen's Gold Medal. By his early fifties, universities began awarding him honorary degrees.

He was asked to serve on literary panels and prize committees, and became a rather effective literary bureaucrat. He was the subject of a BBC television program, and a reading of his work by others was staged in London under the title "An Evening Without Philip Larkin." He was made a Companion of Honor by Prime Minister Thatcher. Earlier, W. H. Auden and John Betjeman offered to nominate him for the poetry professorship at Oxford, which he would easily have won but which he turned down. He also refused the poet laureateship. In a birthday volume entitled *Larkin at Sixty,* the playwright Alan Bennett, commenting on Larkin's famous distaste for public celebration, wrote that "a birthday party for Philip Larkin is like treating Simone Weil to a candlelight dinner for two at a restaurant of her choice." Although he was never taken in by this kind of success, Larkin realized that, at the table of public recognition, he had been served exceedingly well.

Larkin was especially artful at that greatest of all modern tools of self-promotion, the interview. In those he gave, Larkin drew a picture of himself as a winning curmudgeon, dedicated to attacking obscurity and deflating pretension, and asserting an appetite for simple philistine pleasures. Famously insular, he answered a question about visiting China by saying that he would not mind it if he could return home the same day. When asked, "Do you feel you could have had a much happier life?" he replied, "Not without being someone else."

In these interviews and in his occasional journalism, Larkin presented himself as a man who had the clarity and courage to be against his time—artistically and in almost every other way. He was, he wished it to be known, not in the poetry racket: "I have never read my poems in public, never lectured on poetry, never taught anyone how to write it." In explanation of his refusal to give readings, he said, "I don't want to go around pretending to be me." He also cut himself loose from the academy, which he thought encouraged poetry to be more difficult than it ought to be; this imposed difficulty was part of the legacy of modernism, a road which, in his view, should never have been taken. And, finally, in his political views, he dissociated himself from the liberal leftism that was and remains dominant in literary and academic culture.

In his introduction to *All What Jazz,* Larkin explained his strong dislike of modernism (as represented by such diverse artists as Ezra Pound, Pablo Picasso, and Charlie Parker) in these words:

> . . . I dislike such things not because they are new, but because they are irresponsible exploitations of technique in contradiction of human life as we know it. This is my essential criticism of modernism, whether perpetrated by Parker, Pound, or Picasso: it helps us neither to enjoy nor to endure. It will divert us as long as we are prepared to be mystified or outraged, but maintains its hold only by being more mystifying and more outrageous: it has no lasting power.

Do Larkin's own poems have this power? People in a position to say always seemed to think they did. His American contemporary Robert Lowell much admired Larkin's poetry. (Larkin, on the other hand, thought Lowell "simply barmy.") Another American, the poet and critic Randall Jarrell, although he never wrote about Larkin publicly, similarly championed his work in his letters. ("I'm crazy about him," Jarrell wrote to Lowell.) Auden and Betjeman greatly valued Larkin's poems. But, quite as important, many readers who had long before given up on poetry as too abstruse, specialized, private—to borrow Marianne Moore's words, an imaginary garden inhabited by altogether too many too real toads—found themselves reading Larkin with amusement and appreciation.

A funny game, poetry: as Jarrell once pointed out, a poet has only a half-dozen or so times to strike lightning—that is, to write the perfect poem—and he is assured immortality. Yet how few have done it! Jarrell himself did not. It is unclear whether Robert Lowell can be said to have done it more than once or twice. Among modern poets of an earlier generation, T. S. Eliot did; so, too, did Wallace Stevens; by no means is it plain that William Carlos Williams or Marianne Moore did. Auden did, as did Robert Frost, perhaps more convincingly and in greater profusion than any other modern poet.

By this measure—the composition of a handful of resounding and flawless poems—Philip Larkin appears to have succeeded, too. In "At Grass," "Church Going," "Mr. Bleaney," "Dockery and Son," "Old Fools," "Aubade," poems where the tiles slide perfectly into place and the finished work closes with a satisfying click, he produced major poems, perfect of their kind. In "Annus Mirabilis," "Verse de Société," "Naturally the Foundation Will Bear Your Expenses," "This Be the Verse," and a great many more he wrote strong comic poems, usually with a sharp bitter twist. Larkin is a poet who is not only readable but rereadable and—the third and ultimate test—memorable. His genius was to have taken the imperfections of his life, perhaps his chief subject matter, and turned them into perfection in his work.

When Philip Larkin died of cancer of the esophagus in 1985, his fame was great and his claims on immortality considerable. But a funny thing happened on the way up Parnassus. Among Larkin's literary executors are Anthony Thwaite and Andrew Motion. Thwaite is a literary journalist and a former editor of the (now-defunct) monthly *Encounter,* while Motion is an academic and critic of poetry; both are also poets. Between them they divided the literary spoils. Thwaite brought out a *Collected Poems* (1988) and in 1992 the *Selected Letters of Philip Larkin, 1940–1985,* while Motion wrote what is intended to be the definitive biography, *Philip Larkin, A Writer's Life.*

Taken together, these three books have come near to sinking Philip Larkin's reputation. All his life Larkin feared death, and he turns out to have been correct, but in a way he could not have known—for what has happened to him after death is much worse than anything in his life. "A couple of years ago Larkin was still our best-loved postwar poet," Martin Amis has written in dismay; "now, for the time being, he is the most reviled."

The *Collected Poems* did the least damage. The complaint about it was that everything good in the book was not new and much that was new was not good, and so should have been excluded. As editor, Anthony Thwaite chose to print several of Larkin's youthful poems—those written between the ages of seventeen and twenty-three—many of which Larkin himself referred to as "pseudo-Keats babble." Thwaite also included a small number of poems that Larkin considered unfinished. A perfectionist with the patience to go with his proclivity, the mature Larkin, as Thwaite notes, "could not bring himself to publish anything about which he felt any doubt." Yet since Larkin felt doubt about almost everything having to do with himself, Thwaite overruled him in death and printed a number of poems which in his view "deserve to stand with [Larkin's] best already known work." Some, in my view, do; some, regrettably, do not.

But such controversy as the *Collected Poems* brought was confined to poets and critics of contemporary poetry, and was an intramural affair at best. The same cannot be said for the publication of the *Selected Letters* and Andrew Motion's biography. In England the *Letters* came out before the *Life;* here the *Life* preceded the *Letters.* In some ways it is best to read the *Letters* first—as it happens, I did not—because they tend, if not to refute the *Life,* at least to complicate and hence to soften it.

Behind Andrew Motion's biography of Philip Larkin lurks what feels like one of those Henry James stories about betrayal among artists. Although Motion contends that he had nothing of the sort in mind, and claims too that his biography is sympathetic to its subject, his life of Larkin is, in fact, oddly prosecutorial. (In the *Selected Letters,* it is worth remarking, Larkin's own comments about Motion tend to be mildly derisive.) The Philip Larkin who emerges from Motion's book is ungenerous, neurotic, bigoted, utterly self-regarding, and damned unpleasant generally. Think how he might have emerged in a biography not written by a friend.

Forgiveness is at the heart of biography. The biographer either will or will not find it in himself to pardon his subject the transgressions he is almost certain to discover once he begins digging around in the life. Especially is this the case in biographies of modern artists. The modern artist, after all, has long had a warrant, a sanction of a sort, to be a miserable son of a bitch. Driven to distraction by the difficulties of his work—so the warrant reads—the artist, if he is not a little mad to begin with, must be allowed a wider berth than the rest of us to leave more human rubble in his wake. It is an old story: the wound and the bow, and all that.

The roll of artists in the modern age is filled with alcoholics, misanthropes, megalomaniacs, major-league neurotics, creeps, drips, and simple bad hats. The list of those noted for kindness and acts of unmotivated goodness is shorter than the list of four-star restaurants in Duluth. When yet another artist with a difficult personality presents himself to be written about, the biographer must choose either to sympathize, understand, and explain away the unpleasantness, or nail the fellow to the wall.

Philip Larkin had what I should call a troubled rather than a difficult personality, and Andrew Motion is at some pains to explain the origins of his troubles. A shy and stammering boy with poor eyesight, homely, awkwardly tall, not notably gifted in the skills appreciated by the young, brought up in a loveless marriage, Larkin had rich ground in his early life for psychological complication. "I never left the house," he later wrote, "without the sense of walking into a cooler, cleaner, saner, and pleasanter atmosphere, and, if I had not made friends outside, life would have been scarcely tolerable." As Motion shows, Larkin was one of those boys whose keenest pleasures tended to be lonely ones: reading, going to the movies, listening to jazz records. Sex, he would later aver, was really too good to share with anyone else.

Larkin thought his mother a passive, tidy-minded, dreary woman who felt her life always slipping out of control. His father, Sidney Larkin, rose to be the city treasurer in Coventry and was a much more complex case. "Everything Larkin disliked or feared in his father," Motion writes, "was matched by something he found impressive or enviable." Among those impressive or enviable items were self-reliance, immense competence, respect for education, knowing one's own mind, wide reading. Sidney Larkin shaped his son's literary tastes, guiding him to G. B. Shaw, Thomas Hardy, Oscar Wilde, Arnold Bennett, and Samuel Butler as well as D. H. Lawrence, Aldous Huxley, and Katherine Mansfield. Sidney Larkin was also pro-German—he was, as Philip later described him, "the sort of person that democracy didn't suit"—and possibly even pro-Hitler. This last fact would be used, if not by Motion then by others among Larkin's recent contemners, to count against the son's own politics.

Although in his introduction Motion speaks to the contradictory qualities that comprised Larkin's personality—his selfishness and his kindness, his shyness and his skill at self-promotion, his reactionary attitudes and his personal tolerance—the more generous and admirable aspects of the man somehow fall away over the long haul of this biography. They do so because Motion cannot finally forgive Larkin for two things: his relations with women and his political opinions.

Larkin was one of nature's bachelors. His own family life probably put paid forever to the idea of his marrying. As he once noted in his diary: "Let me remember that the only married state I intimately know (i.e., that of my parents) is bloody hell. Never must it be forgotten." And in an autobiographical fragment, he wrote: "Certainly the marriage [of his parents] left me with two convictions: that human beings should not live together, and that children should be taken from their parents at an early age." Or, as he put it more concisely in the last quatrain of "This Be the Verse":

> Man hands on misery to man.
> It deepens like a coastal shelf.
> Get out as early as you can,
> And don't have any kids yourself.

In life, it was not quite so simple. While Larkin never spoke of a longing for children—he wrote that he lost his interest in religion when he learned that in heaven one would return to the state of childhood—he did long for women. In letters to unmarried male friends, he spoke of women, as bachelors will, in the standard degrading way, with his own twist of Larkinesque humor: "I *don't* want to take a girl out and spend circa £5 when I can toss off in five minutes, free, and have the rest of the evening to myself." To his friend Jim Sutton he wrote that "my relations with women are governed by a shrinking sensitivity, a morbid sense of sin, a furtive lechery." Women liked scenes, wanted children, wore their emotions like clothes, were possessive. "Above all they like feeling they 'own' you—or that you 'own' them—a thing I hate."

All this makes Larkin sound like a man who would be quite ruthless with any woman who came his way; or perhaps like a man who would do better to steer clear of women altogether. In fact, against the advice of the metaphysical poet, he could neither wholly abstain nor wed. His adult life was an almost perpetual entanglement with women whom he could neither marry nor easily break away from. He yearned for female companionship, then he wanted to be free of it; he was unhappy without a woman in his life but always uncomfortable when enmeshed in a love affair. As he jotted in one of his notebooks:

> Not love you? Dear, I'd pay ten quid for you:
> Five down, and five when I got rid of you.

He never sorted it out. In his twenties, he was engaged to a woman who lived in Wellington, the site of his first library job. He had a long relationship with an attractive woman, an English-literature academic named Monica Jones, who lived in Northumberland, a freedom-giving distance away from Hull. He had an unconsummated relationship with a recent graduate of Queen's College in Belfast, with whom he worked at that school's library. Off and on, he saw a woman who worked at the library in Hull and whose earnest Catholicism brought sexual complications. He had an affair that sounds more like a fling with the divorced wife of a former friend. Much later in life, Motion informs us, he slept with his secretary. The clever title of a review of Larkin's *High Windows,* "Don Juan in Hull," drips with sad irony.

Apart from his quite genuine attachment to Monica Jones, Larkin seems to have been the sexual equivalent of a human type known as the permanent transient: wherever he was, he thought of elsewhere. In Larkin's case, whomever he was with, he longed for the company of another. On holiday with one of his lady friends, he was certain to correspond with another. "You see," he wrote to Jim Sutton, "my trouble is that I never like what I've got."

To justify this refusal of final commitment, Larkin invoked his work. "How will I be able to write," he asked the woman he was engaged to in his twenties, "when I have to be thinking of you?" The composer Maurice Ravel took the line, which Larkin would have approved, that it is probably best for an artist not to marry: "He lives like an awakened dreamer," Ravel said, "and that's not amusing for a woman who lives with him." Larkin, in his middle forties, wrote to Monica Jones in his characteristically abashed tone to apologize for holding things at bay between them in order to get his writing done. "Anyone would think I was Tolstoy, the value I put on it," he said, adding: "It hasn't amounted to much."

Andrew Motion has a theory that Larkin's conflict with women was at the center of his power to write poems. "When he approached the middle of his life he stopped seeing the conflict as something that must be resolved, and regarded it instead as the means of self-definition." True enough, this conflict gave Larkin the subject matter for some of his sadder poems—"Self's the Man," "Talking in Bed"—about loneliness and the impossibility of striking any enduring human connection. "I believe that human beings can do nothing for one another except provide amusement, which is pleasant but does not last," he wrote when still a young man. Yet there was no pleasure in any of this for Larkin himself, who felt that when he was old he would regret having wasted his life and "therefore, in addition to being afraid of death, I shall feel cheated and angry."

If Philip Larkin never quite sorted out his relations with women, neither, quite, does his biographer. When all the many details Motion provides have worked their way into the reader's mind, they lead to the conclusion, in the crude thinking of our day, that Philip Larkin was a misogynist, his selfishness amounting to cruelty. It does not help matters to learn that Larkin also had a taste for soft pornography. Yet the tenderest of his letters are those written to women, and by no means all of them to women in whom he had a sexual interest. He was able consistently to strike the note of intimacy with women in a way he could not do with men. With women he is often at his best.

The point that one has to consider is that what Larkin sometimes said, he did not necessarily always mean; and even in those instances where he might have meant the unpleasant personal views he uttered, he never acted upon them. In middle life, in an autobiographical fragment, Larkin might refer to his mother, with her compulsiveness and irritating passivity, as a "sniveling pest," but in fact throughout her old age (she lived to be ninety-one) he stood by her, writing to her almost daily, traveling to visit her on a regular (and frequent) basis, and seeing her through to the end as the dutiful son he was. He may have been grudging in his dutifulness, but such duty is hard, and in the end the chief thing is that he performed it.

The separation of word from deed is not always simple, but it is one that becomes crucial in a culture like ours where opinions are allowed to eclipse or even negate accomplishments. Which brings us to the second of Andrew Motion's problems, and almost everyone else's who has written about his book and Anthony Thwaite's edition of the *Selected Letters:* Philip Larkin's politics and the social opinions behind them. In one view, Larkin's politics were right-wing; in another, my own, they were thoroughly anti-Left. It is not quite the same thing.

Larkin thought the left-wing politics of the Labor party, of the British trade unions, and of university students in the sixties and the teachers who chose to go along with or abet them, were destroying England. As he wrote to a friend:

> You can't be more depressed than I about the state of the country. To my mind it is only a question of time before we are a sort of sub-Ireland or Italy, with the population scratching a living by sucking up to tourists and the Queen doing two performances a day of *Trooping the Colour* for coach loads of Middle-Westerners and Russian Moujiks. God, what an end to a great country.

In the *Selected Letters,* such sentiments, often expressed less politely, have landed Larkin in deep posthumous trouble. In British reviews of the *Letters* and of Andrew Motion's *Life,* Larkin has been accused of "racism, misogyny, and quasi-fascist views." He has been referred to as a "foul-mouthed bigot"; had his masculinity questioned; and declared "really a nutcase." The publication of the *Life* and the *Letters,* opening Larkin's political views to the public, has also led to a reassessment of him as a poet. A man holding the views he did, it has been suggested, cannot be other than a minor artist with an inflated reputation, which it is now time to deflate.

On the charitable side, critics have written that, though Larkin's views may have been hideous and he a terrible fellow, nonetheless the poems remain and it is for the poems alone that he should be remembered and for which we should be grateful. This general line rather echoes Larkin himself on the World War I poet Wilfred Owen, of whom, in a letter to Robert Conquest, he wrote: "W.O. seems rather a prick, really, yet the poems stay good."

Meanwhile, the self-appointed members of the thought police in our universities have before them the happy task of raking Larkin's poems for evidence of unacceptable opinions. Odd, is it not, that an on-the-make character in one poem, "Posterity," should be named Jake Balokowsky, a Jew? Misogny is easily enough sniffed out. Racism may present a tougher job; but maybe not, for is not any admiration for the British empire, as in "Homage to a Government," evidence of racism? And what about homophobia? Stay on the case: it must be there somewhere. Academics exist who will find all this not in the least tiresome work.

But how bad are the opinions expressed in Larkin's letters? Some are pretty bad, others are bad but funny, a few are of a kind that admirers of Larkin will wish were never voiced. Ironic derision is a note often struck in these letters. Larkin loved to spot a phony, to call a spade a freakin' shovel. Thus, he refers to Joseph Heller's *Catch-22* as "the American hymn to cowardice," and to the IRA as "these mad murdering Irish swine." He notes that the universities are "educating the children of the striking classes." Of a poetry competition he is judging, he writes: "About half the entrants are Yanks, all worrying about Vietnam and being Jewish." He calls the British critic A. Alvarez "El Al" and Salman Rushdie "Salmagundi." Italy is "wopland" and Morocco "coonland." Mocking the movement, so popular in the early eighties, to rid university portfolios of any investments in South Africa, he derides the "years-long wrangle over South African shares, or shares in companies that have South African interests, or shares in firms that employ chaps who once ate a South African orange, or something."

Humor has always taken its seasoning from the forbidden, from deliberate indiscretion, and if one cannot be indiscreet in correspondence with dear friends, then we are all in sad shape. ("Letters," the young T. S. Eliot wrote to his college friend Conrad Aiken, "should be indiscretions—otherwise they are simply official bulletins.") Yet, such is the touchiness of the time in which we live, a famous literary man now has to be warier of what he writes than a millionaire playboy wooing a trial lawyer's daughter.

There is worse. "Keep up the cracks about wogs and niggers," Larkin wrote to his friend Kingsley Amis. (One hopes Sir Kingsley is even now at the document shredder.) To certain correspondents—Amis, Conquest, a man named Colin Gunner—Larkin reciprocated in kind. The "cracks" range in meanness from a reference to the "bloody Paki next door" to "And as for those black scum kicking up a din on the boundary [of the cricket field at Lord's]—a squad of South African police would have sorted them out to my satisfaction."

I wish Larkin had never said such things because they can only be used against him by people who, along with being impressed with their own virtue, cannot stand too much complication in human character. The truth about the *Selected Letters of Philip Larkin* is that their author was a good-hearted man who could write with exquisite tact to a woman who had sent him a novel about the death of her son in a tragic accident; who could bemoan killing a hedgehog and later write a poem, "The Mower," about it (". . . we should be careful / Of each other, we should be kind / While there is still time"); who could soothe friends in their grief, stick by them in their suffering (see the letters to Barbara Pym), entertain them in their boredom, delight them with his faithful attention. The occasional politically incorrect opinions have obscured the fact that there is scarcely a letter in the *Selected Letters* that does not contain something charming, touching, funny, or generous.

This is all the more impressive because Larkin seems to have been a genuinely unhappy man. In a review of *The Oxford Book of Death* he wrote that "man's most remarkable talent is for ignoring death." Certainly, he could never for long get it out of his own mind. Time was a perpetual slow leak, and the years were precious air always escaping him. His twenties, his thirties, his forties, his fifties, all seemed to him to have been wasted, to have gotten away in an "uneventful progress toward the grave."

Larkin's last years were a vast wet blanket of sadness. He was a fully blocked writer, who told a journalist that he "would sooner write no poems than bad poems." He had put on weight, and could not forbear remarking on his "sagging face, an egg sculptured in lard, with goggles on—depressing, depressing, depressing." "So we face 1982," he wrote to Kingsley Amis, "sixteen stone six, gargantuantly paunched, helplessly addicted to alcohol, tired of livin' and scared of dyin', world-famous-unable-to-write poet, well you know the rest." When in January 1985 he acquired a new Parker 61 fountain pen, he noted to an old friend that parts would be available for it for the next ten years, adding: "That'll see me out." He died before the year was done.

At the close of a brief paragraph of complaint in a letter to the writer John Wain, Larkin said sardonically about himself: "What I like about Phil, he always cheers you up." Yet the strange fact is that reading Philip Larkin always does cheer one up—such, at least, is his effect on me. Sad though the subjects of his poems indubitably are, empty though his letters struggle to convince one that his life was, he himself remains an oddly stirring figure. There is something splendidly impressive about a man unable to lie about his experience and who, no matter how dark or even pathetic that experience, finds reason to laugh about it. Larkin's poetry and life show that to be "less deceived," though it may not be enough, is at least a start. They also show that just because life seems almost unrelievedly depressing—dour, laden with disappointment, with death waiting at the end—that is no reason to let it get you down.

"
.

Mary McCarthy in Retrospect

———————◦━━◦━━•━━◦━◦———————

"I didn't have the two top things—great animal magnetism or money," F. Scott Fitzgerald once remarked. "I had the two second things, though, good looks and intelligence." Mary McCarthy (1912–1989), like Fitzgerald—like him, too, in being half-Irish on her father's side—could say the same. Only those two qualities, good looks and intelligence, can take on a very different significance in a woman. Good looks in a man, especially in a man doing intellectual or artistic work, can prove a mixed blessing; they can issue in narcissism or petty vanity and often even suggest an underlying weakness. But good looks in a woman, especially an intellectually gifted woman, can seem more than a touch anomalous: it is almost as if beauty would make a woman's possession of intellectual ability appear surprising. To have both, surely, is an insult to Freud's theory of sublimation, which holds that artists give up money, fame, and beautiful lovers for their art, through which they hope to win—yes, you will have guessed it—money, fame, and beautiful lovers.

The two intellectual women whose careers have had the greatest publicity in America over the past half-century, Mary

McCarthy and Susan Sontag, have both been striking-looking: Mary McCarthy on the model of the natural American beauty, Susan Sontag, more academically, on the model of the bohemian graduate-student lover every bookish man feels he ought to have had. If all this sounds unbearably sexist, or plain masculine stupid, do stop a moment to consider whether Miss McCarthy's or Miss Sontag's career would have been the same if either had been 4 feet 10 inches, weighed 165 pounds, had sandy-colored frizzy hair, and wore largish round spectacles.

Whether she was writing criticism, fiction, or political pamphlets, Mary McCarthy always wrote, my guess is, with the authority of beauty on her side. When she grew older, her looks disappeared and she came to resemble a rather harrowing Irish old-maid public-school principal, but what never disappeared, I would guess again, was the consciousness of having once been beautiful. Dark, with good facial bones, a fine forehead, and a heart-stopping smile, she was, from the outset of her career, a star: she was this beautiful woman who wrote in a knowing way about so much, not least about sexual experience—her own sexual experience, one always assumed, which made the whole proposition even more enticing.

So intrinsic were Mary McCarthy's good looks to her career that everything about the literary persona at the center of that career seemed to proclaim: "I am not your standard emotionally crippled, intellectual female who has drifted into art or criticism because nothing better was available to her." In the best of her stories, "The Man in the Brooks Brothers Shirt" (1941), Miss McCarthy made plain, through her transparently autobiographical heroine, Margaret Sargent, her own queenly standing in the first world she chose to dominate, that of the New York intellectuals in the 1930's.

As for the men who sought her favors in this group, in one way or another, the narrator of the story reports, "They were all of them lame ducks":

The handsome ones, like her fiancé, were good-for-nothing, the reliable ones, like her [about-to-be-ex-] husband, were peculiar-looking, the well-to-do ones were short and wore lifts in their shoes or fat with glasses, the clever ones were alcoholic or slightly homosexual, the serious ones were foreigners or else wore beards or black shirts or were desperately poor and had no table manners. Somehow each of them was handicapped for American life and therefore humble in love. And was she too disqualified, did she really belong to this fraternity of cripples, or was she not a sound and normal woman who had been spending her life in self-imposed exile, a princess among the trolls?

One thing that needs to be said about this passage is that it was written about people, the editors and writers around the magazine *Partisan Review,* who had given Mary McCarthy what literary success she had had up to the time she wrote it. What was more, she still wrote for *Partisan Review,* still saw socially the people she was mocking so thoroughly, and still thought of them as friends. "Dear Jesus," a frightened Margaret Sargent says in another context, "I'm really as hard as nails." Although she teetered on the edge of nervous breakdown at various times in her life, Mary McCarthy was herself hard as nails; and over the years, as she lost the trepidation she once had, she became even harder. From a princess among the trolls, it could be argued, she turned into a queen of the trolls.

In her defense, it ought to be noted that Mary McCarthy played in a league with some fairly tough guys. The true art form of the intellectuals around *Partisan Review* was the crushing put-down—of one another. William Phillips, for example, once called Mary McCarthy, when she was living with Philip Rahv, his co-editor on *Partisan Review,* Rahv's "alter-Iago." Mary McCarthy herself referred to the garrulous art historian Meyer Schapiro as "a mouth looking for an ear." When McCarthy published her collection of stories, *The Company She Keeps* (1942), the poet Delmore Schwartz suggested it ought to be retitled "Tidings from the Whore."

In his memoir *The Truants,* William Barrett, the best chronicler of New York intellectual life in this period, though far from admiring of McCarthy, does allow that she had entered a man's world and was able to "hold her own with men—both intellectually and sexually." Refusing to admit what others might have thought the natural vulnerability of a woman, Mary McCarthy gave rather better than she got.

How much she gave and what she got in return we now know in extensive detail, thanks to Carol Brightman's *Writing Dangerously: Mary McCarthy and Her World.* This is the third full biography devoted to Mary McCarthy but the first to have appeared since her death—and the first, therefore, able really to dish the dirt, as McCarthy's generation of Vassar girls might have put it. As she herself made clear in her fiction, Miss McCarthy's was not a scandal-free life, and though not all the players in her personal pageant have shuffled off the stage, many things about her life could not have been written about until after her death. Miss Brightman, a Vassar girl herself, is not at all chary of playing kiss-and-tell in the manner of contemporary biographers— that is, her subject did all the kissing and now she does all the telling.

Carol Brightman interviewed Mary McCarthy many times before her death in 1989, and, she gives us to believe, became quite friendly with her. As a biographer, though, she takes the odd position of seeming to admire her subject in general while reserving the right to dislike her in most of her particulars. She realizes, for example, that much of Mary McCarthy's fiction is quite stillborn, and she is not afraid to say so, or to offer reasons why this might be.

Miss Brightman also brings her own politics to this biography of an intellectual who spent so much of her own energy on politics. Miss Brightman's politics are for the most part standard New Left—she edited the journal *Viet-Report* during the Vietnam war—with a special emphasis on anti-anti-Communism. In some circles, apparently, even after the fall of Communism—a doctrine that made for more human misery, individual and collective, than any in the history of the world—to be an anti-Communist can still be held as a mark against an intellectual, and it is in these circles that Carol Brightman travels.

Mary McCarthy was an anti-Stalinist, and, except for a brief Trotskyite phase and with certain qualifications, an anti-Communist she remained until the Vietnam war, when her politics took a sharp turn and her anti-Communism was displaced by her anti-Americanism. Only after this displacement has been made does her biographer begin to feel a full political kinship with her—a kinship she distinctly does not feel with other intellectuals around *Partisan Review* or with members of the Congress for Cultural Freedom or indeed with anyone who saw Communism as a distinct menace, both in itself and to the world. Miss Brightman's notion of a truly malevolent character is Sidney Hook, her notion of evil incarnate is the CIA.

One of the cleverest methods for putting off a biographer is to write a brilliant autobiography. Mary McCarthy did not quite manage this. She wrote three different autobiographical volumes: *Memoirs of a Catholic Girlhood* (1954), *How I Grew* (1987), and *Intellectual Memoirs* (posthumously published in 1992). The best of these is *Memoirs of a Catholic Girlhood,* where she tells of her parents' death in the flu epidemic of 1918, leaving her, then six years old, and her three brothers orphans. Her account of her tyrannous Aunt Margaret and Uncle Myers, under whose roof in Minneapolis she spent six years, and then of her life in Seattle with her more cultivated Preston grandparents (her Preston grandmother was Jewish) remains an impressive piece of work and probably her best book.

The other two autobiographical volumes are drier, sketchier, less satisfying. *Intellectual Memoirs,* however, is notable for its pages on Miss McCarthy's sex life; it includes a brief exegesis on the size and shape of various male members (not of parliament) and her account of having once slept with three different men within a twenty-four-hour period, which in hockey and among libertines is known as the hat trick.

The daughter and granddaughter of the most beautiful women of their respective generations in Seattle, Mary McCarthy was herself, in the old botanical metaphor, deflowered at the age of fourteen by a man nearly twice her age. She went on to have four marriages and claimed to have slept with more than 100 different men. This notable propensity on her part for contemplating the ceiling is psychologically interesting, because Mary McCarthy did not, as Carol Brightman points out, seem to take all that much pleasure in sex. Nor do the various heroines in her fiction. In her best-known novel *The Group* (1963), the uncomplicated enjoyment of sex seems to be reserved for the healthily insentient. When, in "The Man in the Brooks Brothers Shirt," Margaret Sargent decides to sleep with the stranger she has met on the train, Miss McCarthy describes her decision thus: "She had felt tired and kind and thought, why not?"

Like most talented women, Mary McCarthy was no feminist, either when young or in her later years. She felt feminism "bad for women," for she thought it born of desperation and that "it induces a very bad emotional state." What she was instead was a liberated woman—liberated chiefly in the sexual realm, but not there alone. Among her Vassar classmates (class of '33), Miss McCarthy was considered smart, sarcastic, sophisticated, very daring. While a freshman, she spent weekends in New York living with Harold Johnsrud, an actor and would-be playwright who was to be her first husband; the summer of her senior year, she moved in with him. This was an audacious thing to have done in that day, though a classmate later suggested that, having no parents, Miss McCarthy had less to fear socially than other Vassar girls.

Vassar was a key experience for Mary McCarthy. It was a

place of greater prestige than it became after admitting men in 1969 and diluting its snobbery. Even as late as the 1950's, a Vassar girl was a condition, a station in life. "Vassar girls, in general," thinks one of the characters in *The Group,* "were not liked by the world at large; they had come to be a sort of symbol of superiority." At Vassar, even someone as rebellious as Mary McCarthy kept the fact that she had a Jewish grandmother from her classmates; it was, in those purlieus, bad enough to be half-Irish. On weekends at the country estates of her classmates, McCarthy had a chance to see how the other 1 percent lived.

"Vassar," writes Carol Brightman, "supplied Mary McCarthy with a pedigree, by osmosis." Today Mary McCarthy's name is to Vassar as F. Scott Fitzgerald's is to Princeton: two quite uncharacteristic students whose later success has come to identify them thoroughly with their respective schools. Astonishing to report, such was her fame later in life that Miss McCarthy was offered the presidency of Vassar in 1985.

Mary McCarthy graduated Phi Beta Kappa and *cum laude* in 1933. She married Johnsrud that summer, and immediately felt "I had *done the wrong thing.*" She felt something similar when, five years later, she agreed to marry the famous critic Edmund Wilson, the motive for doing which, nearly forty years after the fact, she claimed still not to be able to puzzle out. In her essay "My Confession" (1953), she notes:

> The "great" decisions—those I can look back on pensively and say, "That was a turning point"—have been made without my awareness. Too late to do anything about it, I have chosen.

She goes on to say that this is all the more striking when the choice has been political or historic, but to make two marriages passively seems to me more remarkable still, especially from a writer known above all for her cool analytical power.

Mary McCarthy was someone much impressed by the role of accident in life. In "My Confession," she also discusses the accidental way she came to politics. After her marriage, she did a bit of book reviewing for the *New Republic* and the *Nation,* though for the most part not on heavily political subjects. She had the normal young person's instinct to favor the underdog, and this put her on the side of the convicted anarchists Sacco and Vanzetti and of the radical labor leader Tom Mooney. Her husband, she claims, had "social anger in him," owing to his father's having lost a job in an academic scandal. Being around theatrical people, she and her husband "began to take part in a left-wing life, to which we felt superior, which we laughed at, but which nevertheless was influencing us without our being aware of it." She and Johnsrud, in evening clothes, picketed on behalf of striking waiters at the Waldorf. But the Communist-party members and fellow travelers they saw, she allows, "knew we were . . . unserious, politically."

When the Moscow trials were in the news in the mid-thirties, Miss McCarthy was off in Reno, waiting out a divorce—she and Johnsrud each had many love affairs on their marriage's road to ruin—and knew nothing about them. At a party upon her return to New York, in what she thought was a standard cocktail-party argument, she said that Leon Trotsky was entitled to a fair hearing to defend himself against the accusation that he had betrayed the revolution. A few days later, she found her name on the stationery of the Trotsky Defense Committee. Offended, she was about to write to ask that her name be removed when she was suddenly harassed by late-night phone calls from Communist party sympathizers advising her to disassociate herself from the Committee. Being naturally contrarian in spirit, she decided to remain a member.

Where before she had been either indifferent or vaguely pro-Communist, she was now anti-Stalinist. She found herself arguing Trotsky's case at parties. To argue it better, she had to read up on the Moscow trials and, from there, on the history of Communism. She never became a Marxist, and in "My Confession" remarks, in a nice Mary McCarthy touch, that Marxism "was something you had to take up young, like ballet dancing." In "My Confession," too, she claims that, never having been a Communist, she came by her anti-Communism naturally, through thoughtfulness and reason, so that it had nothing of the "vindicating or vindictive character" of someone who had been badly deceived by the party.

Mary McCarthy describes her siding with the Trotskyites as *the* pivotal decision of my life." Politics certainly changed her social life. She ceased to see conventional people, who "included anyone who could hear of the Moscow trials and maintain an unruffled serenity." Many of the social habits of the recent Vassar graduate were now set aside. She read the *New York Times* instead of the *Herald-Tribune,* and

> soon I stopped doing crossword puzzles, playing bridge, reading detective stories and popular novels. I did not "give up" these things; they departed from me, as it were, on tiptoe, seeing that my thoughts were elsewhere.

Still, there were people who thought that Mary McCarthy was not fundamentally in earnest about politics. Nancy Macdonald, the first wife of Dwight Macdonald, the intellectual journalist, told Brightman that Mary "liked the *idea* of being political, but I don't think she was terribly serious about it." Brightman's own view is that "a curiosity born of social ambition" propelled her into radical politics.

Through James T. Farrell, whose novel *Studs Lonigan* she had reviewed, Mary McCarthy met the editors and writers who had recently captured *Partisan Review* from the Communist party. Her Trotskyite dalliance naturally put her into the *Partisan Review* orbit; the Trotskyites, McCarthy herself said, had all the beautiful girls. "My dear," she wrote to a Vassar classmate, "I've got the most Levantine lover!" She was referring to Philip Rahv (born Ivan Greenberg), as a boy brought to this country from Russia via a short detour in Palestine, with whom she soon moved in. It was, pronounced Rahv of the arrangement, making a nice little Trotskyite joke, "class war in one apartment." Among the *PR* crowd, McCarthy later wrote, "the only pleasures that were taken seriously were sex and arguing." Marxism and modernism were their meat and drink; Payne Whitney, the psychiatric clinic, their Grossinger's.

Sustained by a belief in the importance of art and ideas—the editors of *Partisan Review* argued about whether they were for or against World War II as if they were themselves, say, the government of Sweden—these intellectuals turned *PR* into a magazine of great significance. To have appeared in its pages with sufficient brilliance could be the making of a young writer: and such it was for, among others, Delmore Schwartz, Saul Bellow, Clement Greenberg, and Mary McCarthy. At Vassar, one of McCarthy's favorite teachers had suggested that she eschew imaginative literature in favor of criticism, and it was as a theater critic that, urged on by Rahv, she first appeared in *Partisan Review*. The provocative dash of her writing, appearing alongside work by André Gide, George Orwell, T. S. Eliot, and Wallace Stevens, was plainly the making of Mary McCarthy. In her reviews she first established her formidability as someone sharp, authoritative, clearly not to be fooled with.

It was also in *Partisan Review*'s office in 1937 that Miss McCarthy met Edmund Wilson. He was then forty-two, she twenty-five. He was already established as the most powerful literary critic in America. She was a girl with an eye perpetually peeled for the main chance. If there is a literary-criticism equivalent of the old Hollywood producer's casting couch, Miss McCarthy landed on Wilson's. Having done so, she decided to go ahead and marry him, or so she later reported in connection with her disavowal of any love felt for him then or at any other time. Rahv, with whom she was then living, was astonished to learn that she now planned to marry Wilson. It is not clear that he ought to have been. William Phillips later claimed not to be; in an interview with Miss Brightman, he reported: "I just assumed that [Mary] thought Wilson a more interesting figure than Rahv."

Death often turns the hard-hearted sentimental, and so Mary McCarthy turned when Rahv died in 1973. In the *New York Times Book Review,* she wrote about the tender, feminine side of his mind and his childlike sense of wonder at the world, comparing him at the close of her piece to Tolstoy's Pierre Bezukhov, that dear, good-hearted, and awkward idealist in *War and Peace.* But in her novel *The Oasis* (1949), under the transparent veil that fiction would almost always be to her, she describes a character named Will Taub (not much of a disguise, even syllabically, for Phil Rahv) as a pure type of the operator and opportunist, a thoroughly dreary and, but for his comic ineptitude, possibly dangerous fellow whose powers of understanding were defied by such things as "children, birds, cows, water, snakes, lightning, Gentiles, and automobiles." So great was Rahv's fury at this portrait that, according to Miss Brightman, he initiated a lawsuit, alleging 132 violations of his rights, which he later dropped.

In *Intellectual Memoirs,* McCarthy reports Wilson telling her that "Rahv doesn't *do* anything for you," while marrying him would "do something" for her. Her own explanation for marrying Wilson is a quasi-Marxist one: he seemed closer to her own social class. Miss Brightman weighs in with a quasi-Freudian explanation: that the older Wilson seemed a possible replacement for her recently deceased Preston grandfather, though, as it turned out, in Wilson she came closer to finding a replacement for her villainous Uncle Myers.

The Mary McCarthy–Edmund Wilson marriage has long been a subject of literary curiosity. How could two such strong temperaments possibly get along within the constrictions of a marriage? The answer is that they could not. Screaming was their normal mode of discourse. Wilson beat her up; she kicked and scratched him. When she became pregnant with his child, Wilson tried to talk her into an abortion. The summer that Wilson taught at the University of Chicago, their neighbors in Hyde

Park twice had to call the police to stop the couple's violent arguments. As a final touch, Wilson had McCarthy briefly committed, as insane, to Payne Whitney, in a manner she describes in *The Group,* where she switches the blame for this act to her first husband. The marriage lasted seven years, which, in retrospect, given the hell each made for the other, seems remarkably long-lived.

Still, as the punchline from the old Jewish joke has it, "It wasn't a total loss." Wilson thought Mary's talent lay not in criticism but in imaginative writing, and McCarthy herself later remarked that "I would never have written fiction if it hadn't been for [Wilson]." Writing fiction gave her a literary cachet that she could never have earned through criticism alone—though today, with the exception of some of the stories in *The Company She Keeps,* McCarthy's fiction seems almost exclusively of narrow, by now largely historical, interest. Because of her propensity for plagiarizing from life in her fiction, she acquired the reputation of being a scandalous writer. But more important, had she not written criticism, her fiction would never have received the attention it did; and had she not written fiction, her criticism would not have had quite the authority it did.

Mary McCarthy married twice more after her marriage to Wilson: first to Bowden Broadwater, a man eight years younger than she with a nice nose for scandal who lived on the edges of New York cultural life and who she later claimed not to have known was bisexual; and, finally and apparently happily, to a minor American diplomatic official named James West. In both marriages, she was clearly the primary party: daily life was organized around her needs, concerns, whims. This was owing to her growing fame and the power it carried with it. By the late 1940's, her work began appearing in *The New Yorker,* and she was becoming a writer of national reputation, a personage, a figure, a force.

During the late 1940's and early 1950's, too, Mary Mc-

Carthy began to Europeanize herself. The Italian writer Nicola Chiaromonte became a great friend of hers; so, too, did Hannah Arendt, the German-Jewish philosopher then living in America whom McCarthy's son would later call his mother's intellectual conscience, which does not say much for either of them. She took teaching jobs at Bard and Sarah Lawrence. She made the inevitable connections with Bernard Berenson and Isaiah Berlin, intellectual figures with great social prestige. She shucked off the last vestiges of intellectual bohemianism and began to dress expensively. Along the way, Paul Tillich, the theologian, made passes at her, Igor Stravinsky pursued her; she had an affair with a now-forgotten London journalist named John Davenport, and dropped her third husband (Bowden Broadwater). She wrote intellectually thin books about Venice and Florence. ("But, my dear," said Berenson, "what do you *know* about Florence?") Under the strain of all this, she underwent depression and near nervous breakdown, waking up one morning in Florence believing that she *was* the English publisher George Weidenfeld.

According to Miss Brightman, Mary McCarthy's reputation really took off with the publication of *Memoirs of a Catholic Girlhood* in 1957. Publishers began to besiege her. She no longer needed to think of herself as part of a narrow band of New York intellectuals—"the boys from over the bridges," as Hannah Arendt, with a fine touch of snobbery, called the *Partisan Review* crowd, referring to their origins in Brooklyn and the Bronx. William Shawn, of *The New Yorker,* wanted to send her to Jerusalem. She was sought out for interviews.

The Group, published in 1963, was the big Mary McCarthy novel everyone had been waiting for but not many important critics—important, that is, to her—much liked it. Important critics did not, however, keep it from being a best-seller through much of 1963 and well into 1964. It was widely translated, and, according to Miss Brightman, as of 1991, "more than 5.2 million copies had been sold worldwide." Part of the book's immense popular success was owing to its scandalousness (for its day): it was early out of the gate in describing sex from a woman's point of view; it provided an interesting sociology of the diaphragm (not the first appearance of this device in Mary McCarthy's fiction); it offered an upper-class American lesbian as a main character. The novel also presented some extended glimpses into upper-class life, viewed with appropriate wonder, of a kind not uncommon in fiction written by the American Irish.

The Group chronicles portions of the lives of six graduates of the Vassar class of '33. It begins with the wedding of Kay Strong (the Mary McCarthy character) and ends, roughly eight years later, at her funeral. (She dies falling out of a window at the Vassar Club in Manhattan.) Kay's death is not merely the chief but perhaps the only surprise in the novel. McCarthy's main effort is bent on showing how her characters live, which includes what they wear and eat and how they act and make love. The book is richly laden with facts, but there is something hollow at its center. It is more intent on sociology than on fiction. But today's sociology turns out to be yesterday's news, and yesterday's news is what *The Group* reads like today.

Carol Brightman believes that Mary McCarthy's "limitation as a novelist is a failure of imagination," by which she means that McCarthy never really was able to let go, to "reach beyond personal experience into the impersonal realm of the imagination." I prefer the explanation offered by Randall Jarrell in his novel *Pictures from an Institution*. There, Jarrell has a novelist whom he names Gertrude Johnson and who, though Jarrell never admitted it, seems to have been modeled on Mary McCarthy. Gertrude knows a great many facts but nothing of human emotions: she can tell you the name of the furniture polish a child has swallowed but not how the child feels as it seizes and swallows the polish. Of Gertrude, Jarrell, devastatingly, writes:

> If she was superior to most people in her courage and inde-
> pendence, in her intelligence, in her reckless wit, in her ex-
> traordinary powers of observation, in her almost eidetic
> memory, she was inferior to them in most human qualities;
> she had not yet arrived even at that elementary forbearance
> upon which human society is based.

Edmund Wilson, when he was married to her, prophesied that Mary McCarthy would become the female Stendhal.
But in her fiction the magic never kicked in. She was instead
content to use fiction to settle old scores or to preach her opinions—establishing, once again, her own superiority. This
propensity grew even greater as she grew older, and mars her
last two novels—*Birds of America* (1971) and *Cannibals and Mis-
sionaries* (1979)—to the point of making them quite unreadable.
Writing about George Orwell, Mary McCarthy speculated that
"maybe he did not have enough human weakness to be a real
novelist." Insufficient human weakness was not Miss McCarthy's
problem; escaping her weakness in the realm of art was.

With the money earned from *The Group,* Mary McCarthy
was able to transform herself from the hard-hearted vamp into
the *grande dame* of American letters. With her fourth husband,
she now took up permanent residence in Paris, returning only
for the summer months to a house she had bought in Castine,
Maine. The French press referred to her as *"la Simone de Beauvoir américaine,"* which, since she detested Simone de Beauvoir,
must have rankled. In her book *America Day by Day,* de Beauvoir
referred to Mary McCarthy, without mentioning her by name,
as "that beautiful and cold novelist who has already gone through
three husbands and several lovers in the course of a cleverly laid
out career."

The Vietnam war came along just in time to revivify Miss
McCarthy. She had in any case been drifting away from anti-
Communism, and revelations that the CIA had helped support
the English monthly *Encounter* and other liberal anti-Communist

endeavors put her further outside its traditional orbit. When the *New York Review of Books,* which had positioned itself as an anti-anti-Communist paper and of which McCarthy was one of the great figures, offered to send her to Vietnam to write six articles on the war for $1,000 an article, she agreed to go.

In "The Genial Host," one of the stories in *The Company She Keeps,* the Mary McCarthy character remarks that behind her own politics was a temperamental attraction to unpopular causes:

> When you were young, it had been the South, the Dauphin, Bonnie Prince Charlie; later it was Debs and now Trotsky that you loved. You admired this romantic trait in yourself and you would confess humorously: "All I have to do is be *for* somebody and he loses."

This time, in taking up the position she did on the war in Vietnam, she had chosen both a popular and a winning cause.

Read today, Miss McCarthy's little book *Hanoi* makes fairly plain that she had taken the short but decisive step from being against the Vietnam war to being *for* North Vietnam. She is probably correct when she remarks, in the polemical preface to this book, that "the power of intellectuals, sadly limited, is to persuade, not to provide against contingencies." But intellectuals, as a type, are never more repulsive than when deciding, at least in print, the fate of thousands on no greater basis than the yearning for the tidiness of their own logic.

A very poor performance, Mary McCarthy's in *Hanoi,* as she describes the cheerful, bustling people of North Vietnam, persevering in the face of American monstrousness. Conditions in Hanoi are ever judged superior to those in Saigon. Auschwitz is brought up in connection with American bombing. In a letter to Dwight Macdonald she had characterized Communism in North Vietnam as "virtuous tyranny," adding that "I have enough tyranny in me to respond to the appeal."

But she really felt that she had a great deal of virtue, too. For in accounting for her motives in going to Hanoi, she writes: "I could not bear to see my country disfigure itself so, when I might do something to stop it." But then her love for her own country would seem to be rather ambiguous, for in her preface she stipulates that "the alternatives to Communism offered by the Western countries are all ugly in their own ways and getting uglier."

So important did correct views on Vietnam come to loom for her that she even judged dead writers on what positions, had they been alive, they might have taken on the war there. In her essay "The Writing on the Wall," George Orwell, the most important political writer of her generation, flunked the test. She found his "belligerent anti-Communism" disqualifying and, in an early act of political correctness, read him out of the canon of acceptable writers.

As long as she remained alive, Mary McCarthy was a formidable presence in American literary life, even though her books garnered fewer and fewer praising reviews and seemed less the intellectual events they once had been. She wrote about the trial of Captain Ernest Medina, the American officer who commanded the troops responsible for the My Lai massacre, and, later, about the Watergate hearings, both of which gave her plenty of opportunity to vent her distaste for American life. At her summer home in Maine, she played the *grande dame* to the full, insisting on formal ritual; "The Duchess of Castine" is the title of Miss Brightman's chapter on her life in Maine. She made a tremendous fuss about food, and saw in American white bread and supermarkets the fall of the West.

Past sixty now, not always a fine age for a once-beautiful woman, she wrote memoirs, learned nearly monthly of the death of former friends, attended to her own illnesses. Her last few years were haunted by a lawsuit for libel that the playwright Lillian Hellman—whom McCarthy had detested for decades both as a writer and as an old apologist for Stalinism—launched against her for saying, on the Dick Cavett television show, that "every word [Hellman] writes is a lie, including 'and' and 'the' "; the suit was only dropped when Hellman died. Many people felt the two women richly deserved each other.

"I still haven't *succeeded*," Mary McCarthy told Miss Brightman two years before lung cancer swept her off the board at seventy-seven. But Miss Brightman does believe hers was a success of sorts. "It is her respect for words and their mysteries that makes her literary example worth pondering," writes Miss Brightman, trying to save something from the long life of her subject. "The peculiar intensity of McCarthy's prose, the authority one feels behind its observations and judgments, comes in part from a scrupulous commitment to accurate expression." The critical essay rather than the novel, everyone seemed to agree, was her true form. "She was our most brilliant literary critic," Gore Vidal wrote, in a compliment with a dagger of malice added, because she was "uncorrupted by compassion."

Yet Hazlitt says that true taste is demonstrated by enthusiasm, and by this test Miss McCarthy, as a critic, does not fare very well. Her friend Dwight Macdonald once remarked that every time he said yes he got in trouble. Mary McCarthy did not do much better. As a critic, she became a champion of William Burroughs's novel *Naked Lunch* (not at her house in Castine was lunch likely to be so served); she thought Günter Grass's *The Tin Drum* "a new genre"; she claimed to admire the fictional experiments of Nathalie Sarraute; she wrote an elaborate explication of Vladimir Nabokov's overly elaborate box-within-a-box novel *Pale Fire;* she tried to make a case for the greatness of Ivy Compton-Burnett. But it is by her devastations—of the American playwrights, of J. D. Salinger, of Simone de Beauvoir—that she is best remembered, though probably not for much longer, in good part because, ironically, she herself helped to kill interest in these subjects.

Although Mary McCarthy seems to have given more pain

than pleasure in her daily dealings with the world, considered as the adventures of a woman essentially alone in life, hers is a career worthy of contemplation. In *Memoirs of a Catholic Girlhood,* she speaks of the importance for her, as a little girl, of wanting to be noticed. For several decades, with the aid chiefly of strong clear prose and clean good looks and the force of personality, this woman was able to command the attention of whatever world she happened to reside in at the moment. She made a great stir in her day but now that the stir is over and the attention withdrawn, interest in her work is all but completely drained. Her life, viewed in retrospect, seems rather sad, but not without meaning: good looks and intelligence, those ostensibly great gifts, if not accompanied by an understanding heart, are by themselves not enough, either in literature or in life.

Ambrose Bierce,
Our Favorite Cynic

—◆◆—

In a small but highly selective neighborhood in Hell reside the cynics, among whom Ambrose Bierce must surely have long ago taken up residence. His neighbors there are likely to include Juvenal, La Rochefoucauld, Chamfort, Swift, Heine, Strindberg, Mencken, and (a recent arrival) the Romanian-born French writer E. M. Cioran. If superior talk is your idea of a good time, it's not really such a bad place to end up, this neighborhood. "Heaven for climate," as J. M. Barrie once wrote. "Hell for company."

One of the reasons cynics deserve Hell is that most of them seem to have had a preternaturally good time on earth. If behind every comedian there is a sad, if not heartily depressed, figure, behind every cynic there is just as often someone laughing at the spectacle of human earnestness. "The poor wish only to be rich, which is impossible, not to be better," Bierce wrote. "They would like to be rich in order to be worse, generally speaking." How vicious, uncharitable, unsympathetic—indecent, really—and, alas, probably quite true! If it didn't often contain that kernel of obstinate, objectionable truth, cynicism would be of no interest whatsoever.

Ambrose Bierce is today best known for *The Devil's Dic-*

tionary and the much anthologized short story "An Occurrence at Owl Creek Bridge," and for everything that we do not know about his death. What we do know is that in 1913 Bierce, who was then seventy-one and was the country's most famous iconoclast, decided to chuck it all and see what was going on with Pancho Villa in Mexico. Endless are the theories of what became of him there, including one that holds that he never went to Mexico at all but killed himself in the Grand Canyon, which is the view favored by Roy Morris, Jr., in his workmanlike biography, *Ambrose Bierce: Alone in Bad Company.*

Whether death was a good career move for Bierce is another much debated subject. Some say that the mystery of his death added to his legend—the legendary Bierce appears in Carlos Fuentes's novel *The Old Gringo,* and the subsequent movie version, in which he is played by Gregory Peck—and that it has kept interest in his writing alive. Others say that the only effect of the legend has been to distract attention from where it belongs—on Bierce's writing, which carries its own vexing complications.

"It is only a question of time, and perhaps of not much time," Wilson Follett wrote of Bierce, "when we shall see him emerge from the mists of his legend and appear not only as an American writer of the very first stature, but also as a world figure." Follett made that prediction in 1937, and it hasn't come true yet. Years earlier, Bierce had written, in a letter to a friend, "How many times, and covering a period of how many years, must one's unexplainable obscurity be pointed out to constitute fame? Not knowing, I am almost disposed to consider myself the most famous of authors. I have pretty nearly ceased to be 'discovered,' but my notoriety as an obscurian may be said to be worldwide and apparently everlasting." Poor Bierce, he sounds like the poet Robert Southey, who was assured that his reputation would be secure long after Homer and Virgil were forgotten—but not until.

Cynics aren't born but made, and though the origin of

Bierce's cynicism has been disputed, its depth has not. Even H. L. Mencken, a practitioner and genuine connoisseur of these matters, claimed, after spending time with Bierce, to have been appalled by the darkness of his views. Bierce said that, as a journalist, he was in the business of dispensing abuse, and at this he worked overtime. He may have been something of a Johnny-one-note, but with that single note his repertoire included ridicule, invective, vituperation, rage, and more than occasional fury. His steady hatred was mildly ameliorated only by his amusement at the passing travesty called the human show.

Whence did such cynicism derive? In *The Devil's Dictionary,* which contains chiefly lexicographical entries, written in terse, sometimes aphoristic prose, the entry under "Birth" begins, "The first and direst of all disasters." Bierce's own birth wasn't really so dire, although he made it out to have been. He was born in 1842 in Horse Cave Creek, Ohio, the tenth child of Marcus Aurelius and Laura Bierce, all of whose children were given names beginning with the letter "A." English puritan in its genealogy and spirituality, the family moved when Ambrose was four to northern Indiana, where Marcus Bierce worked, not very successfully, at farming, among other trades. In later life, Bierce referred to his parents as "unwashed savages," which is laying it on with a crane: the father may not have had much business sense, but he was bookish, and the son had the run of his library. Bierce's real grudge seems to have been against his mother, the charge here being insufficient affection.

There is no entry in *The Devil's Dictionary* for "Mother"; had there been, it might have read, "First among betrayers." Certainly Bierce grew up in nothing like the suffocating atmosphere of ignorance, superstition, scandal, and shame that was visited upon Theodore Dreiser growing up in Indiana thirty-odd years later. Lack of love in the home may help but doesn't of itself qualify one for a lifetime of cynicism. Mencken was able to achieve his cynicism despite being something of a mother's boy.

Scratch a cynic and underneath, as often as not, you will

find a dead idealist. Although he never spoke of it, Bierce's ide-alism apparently exhausted itself in his abolitionism. His fam-ily was abolitionist, and his Uncle Lucius, who as a lawyer and a political figure in northern Ohio was easily the most successful of the Bierces, was so ardent in his belief that he bragged of hav-ing supplied swords to John Brown and his fanatics for their raid on Harpers Ferry. Young Ambrose got a job, at sixteen, on an abolitionist newspaper in Warsaw, Indiana. Probably owing to his uncle's efforts, Bierce soon afterward spent a year at the Ken-tucky Military Institute. "It was here, presumably," Morris spec-ulates in his biography, "that Bierce acquired his characteristic military bearing and the useful skills of draftsmanship and car-tography that would stand him in good stead in the years to come."

The years to come were, of course, those of the Civil War. Bierce, at eighteen, was the second man in Elkhart County to sign up with the Ninth Indiana Volunteer Infantry Regiment. No sensible cynic would even consider such an act. But Bierce did hard time in the war. He served as a foot soldier, a scout, and a topographical engineer. He was taken prisoner, but es-caped. He fought in three of the war's bloodiest battles: Shiloh, Stones River, and Chickamauga. Leading a skirmish line at Ke-nesaw Mountain, in 1864, he took a bullet that left his head, as he later said, "broken like a walnut." By the war's end, he was a first lieutenant; he had been cited many times for bravery.

Bierce often said that a part of him died in the Civil War. That part, clearly, was the idealist. As a young soldier, he saw every kind of vanity and stupidity. He saw men with the power of rank send men without any power whatsoever to their cer-tain deaths, chiefly to please yet other men, who would never fight for anything but the objects of their own ambition. He saw squalor and cowardice and death—and in wholesale lots. In "What I Saw of Shiloh," written in 1881, Bierce recounted how burned woodlands sent flaming leaves down on wounded sol-diers, leaving them "in postures of agony that told of the tormenting flame. Their clothing was half burnt away—their hair and beard entirely; the rain had come too late to save their nails. Some were swollen to double girth; others shriveled to manikins. According to degree of exposure, their faces were bloated and black or yellow and shrunken."

While the Civil War ended Bierce's idealism (it did something similar to Oliver Wendell Holmes, Jr., who was severely wounded in it), it probably also gave birth to the writer in Bierce, even though he would not write directly about it until many years afterward. In that war, which he came to view as, at least partly, a time of grandeur, "when there was something new under the sun," he acquired memories that, like sins, could be expiated only through the secular form of confession known as literature.

If the Civil War may be said to have put the blacking on Bierce's general outlook, his career in journalism supplied the polish. At the war's end, Bierce pushed on out West on a fact-finding tour of Army posts under his former commander, Major General William B. Hazen. At the tour's end, Bierce remained in San Francisco, first taking a job at the United States Mint, then falling—lapsing, he might have said—into journalism. In 1871, he married Mollie Day, the daughter of a successful mine owner. The couple went off to London for three years, where he sharpened his writer's skills at humor magazines with names like *Fun* and *Figaro.* Apart from an unsuccessful attempt to manage a mine in the Black Hills, near Deadwood, in what was then the Dakota Territory, and a ten-year stint toward the end of his career working for William Randolph Hearst in Washington, D.C., Bierce spent the better part of his days in journalism in San Francisco.

Working on various papers there, he wrote columns under such rubrics as "Town Crier" and "Prattle," in which he knocked off sketches of West Coast types and blasted anyone he damn well pleased. In those days—the late 1860's and the early 1870's—a journalist was well advised to carry a gun, for people did then to journalists what they only wish to do now: they shot them. (Bierce toted a loaded Colt revolver after insulting, in print, the actress wife of a man named Henry Widmer.) Bierce also wrote some fairly forgettable verse, and essays for *The Overland Monthly,* then edited by Bret Harte. His recent reading in the classics and in English literature was rather too prominently on display in his early writing. This would change.

What wouldn't change was his utter comfort and ease while on the attack. He seemed to be happiest when letting his most bitter sentiments rip. He wrote *de haut en bas,* casting, as he might have averred, artificial pearls before real swine. The man Bierce had made himself into was an aristocrat of the mind: high, haughty, magisterially amused at the spectacle of the rabble—rich and poor rabble alike—swirling below. Even so, as Roy Morris makes clear, he tended to take the side of the underdogs, the Mormons among them. "Excepting the Jews and the Chinese," Bierce wrote, "I know no worthier large class of people than they." In most conflicts of his time, he took his place far above the ruck, always saving a sufficiency of cold contempt for "that immortal ass, the average man." It wasn't at all a bad show.

Although Bierce was the father of three children, he was not, unsurprisingly, much of a family man. He lived with his wife only intermittently, and when he discovered that she was interested in another man he separated from her, announcing, "I don't take part in competitions—not even for the favor of a woman." The older of his two sons killed himself over the loss of a girl when he was not yet seventeen; the other son died, of alcoholism, at twenty-six. Bierce was thus twice a member of the sad society of those who have buried their own children. These events doubtless chilled further his already bleak views. Still, he continued, warning his enemies that he was around for the duration: "While the public buys my rebuking at twice the price your sycophancy earns—while I keep a conscience uncorrupted by religion, a judgment undimmed by politics and

279

patriotism, a heart untainted by friendships and sentiments un-soured by animosities—while it pleases me to write, there will be personalities in journalism, personalities of condemnation as well as commendation."

Some feel that Bierce wasted his talent in journalism; others feel that his talent was precisely for journalism. The latter cite his brilliant attacks on the big four of California capitalism—Leland Stanford, Mark Hopkins, Charles Crocker, and, especially, Collis P. Huntington, the Southern Pacific Railroad man. Huntington, it is said, once asked Bierce to name his price to leave him alone. "My price is seventy-five million dollars," Bierce responded, referring to the railroad's public indebtedness, which Huntington and his lobbyists were attempting to avoid. "If, when you are ready to pay, I happen to be out of town, you may hand it over to my friend, the Treasurer of the United States."

Bierce might have remained no more than another cut-and-slash journalist and critic but for a revival of his interest, in the late 1880's, in the Civil War, which, as Morris recounts, "began a remarkable three-year stretch of creative endeavor, one that, within the limits of its author's narrow but not inconsiderable talents, has seldom been surpassed in American literature." During this period, Bierce wrote "An Occurrence at Owl Creek Bridge," "Chickamauga," and many of the other stories in his 1892 collection, *Tales of Soldiers and Civilians.*

M. E. Grenander, who is Bierce's most intelligent critic, has rightly remarked that Bierce "has always hovered on the margins of America's literary canon." Part of the reason is that Bierce was never a very careful caretaker of his own career. He published badly, often bringing out trivial books or not finding good publishers for his better books, and then, in 1909, late in his life, he allowed a friend to talk him into amassing a twelve-volume *Collected Works of Ambrose Bierce.* This packed the best and the rather ampler worst of his writing in one place. In 1946, Clifton Fadiman brought out a single volume, *The Collected Writ-*

ings of Ambrose Bierce, which, at 810 pages, went a long way toward slimming things down, yet, in presenting all of *The Devil's Dictionary,* and filling the remainder of the book with Bierce's sometimes quite negligible stories, it, too, gave a less than complimentary view of Bierce's particular—perhaps one should say, instead, peculiar—talent.

Bierce would be an important figure if only for the lines of influence he radiated, both as a writer of fiction and as a journalist. As the first American to write dispassionately and precisely—which is to say truthfully—about war, Bierce influenced Stephen Crane (who in *The Red Badge of Courage* wrote the great Civil War novel, even though he was born six years after its conclusion) and also Ernest Hemingway. Crane said that "nothing better exists" than Bierce's story "An Occurrence at Owl Creek Bridge." Bierce, in his habitual manner of returning a compliment, once said he "thought that there could only be two worse writers than Stephen Crane, namely two Stephen Cranes."

The other line of influence that becomes immediately apparent is that extending from Bierce to Mencken. Mencken was much smarter than Bierce about managing his career. But the two men held in common an ability to twirl the knout with stylish dexterity, smashing whatever it took their fancy to smash. Mencken wrote of Bierce, "He was the first American to lay about him with complete gusto, charging and battering the frauds who ranged the country."

Literary influence is one thing, actual literature another. Did Bierce write anything that still lives? Yes, if one concedes that he needs to be taken, like all strong purgatives, in careful dosages. Read too much of him and his cynicism seems too consistent, too predictable, too easy, almost as if it had been written on automatic pilot. Clifton Fadiman, after acknowledging Bierce's talent as "a minor prophet of hopelessness," put it well: "He is a pessimism-machine. He is a Swift minus true intellectual power, Rochefoucauld with a bludgeon, Voltaire with stomach-ulcers." Even his stories come to seem a rather rote performance.

These stories, almost all of which are less than ten pages in length, are splendidly exact in the telling. Bierce relied little on the layering of subordinate clauses or the embellishment of elaborate punctuation; his sentences seem so many obedient soldiers, at attention and smartly turned out, each understanding its assigned task. Almost every Bierce story turns on a grotesque twist at the close. He had an insatiable appetite for the ghastly. Whether about the Civil War or about civilian life, a Bierce story reads as if it were sired by O. Henry out of Hubert Selby, Jr. Read them all and you feel as if you had read one, as Kenneth Tynan once wrote about the plays of Ionesco.

The most horrific Bierce story, "Chickamauga," is about a deaf-mute child who mistakes the stream of blood-soaked soldiers returning from the battle for a bizarre circus parade of sorts, which he, with a wooden sword, sets out to lead. All goes along grotesquely enough till the close, when the child is excited by a fire that turns out to be flames from his own house, outside which he discovers a female body: "The greater part of the forehead was torn away, and from the jagged hole the brain protruded, overflowing the temple, a frothy mass of gray, crowned with clusters of crimson bubbles—the work of a shell." The body, no regular reader of Bierce would be much surprised to learn, is that of the child's mother. All that remains is the child's strangled cry—"something," Bierce almost gleefully reports, "between the chattering of an ape and the gobbling of a turkey."

Imagine the worst and you will have grasped the ending of almost every one of Bierce's Civil War stories: a man shoots his father, twin brothers kill each other, one officer kills his dearest friend, another fires artillery on his own house and family—all in the line of duty. In Bierce's ghost stories, one character after another kills himself out of fear. Sometimes a comedy of understatement crops up. "Early one June morning in 1872," the story "An Imperfect Conflagration" begins, "I murdered my father—an act which made a deep impression on me at the time." Another, with the title "My Favorite Murder," begins, "Having murdered my mother under circumstances of singular atrocity, I was arrested and put upon my trial, which lasted seven years." Neither these nor, alas, many of Bierce's other stories manage to stay long in the mind, chiefly because Bierce, in his fiction, was so little interested in character, or even in psychology. Nearly all his stories are devoted to demonstrating the hopelessness of humankind, which is ultimately and everywhere the victim of a plan it doesn't come close to understanding.

Exactly what this plan is Bierce never spells out, except to make plain that men and women are its dupes and never more dupish than when they think they are not. He makes this general point in all its powerful particularity throughout *The Devil's Dictionary,* a work that still gives off many of those sharp, unpleasant pings of truth which most people would prefer not to hear. Sometimes it is nicely comical, as in the definition of "urbanity," which is "the kind of civility that urban observers ascribe to dwellers in all cities but New York"; or as in the definition of "self-esteem," which is "an erroneous appraisement."

More often, *The Devil's Dictionary* is given over to flaying the thick skin covering human illusions. Thus, "liberty" is "one of Imagination's most precious possessions"; "politics" is "a strife of interests masquerading as a contest of principles"; "happiness"—shades of La Rochefoucauld here—is "an agreeable sensation arising from contemplating the misery of another"; a "conservative" is "a statesman who is enamoured of existing evils, as distinguished from the Liberal, who wishes to replace them with others"; and "year" is "a period of three-hundred-and-sixty-five disappointments."

The larger vision that emerges from *The Devil's Dictionary* features Bierce's scorn for marriage, family, sex, religion, government, politics, law, journalism, philosophy, most scholarship, and all art served up with the least pretension. Much of this may have been the reflex action of a lifelong provocateur, for in the end the style a person takes on can become his dominant—in fact, domineering—reality. Yet Bierce did indisputably hold the dark views he promulgated in his writings.

It is far from clear that these views made his life miserable. Bierce, as Morris notes, was full of contradictions. Although he ceaselessly mocked women in print, he tended to be courtly and kind to the women he encountered in life. Anticapitalist though he was, he thought socialism little more than a joke. He hated war, yet looked back on his own soldiering days as among the finest of his life. He found it easier to be kind to strangers—among them aspiring young writers—than to those he loved. Believing that the lot of human beings could not be improved didn't prevent him from staying on the attack against those he thought were out to make it still worse.

What does it take to make a cynic smile? Watching the rest of us struggle for either personal or social improvement generally turns the trick. The largest smile of all, perhaps, is reserved for attempts to obtain justice, which—so your own neighborhood cynic will be delighted to inform you—simply isn't available. Going against their subject's own grain, the small cadre of critics and biographers who have been writing about Bierce since his death have, for more than eighty years now, been trying to bring him some kind of rough literary justice. At odd intervals, his work gets revived, though generally in a low key: a volume of critical essays about him is published; Edmund Wilson devotes a rather dismissive chapter to him in *Patriotic Gore;* a book of his poems is brought out; new biographies appear. None of it, however, to much avail, which probably wouldn't have surprised Bierce. He thought posthumous fame the greatest joke of all. "The invention of a humorist," he called it, adding, "If the gods ever laugh, do they not laugh at that?"

Were he alive, Bierce might well be perfectly satisfied with his current position in American literature—as a secondary figure, an odd man out, a curiosity set in a dark lacquer cabinet somewhere along the back wall. It would not suit his Olympian detachment, after all, to be highly regarded by those whom his views required him to despise. Even if the world took Ambrose Bierce for a great writer, it still wouldn't undermine his cherished belief in its profound and immitigable idiocy.

Mistah Lowell—He Dead

In some ways you are the luckiest poet I know!—
in some ways not so lucky, either, of course.
—ELIZABETH BISHOP

Sometimes it seems that the only real thing about Robert Lowell was his madness. This was all too real, and, for those who had to live with it, in the end it proved quite impossible. Poor Robert Lowell, born to nearly every advantage but lacking the crucial element of full-time sanity. Madness and art is an old story, of course, and in Lowell's generation it was pitilessly retold. Call the roll: Robert Lowell, Randall Jarrell, Delmore Schwartz, Theodore Roethke, Elizabeth Bishop, John Berryman, Sylvia Plath (a bit younger than these others). Now add up the staggering cost of mania, depression, paranoia, alcoholism, heart attack of a kind almost inseparable from broken heart, and suicide. "We poets in our youth begin in gladness; / But thereof comes in the end despondency and madness." Wordsworth wrote it, but these poets lived it. A grimmer and sadder story no one could have devised.

"He never realized, don't you know—he never suspected that to be stark raving mad is somewhat of a handicap to a writer," said Max Beerbohm, with his usual delicate comic irony, of D. H. Lawrence. Lawrence was literarily, not certifiably, mad, driven to wild extremes by wretched ideas. Robert Lowell, who had no ideas whatsoever but who was genuinely mad, knew what a distinct disadvantage it was. Over and over, in letters to friends, he conveyed the awfulness of his attacks—for such was the word he used to describe his horrendous, almost regular breakdowns, "attacks," as if they came from outside. Taken off in police wagons, straitjacketed, placed in padded cells, electroshocked, heavily Thorazined, confronted by a series of uncomprehending psychotherapists—Lowell had had the whole course, the full catastrophe, underwent every sadness, humiliation, nightmare. He once wrote to John Berryman that they had in common "visiting the bottom of the world." In his poem "In a Dark Time," Theodore Roethke wrote: "What's madness but nobility of soul / At odds with circumstance." Not to put too fine a point on it: Horseshit! What madness is is hell and the worst luck in the world.

Elizabeth Hardwick, Lowell's second wife, who lived with him longer than anyone, wrote to Allen Tate in 1959 after another of her husband's breakdowns—his fifth in ten years, with many more to come—that they brought "real suffering." She added: "And for what? I do not know the answer to the moral problems posed by a deranged person, but the dreadful fact is that in purely personal terms this deranged person does a lot of harm."

The rhythms of Robert Lowell's breakdowns are by now perhaps more famous than those of his poems. Things would begin to "speed up" for him; he would burble on, not infrequently about Alexander the Great, Napoleon, Hitler (a sentimental favorite); streams of wild manic energy coursed through him; he would find a new young woman—a student, a nurse, an Italian, a Lithuanian—who held out the promise of a new life, a fresh start, and to whom he would inevitably propose marriage, his wife and daughter at home mere details to be taken care of later; and finally, spun quite out of control now, violent and dangerous, the 911 call goes out, the police come in, and the ambulance is on its way to Bellevue, Payne-Whitney, MacLean's, or some other insane asylum; whence commences the nightmare of the coming down, through electricity and chemicals and the talking cure; then, the fragile self is brought home, packed in cotton, dominated by depression, filled with remorse. *"Du calme, du calme,"* the physician in "Heart of Darkness" advises Marlow before he is about to plunge into the tropics; and so did Lowell have to remain during his long months of recuperation. He had to stay calm while awaiting his next plunge into madness, which showed up a vast deal more promptly than Godot, and after which, as Lowell wrote to Randall Jarrell, when the latter was recovering from a breakdown of his own, there was the "groveling, low as dirt purgatorial feelings with which one emerges."

I have just read through Ian Hamilton's *Robert Lowell, a Biography* and *Lost Puritan, A Life of Robert Lowell* by Paul Mariani, both of them sympathetic to their subject, Mariani perhaps a bit more than Hamilton, but both featuring Lowell's madness. Mariani's was written partly to de-emphasize the strong role played by madness in Hamilton's book, but does not quite succeed in doing so. It could scarcely have been otherwise. Madness was the theme, the plot, the story, the background music of Robert Lowell's life. What is amazing about that life is that he achieved as much as he did in the intervals between his breakdowns. Along with a substantial body of poems, Lowell left a modest collection of critical prose, a book of translations, two moderately successful theatrical adaptations (of Melville's "Benito Cereno" and Hawthorne's "My Kinsman, Major Molyneux"), translations for the stage of *Phèdre* and *Prometheus Bound,* and a lengthy teaching career. He juggled all this and his madness, too, until one afternoon in the early autumn of 1977, in Manhattan, when he was returning from abroad to his daughter and Miss Hardwick, sitting in the back of a cab, clutching a wrapped-up Lucien Freud portrait of his still current wife, Caroline Guinness Blackwood, his heart finally gave out.

Dead at the age of sixty, Robert Lowell had a dreadful life and an astonishing career. After serving a fairly brief apprenticeship, he was immediately elevated to the very grand heights. *Lord Weary's Castle* (1946), published when he was not yet thirty years old, was greeted with the literary equivalent of trumpets and a twenty-one-gun salute. Selden Rodman's review in the *New York Times Book Review* gives something of the tone of its reception: "One would have to go back as far as 1914, the year that saw the publication of Robert Frost's *North of Boston* or to T. S. Eliot's *The Love Song of J. Alfred Prufrock* to find a poet whose first public speech has had the invention and authority of Robert Lowell's." Randall Jarrell chirped in with: "A few of these poems, I believe, will be read as long as men remember English." Louise Bogan wrote about Lowell's "moral earnestness . . . it is extraordinary to find it at present in so pure a form."

Give that man a Pulitzer, and in 1947, when Lowell was thirty, they did. That same year they also gave him a Guggenheim, an award from the American Academy of Arts and Letters, and a few pages of photographs in *Life,* at a time when *Life* was more widely read than any other magazine in America. That summer Lowell was also offered the job of Consultant in Poetry at the Library of Congress, which he took up after spending two months at Yaddo, the artists' colony in Saratoga, New York. In his biography, Ian Hamilton quotes a headline in the *Sunday Globe* in Boston that read, "Most Promising Poet in 100 Years . . . May Be Greater Than James and Amy." The prizes would never stop, the plaudits never cease. In future years, Robert Lowell might have been thought to have slipped with the publication of this book, made a mistake with the publication of that book, but all criticism of him would be in the context of his being America's greatest contemporary poet, the successor to Eliot, Frost, Pound, and Stevens.

One reads *Lord Weary's Castle* today and wonders how this quite came about. Its poems are all formal, in meter and structure, most employ rhyme but frequently not of an end-stopping kind. Few are the memorable phrasings in the poems. They don't, in any persuasive way, seem to issue out of "lived experience," which Lowell would later claim was the quality that marked all his poems. They are dour and dark enough, God knows, though what precisely has brought all this dolorosity about is not always clear from the words on the page. Classical allusions and references to Jesus are admixed with some regularity—stir and season, as the cookbooks say, to taste. These poems, in other words, feel willed, as if written to order, and the customers all resided in a little town called New Criticism.

Lowell himself perhaps best expressed his own doubts about this book. In an interview of 1964 with Stanley Kunitz, he allowed that he couldn't quite explain "why that much attention has been paid me." He brought up *Lord Weary's Castle,* a book, he thought "out of the mainstream, a rather repellent, odd, symbolic Catholic piece of work. It may be that some people have turned to my poems because of the very things that are wrong with me. I mean the difficulty I have with ordinary living, the impracticality, the myopia. Seeing less than others can be a great strain."

In a strong sense, Robert Lowell was New Criticism's child. Soon after he discovered his vocation as a poet, in 1937, he left Harvard and set off for Tennessee to study with Allen Tate; and in what has since become part of the Lowell legend, he set up a Sears, Roebuck tent in the yard at Tate and his wife Caroline Gordon's house, "Benfolly," in Clarksville. In Tennessee, he studied briefly under John Crowe Ransom, who, then in his last days at Vanderbilt, was about to take up residence at Kenyon College in Gambier, Ohio. In his biography, Ian Hamilton writes: "If Ransom was the Southern writers' spiritual chief, Tate was their unflagging impetuous polemicist." Agrarians, Fugitives, Southerners, these men may have been, but they were also international in their poetic connections: Ransom was admired by T. S. Eliot and Tate had lived in Paris and London and Greenwich Village. The summer that Lowell lived in his tent on the Tates' lawn, Ford Madox Ford was a house guest of the Tates.

Lowell followed Ransom to Kenyon, where he fell in with Randall Jarrell (who was three years older than he) and Peter Taylor, later to become the novelist and short story writer. He appears to have studied hard at Kenyon, did a degree in classics, worked at developing a poetic style. Ransom published one of Lowell's youthful poems in *The Kenyon Review.* Intellectual marines arriving in little magazines, the New Critics all had their journals: Ransom had *Kenyon,* Tate was editor of *The Sewanee Review,* down at the Louisiana office, at Baton Rouge, *The Southern Review* was co-edited by Cleanth Brooks and Robert Penn Warren. But for Lowell, Ransom's influence was decisive. "The kind of poet I am was largely determined by the fact that I grew up in the heyday of the New Criticism," he wrote in 1974, in connection with John Crowe Ransom's death. "From the beginning I was preoccupied with technique, fascinated by the past and tempted by other languages." In his early poems, written as if for New Critical analysis, Lowell supplied enough ambiguity to plaster Mona Lisa's smile permanently on the *punim* of William Empson.

These Southerners must have been not so secretly pleased to have a Boston Lowell in their camp. Robert, to be sure, was a complicated kind of Lowell. He was not one of the fabulously rich and landed Lowells, but of a lesser branch of the family. On the matter of levels of Lowellalia, Paul Mariani reports that Lowell's father was "definitely *not* one of your robust Captains-of-Industry Lowells, having descended through the much thinner line of Unitarian and Episcopalian ministers and poetasters." His mother's family, the Winslows, were rather grander than his fathers' and as both Lowell's biographers make plain the key masculine figure in the young Robert Lowell's life was not his father, a genial but apparently ineffectual man, but his maternal grandfather, Arthur Winslow. Socially and financially, Arthur Winslow was much better fixed than Lowell's naval officer father, about whom, before his marriage, a friend of his mother's said that, if he were hers to deal with, she would have him lobotomized and his head stuffed with green peppers.

Even without Lowell's terrible mental illness, his bipolar condition, the major jigeroo in his brain that sent him flying off the track and rendered him permanently fragile, his mother would have given him enough problems to keep a full phalanx of shrinks off the dole. As if poor Lowell didn't have trouble enough, he was given a mother worthy of a Tennessee Williams play, Boston upper-class division. A spoiled girl who grew into an imperious and interfering woman, she seems to have left her son, an only child, with the feeling that he could only disappoint her: choosing the wrong wives, the wrong work, the wrong life. She was a mother of the kind that gives one very little peace when alive and then after her death leaves one feeling guilty.

Still, a Lowell remains a Lowell, and Robert, whether he wished it or not, handled his lineage the way one is instructed to handle one's American Express card: he never, that is, left home without it. Jean Stafford, Lowell's first wife, reported to Peter and Eleanor Taylor, as early as 1943, that "the greatest snobs in the world are bright New York literary Jews and the name Lowell works like a love-philtre" among them. My guess is that it also worked with George Santayana, who knew his Boston social hierarchies, with T. S. Eliot, and possibly with Ezra Pound, who even in his madness probably retained knowledge of what it meant to be a Lowell. None of these men, there is reason to suspect, would have responded quite so generously to the young Robert Lowell if his name had been, say, Jim Swenson.

Was Robert Lowell aware of the cachet that lay in his own name? I don't for a moment wish to report that he worked it for what it was worth—when he and Elizabeth Hardwick left Boston to take up residence in New York, he might even be said to have walked away from all that—but that he retained awareness of the extraordinary attention his name commanded there can be no doubt. In a letter of 1962 he reported a dream to Elizabeth Bishop in which Philip Rahv, then the editor of *Partisan Review*, who had "just married a society lady and bought a house on Beacon Street . . . was picking up everything I had carefully thrown away all my life—golden keys of social ease, till at the end his two sons [Rahv in fact had no children] had just entered Groton," while in the same dream Lowell's daughter had to settle for public school.

Elizabeth Bishop touched on the point when, in a letter to Lowell in 1959, she wrote, apropos of Byron: "As Pascal says, if you can manage to be well-born it saves you thirty years." A few years earlier, she made the same point with much greater specificity, when she wrote that she and probably most of their contemporaries are "green with envy of your kind of assurance." What she meant was the social assurance that Lowell put into the poems that became *Life Studies*. "I feel," Bishop wrote, "that I could write in as much detail about my Uncle Artie, say—but what would be the significance? Nothing at all . . . Whereas all you have to do is put down the names! And the fact that it seems significant, illustrative, American, etc., gives you, I think, the confidence you display about tackling any idea or theme, *seriously*, in both writing and conversation." To put Bishop's point somewhat differently: Would Lowell's poem "My Last Afternoon with Uncle Devereux Winslow" give off quite the same ping if the poem were titled "My Last Afternoon with Uncle Manny Klein"? Think, maybe, not.

The Lowell name had its own magic even in politics. Lowell's most famous political gesture, it will be recalled, was his affronting Lyndon Johnson in 1965 by refusing to show up for a White House gathering of artists. He claimed that his doing so would implicitly ally him with Johnson's escalation of the war then being fought in Vietnam. Lowell had first accepted this invitation, then backed out; he had at first agreed not to publicize his refusal to attend, then sent his letter to President Johnson to the *New York Times,* which ran it and the story on its front page. After stating that he was "enthusiastic about most of your domestic legislation and intentions," he added that he could "only follow our present foreign policy with the greatest dismay and distrust." He continued:

> I know it is hard for the responsible man to act; it is also painful for the irresolute man to dare criticism. At this anguished, delicate, perhaps determining moment, I feel I am serving you and our country best by not taking part in the White House Festival of the Arts.
>
> Respectfully, Robert Lowell

The following day the herd of independent minds, considered alphabetically from Hannah Arendt to Robert Penn Warren, sent a telegram to President Johnson endorsing, as the *New York Times*'s headline had it, "Poet's Rebuff of President."

The larger question behind this affair is whether any other figure in the arts but Robert Lowell could have brought it off. One is inclined to doubt it. Straightforward snobbery aligned to reverse patriotism works powerful magic. Lowell continued to oppose United States involvement in Vietnam, and one sees something of the appeal of his almost purely Lowellian presence in the socially envious portrait that Norman Mailer drew of him in his book *Armies of the Night.* In this book, about the anti-Vietnam War protest march on the Pentagon—a Pulitzer Prize-winning book in its day that now reads like a comic book—Mailer reports restraining himself from saying to Lowell:

> You, Lowell, beloved poet of many, what do you know of the dirt and dark deliveries of the necessary? What do you know of dignity hard-achieved, and dignity lost through innocence,

and dignity lost by sacrifice for a cause one cannot name? What do you know about getting fat against your will, and turning into a clown of an arriviste baron when you would rather be an eagle or a count, or rarest of all, some natural aristocrat from these damned democratic states?

On two other occasions Lowell's life took a political turn. In the first, in 1943, at the age of twenty-six, not long married to Jean Stafford, he became a conscientious objector in World War II. What is odd about this is that, almost up until the moment he declared himself CO, he was expecting to be drafted; and earlier he had even attempted to enlist so as to be able to go to officers' school. But when he wrote to President Roosevelt, he did so in good part as a Lowell: "You will understand how painful such a decision is for an American whose family traditions, like your own, have always found their fulfillment in maintaining, through responsible participation in both the civil and military services, our country's freedom and honor." Then he signed off: "I have the honor, Sir, to inscribe myself, with sincerest loyalty and respect, your fellow-citizen, Robert Traill Spence Lowell, Jr."

Lowell was, at that time, in his extreme Catholic phase—Allen Tate predicted he would become a monk—and his religion allowed him to twist the meaning of the War as "a betrayal of my country." (In his poem, "Memories of West Street and Lepke," he wrote of this time: "I was a fire-breathing Catholic C.O., / and made my manic statement / telling off the state and president. . . .") This, too, got play in the press: front page in the *New York Times;* "Lowell Scion Refuses to Fight" and "Socialite's Mother To Uphold Son" ran the headlines in the New England press. Other conscientious objectors sentenced at the same time got three years; Lowell got a year and a day, and was paroled after four months, a lighter sentence, according to a CO sentenced along with him, because he was, after all, a Lowell.

The other notable political incident in Lowell's life took

place at Yaddo, while he was staying there as a guest artist in 1949. He accused the director, Miss Elizabeth Ames, of having close ties with the Communists and actually called in the FBI. This was done in one of his manic flights, his "speeding up," as he and his biographers refer to it; this time the speeding up caused him to discover Communists under the bed and ask that Miss Ames be fired from her job. He was still in a high Catholic phase, and there is nothing like religion added to psychosis to make one see evil everywhere. He had begun taking up with Elizabeth Hardwick, also a guest at Yaddo and his supporter in his demand for the firing of Miss Ames. Hamilton gives this sad incident more attention in his biography than does Mariani. The point of it I take to be that Lowell's politics could be wildly erratic, going from conscientious objector to Communist witch-hunter to oral exemplar, *whoosh,* without missing a stitch or even ever being called on it.

In reading about the all-but-unrelieved sadness of Robert Lowell's life, the single best piece of understatement comes from Gertrude Buckman, the divorced wife of Lowell's friend Delmore Schwartz, with whom Lowell had an affair that, as Miss Buckman would later aver, wasn't really all that much fun. Remarking that Lowell was "to the end of his life emotionally undeveloped and irresponsible," she added—and here is the understatement—that "he wasn't husband material."

She was absolutely correct, of course, even though a great many women at first didn't agree. His family name, his rugged handsomeness—a friend of Jean Stafford's described Lowell as "Heathcliff [as] played by Boris Karloff"—his prestige as a distinguished poet combined to provide an aphrodisiac of sorts, at least for a certain kind of woman. Lowell married thrice, and brought much grief to all three wives. Jean Stafford lost her good looks when Lowell, drunk, crashed a car they were driving in, Stafford's face smashing against the windshield, leaving her permanently with the flattened nose of a boxer too long in the ring. Lowell would later break her nose again, this time in a domestic battle. In a story she published not long after his death, "An Influx of Poets," Miss Stafford took a certain measure of revenge. The narrator's husband, a very thinly disguised Robert Lowell, is put down as obtuse, a snob ("he was as vain as a peacock that Copley had painted his distant Cousin Augustus's family"), and "by instinct anti-Semitic," a man who would "never have a Jew as a close friend."

Of his three wives, Elizabeth Hardwick saw Lowell through the most breakdowns, which almost invariably began with his having a new tootsie in tow, sped up and ready to start a new life. Other times he made plain that he thought the true woman for him was Elizabeth Bishop, to whom he was ever ready to propose marriage and whose lesbianism he apparently didn't feel posed a serious obstacle. In the late 1960s, an honorary denizen of Camelot, he put his moves on Jacqueline Kennedy. He had a daughter with Elizabeth Hardwick, and there must have been good times between them, but in the biographies her role in his life reads more and more like that of a twenty-four-hour home health-care worker who, out of richly deserved exasperation, turns into the querulous Blanche Bickerson quite at the end of her tether. Great biographical injustice is visited upon this woman.

Lady Caroline Blackwood, the writer who was Lowell's third wife—she was herself married twice before, first to Lucien Freud, then to a musician named Israel Citkowitz—seemed splendidly unsuitable straightaway; long, or even short, suffering was not much to her taste. They had a son together, and, after much shared argument and squalor, they parted. Lowell was in fact leaving her to return to Miss Hardwick when he died in the cab in Manhattan.

Yet for all the turmoil and torment in his life, Lowell had great powers of concentration. He was able to closet himself away—in his office-apartment in New York, in his barn-studio in Maine—for ten- and twelve-hour stretches, working on his literary projects. Apart from teaching, which he did off and on in a part-time way, Lowell, after his parents' death, did not have to work at a regular job. So he holed up and read, and, when the spirit was upon him, wrote. Along the way, he acquired much genuine literary culture; sometimes, one suspects, too much, so that every event in his life seemed decipherable to him only if an analog for it could be found in literature.

He also, in his quiet but efficient way, hustled his own career along. All the poets of his generation did. "I am so tired of poetry as Big Business I don't know what to do," Elizabeth Bishop wrote to Randall Jarrell in 1950. "What on earth is the happy medium—readers, certainly, but all this recording & reading & anthologizing is getting me." Yet, for all that, the generation of Lowell-Jarrell-Bishop-Schwartz-Berryman-Roethke was not least remarkable in its collective ambition. In their careers—if not in their sad lives—everything was calculated: readings, reviews, blurbs, no detail connected with career advancement was too small to overlook. Happy networkers, as we should now call them, they formed a nearly perfect daisy chain of mutual promotion. (I add "nearly" because, being poets after all, they allowed room to deflate one another's poetry behind one another's backs.) But they were otherwise quite shameless about reviewing and blurbing one another's books, writing one another recommendations, appointing one another to juries and to the National Institute of Arts and Letters, arranging prizes for one another. None of this is to deny that their obsession with poetry was real—it was—but they saw no reason to let this obsession stand in the way of career.

Theirs was a generation that came after the most powerful generation of poets America had ever known—the generation of Eliot, Pound, Stevens, Frost, Moore, Crane, Williams. None of these older poets, please note, ever had a full-time university connection, whereas all the poets in Lowell's generation, including Lowell, who was given tenure at Harvard, did. Poets of the Lowell generation were the first to be thoroughly professionalized, to write poetry, to write about poetry, to teach poetry, to do nothing, really, outside the realm of poetry. The earlier generation had other work: banking, insurance, medicine, editorial work. They may have thought this work secondary, but in a useful way it kept them in the world. The consequences of this were not negligible. It gave them a wider view of things, and a deeper understanding that life was about more than poetic composition. "Well, certainly," Tolstoy wrote to Ivan Bunin, "go on writing if you feel like it, but remember that it can never be the aim of life."

Poets of the Lowell generation must have sensed that they were writing in a sad aftermath, akin perhaps to writing drama in fourth century Athens in the wake of Sophocles, Euripides, and Aeschylus. Lowell was in this connection perhaps the best at keeping up the appearance—though perhaps pretense is the more precise word here—that things were otherwise. Reviewing *Life Studies* in *Partisan Review* in 1959, F. W. Dupe noted of Lowell that "he wrote as if poetry were still a major art and not merely a venerable pastime which ought to be perpetuated." Dupee, be it noted, wrote in a tone of regret, for he felt that, in *Life Studies,* Lowell's career had taken a turn in the wrong direction. The poems in *Life Studies,* he concluded, "represent, perhaps, major poetry pulling in its horns and putting on big spectacles and studying how to survive." Joseph Bennett, in *The Hudson Review,* was much more dismissive, declaring that this book, "lazy and anecdotal . . . is more suited as an appendix to some snobbish society magazine, to *Town and Country* or *Harper's Bazaar,* rather than as a purposeful work."

From the standpoint of reputation, both Dupee and Bennett were wrong. *Life Studies* sent Lowell's reputation soaring. His first book in eight years, coming after the disappointingly slender volume, *The Mills of the Kavanaughs,* it contained, in his

words, his "first unmeasured [that is unmetered] verse," the first
poetry he had written that dispensed with the "hurdle of rhyme
and scansion between yourself and what you want to say most
forcibly." Mariani titles the chapter in which he wrote these
poems "Breakthrough." *Life Studies,* published in 1959, was Lowell's beginning effort at letting loose, letting go, letting 'er rip.
As the country was heading into the 1960s, his timing could
scarcely have been more perfect.

Some books—*Remembrance of Things Past, The Golden Bowl,
Nostromo*—should never be read for the first time. But *Life Studies* may be one of those books one should never read for the second time. Certainly, it seems thinner, dimmer, than the first
time round. It contains "91 Revere Street," the longish prose
piece that was to be the opening for the autobiography Lowell
never got round to writing. Mariani refers to the "polished
Flaubertian surface of *Life Studies,*" and, true enough, much of
the writing in it, prose and poetry, has a handsomely burnished
feel. Memorable phrasings are not wanting: Lowell's formulation in the poem "Ford Madox Ford" of Ford's *The Good Soldier*
as "the best French novel in the [English] language" is one that
has stuck with me for more than thirty years; so, too, has the
lovely line "There is no Jesus and Mary is his mother," awarded
to the subject of "For George Santayana."

Still, many of the poems disappoint. "Inauguration Day:
January 1953," which sees the death of America in the election
of Dwight David Eisenhower—"and the Republic summons
Ike / the mausoleum in her heart"—today seems faintly ridiculous, a literary man's political feverishness. For a professed La-
tinist, it is a trifle dismaying to find Lowell misusing the word
"decimated." Some of these poems deal in cliché abstraction:
"Memories of West Street and Lepke" notes that "These are the
tranquilized *Fifties* / and I am forty . . ."; and "During Fever"
closes with mention of "Freudian papa." Many of the poems—
"Father's Bedroom," "For Sale," "Words for Hart Crane" among
them—disappoint; reading them, one waits for that last tile to

click into place, satisfyingly closing the poem. But it never comes: they have, as Dupee noted in his review, no denouement.

Life Studies is considered a breakthrough book for Robert Lowell because it set him free, in many of its poems, from the tensions of strict meter and extended the range of his verse to include the directly personal. The confessional poet was emerging but not yet altogether out of the box; in this book, at any rate, what he is chiefly confessing to is being a Lowell and, perhaps better, a Winslow. The book also reveals him as a man with a moistened finger carefully extended in the air, checking the literary climate. "He watched its weather," Stanley Kunitz wrote of Lowell, "with the diligent attention of a meteorologist, studying its prevailing winds, regularly charting its high and low pressure areas." As the years went on, Lowell attempted to dramatize the nation's woes as if they were his own.

By the time *For the Union Dead* (1964) appeared, Lowell's reputation not merely as a major poet, but as *the* American poet was well on its way toward being solidified. In the words of Richard Poirier, "Robert Lowell is, by something like a critical consensus, the greatest American poet of the mid-century, probably the greatest poet writing in English." Let pass that T. S. Eliot and W. H. Auden still walked the earth, Lowell was, at the very minimum, thought the coming man, the great white hope, "our truest historian," to adopt the title of Poirier's review.

So solid had Lowell's reputation become that he had arrived in the enviable position of achieving critical approval even for writing badly. In Paul Mariani's documentation of the reception accorded *Notebooks, 1967–68,* we are reminded that William Meredith, in a front-page review in *The New York Times Book Review,* found the book, even though imperfect, a proper response to "the modern god of chaos" under which Lowell was forced to work; and Robert Boyers thought the same book a "comprehensive and essential document" of the conscientiousness of our century. The subtext of these comments, of course, is that Lowell's harried and horrendous times forced him to write badly.

But then nothing Lowell did, no matter how shoddy, failed to garner praise and prizes. *Imitations,* his book of translations, some of them from languages he himself couldn't read, though it was attacked by many reviewers—"schoolboys," wrote Dudley Fitts, "should read it in a salt mine"—was nonetheless praised by Edmund Wilson and A. Alvarez and won the 1962 Bollingen Prize for translation. Toward the end of his life, returning to translations of the poetry of Eugenio Montale, Lowell allowed, to his friend Frank Bidart, that in his translations "I did shockingly turn, twist, some of the translations to my own morbid purposes." No mention is made of returning the money to the Bollingen Foundation.

For a poet who now appears greatly productive, for the better part of his career Robert Lowell was, poetically, rather costive. Poems did not come easily to him, and then he tended to revise and revise and sometimes misrevise them. But in the early 1960s, he loosened still further his own standard, becoming more impressed with poetry of the kind produced under the less strict prosodic notions of William Carlos Williams. The *Dream Songs* of his friend John Berryman, sonnets written in blank verse, eliminated the costiveness problem for good. Logorrhea now set in. Soon he was producing four such sonnets a week, so that during the year 1968 he produced roughly 4,000 (what he considered) publishable lines in this largely improvisational form—"something," as Mariani reports, "by turns loose and strict, rhyming or not, a form forever hungry to devour whatever events washed up along the sands."

A vast amount happened just then to be washing up. These were the years that Lowell had become active in protesting the war in Vietnam; he had become closer to the Kennedy gang in Washington; he had found a soul brother in Senator Eugene McCarthy, who took on Lyndon Johnson in the 1968 election before Johnson dropped out; his marriage was breaking up; he continued to suffer his breakdowns, with their usual hopeless love affairs. One such affair, with an Irish woman named Mary Keelan, employed at the Mexican monastery of the radical priest Father Ivan Illich, netted him, as we learn from Mariani, "a sequence of twelve sonnets." What it netted Miss Keelan we shall let pass.

Reading the poems produced by Lowell's new aesthetic of immediacy, one finds oneself freshly impressed by the paean of W. H. Auden to careful prosody: "Blessed be all the metrical rules that forbid automatic responses, force us to have second thoughts, free us from the fetters of the Self." What Lowell was doing, of course, was fettering, binding, lashing himself to Self. The year before he died he told an interviewer that "the thread that strings it [his work] together is my autobiography, it is a small-scale *Prelude,* written in many different styles and with digressions, yet a continuing story." So continuing was it that, reading the poems in *Notebooks* today, one wonders why, but for the rule that a sonnet may not exceed fourteen lines, any of these poems end quite when they do; otherwise, there appears to be no reason for them to cease. In a remark quoted in Hamilton's biography but not in Mariani's, Jonathan Raban, the English travel writer and a late-life friend of Lowell's, recounts how Lowell's revisions were often made in disregard of actual content. His "favorite method of revision," Raban reports, "was simply to introduce a negative into a line, which absolutely reversed its meaning but very often would improve it." This ought to stop all close readers of Robert Lowell dead in their academic tracks.

Driven by his new style, Lowell's poems became more openly political, as he himself had with the advent of the radical politics of the late 1960's. He wrote sonnets about Kennedy and Nixon—whatever your feelings about the man, there is something about the name Nixon that just doesn't come off in a poem—he slipped in his own nightmares about nuclear war. Whether or not such politics are permissible in a poem is not the issue; what is is whether Lowell brought it off. Some people think he did. Richard Tillinghast, a former student of Lowell's who in 1969 invited him to come out to Berkeley to view the student revolution as a visiting professor (and what better, safer seat from which to view a revolution than that of a visiting professor), thinks that Lowell's "power as a political poet lay in his knack of becoming one with the *Zeitgeist,* and—despite the many things that made him absolutely unlike anyone else—somehow managed to dramatize himself in his poems as a representative citizen."

I don't think Lowell did bring it off, nor that there was anything in the least representative about him. These "public" poems fail the politics test—that is, if you don't agree with the poet's politics, the poems seem empty, pompous, self-dramatizing merely. "In the past five years," Mariani writes, "he had honed a poetics of the quotidian, an equivalent to Mailer's New Journalism, in which whatever chance tossed up he had snatched for his subject." It is far from clear whether Mariani is aware that this is, at best, a deeply equivocal compliment.

But the personal side revealed in the new Lowell poems wrought much greater publicity than the political side, and this of a notorious kind. Long the leading poet of the "anguish school," as Elizabeth Bishop once called him, Lowell now brought his own romances and marriages out into the open in his poems. Jean Stafford would later say that *The Mills of the Kavanaughs* was really about her marriage to Lowell, but there it was at least disguised. In *The Dolphin* (1973), he not only wrote about his domestic life, but quoted directly from letters Elizabeth Hardwick had sent him when he had left her for Caroline Blackwood. All the ethical niceties of this seem to have been lost on Lowell. W. H. Auden threatened not to speak to him because of this book. Elizabeth Bishop pled with him not to publish it; such cheapened use of personal material, she claimed, was for the likes of Mailer, or James Dickey, or Mary

McCarthy—"they don't count, in the long run," she implored, but he did.

In the end, Lowell went ahead and published the book, with its unappealing mixture of fact and fiction, its use of his former wife's letters, its large supply of grist for the mills of scandalmongers and future biographers. Some critics took his head off for it, but none with more verbal violence than Adrienne Rich, an old friend, who wrote, "I think this is bullshit eloquence, a poor excuse for a cruel and shallow book." In the end, the best criticism of *The Dolphin* is probably that of Miss Hardwick, who called it an "inane, empty, unnecessary" book, filled, even after three years of composition and revision, with "so many fatuities, indiscretions, bad lines still there on the page." Even as scandal, the book fails. What it shows is a man unhinged by his own megalomaniacal self-importance. It remains only to add that *The Dolphin* won the Pulitzer Prize, Lowell's third.

Robert Lowell's life came unraveled at its close. After five years without a breakdown, he began to fool with his lithium dosages and the drug began to let him down, as did Caroline Blackwood, who hadn't any interest in being the nurse-mother-wife to him that Elizabeth Hardwick had been. Yet my guess is that he died thinking himself a genius. Why shouldn't he have? People had been treating him with the deference due a genius for thirty years. After the critical success of *For the Union Dead,* he wrote to Elizabeth Bishop: "More invitations to be on dull committees, more books in the mail for blurbs, more tiresome doctor's degrees. Thank god, it can't go very far for a poet." Yet with him it went a long way. Every emolument, every prize, every attention was paid him.

Yet hard living—the boozing, the cigarettes, the huge doses of drugs to stay his illness—took their toll. By his late fifties, he was an old man with a weakened heart, who needed to go slowly on stairs and was offered help out of cabs. He wore his now grey hair long, his clothes were perennially rumpled, and a certain physical grossness set in. A friend of Jean Stafford's sent her a picture of the Lowell of these years, appending the caption, "The Ben Franklin *de nos jours.* Yuck!" Another photograph of him with his last wife, new son, and stepdaughter is pure Walker Evans.

"I think in the end, there is no end," Lowell wrote to Frank Bidart, "the thread frays rather than is cut." To his friend Peter Taylor, he added that he never really quite comprehended his own life, even though it was really the only subject of his poetry. "I think in a way, I never understood it, that it is [merely] addition not to be understood, just completed." Lowell's best book of poems, in my view, is his last, *Day By Day,* an elegiac work in which he tots up the manifold sadnesses of a painful life coming to its close and in which self-knowledge at last comes into play. Heart attack was the cause given on his death certificate, but Robert Lowell was in reality brought down by despondency and madness in his sixtieth year.

If W. H. Auden is correct—and it is by no means certain that he is—in predicting that the world will pardon Rudyard Kipling and Paul Claudel for writing well, what about Robert Lowell, whose reputation has slipped considerably since his death? *Bien-pensant* politics and good old American democratic snobbery were key elements in its formation, and Lowell's may have been one of those literary reputations that needed him to be alive, stoking the fire to sustain its flame. His vocation may have been stronger than his gift. However much one admires his courage in fighting the madness that visited him all too regularly, it must be said that the poetry he used in part to fend it off does not leave much residue of joyousness or originality. One may talk about Robert Lowell as in the line of New England writers (the lost puritan of Paul Mariani's title), or as a late modernist, or as the poetic exemplar of the New Criticism, or anything else one likes, but finally one butts smack up against his terrible illness, his affliction, his madness. "Great poetry is greatly sane, greatly lucid," wrote Donald Davie, apropos of Ivor

Gurney; "and insanity is as much a calamity for poets and for poetry as for other human beings and other sorts of human business."

No one fought harder to maintain sanity than Robert Lowell, using art as his weapon and his shield, but in the end the poor man never had a chance.

Dreiser's Great Good Girl

People read novels for many varying reasons. They look to
novels for information, wisdom, beauty, romantic inspiration, and diversion: sometimes for all these things at once,
sometimes for one of these things preponderantly over all the
others. In *A Legacy,* the excellent novel by Sybille Bedford, one
character says of another that she now reads two novels a day,
adding, "The next stage is chocolates."

For some readers, novels are as chocolates, things to be
gobbled up till love or something better comes along to pass
the time; for others, novels seem scarcely less essential than the
air they breathe, and people exist—I happen to be one of
them—who feel they have been educated chiefly by novels. For
some readers, a novel must have an element of elevation—it
ought, in a non-Rotarian sense, to lift the spirit; for yet others,
novels are best when they are noncommittal and do not go beyond a strong presentation of the facts, the starker and darker
these facts the better. But even among the most serious readers, all of whom are ready to agree on the general importance
of the novel, there is no real agreement about what makes for
a successful novel.

Serious readers of novels are likely to disagree above all

about the novels of Theodore Dreiser. ("My husband reads Dreiser and actually enjoys him," I recently heard a woman "exclaim," a word I use with some precision.) The chief reason for the controversy about Dreiser is that his powerful novels can be a direct affront to the idea that the novel is an aesthetic object. The occasional but quite genuine crudity of Dreiser's prose has often been remarked upon, perhaps by no one more wittily than by H. L. Mencken, who said that Dreiser had "an incurable antipathy to the *mot juste*." Quite a bit to it. Dreiser was at his worst when he was trying to be at his best. Usually this was at those times when he attempted to play either the poet or the wise man. Even his greatest admirers—and Mencken was among them—feel the need to italicize his verbal clumsiness. As Mencken noted: "Every reader of the Dreiser novels must cherish astounding specimens—of awkward, platitudinous marginalia, of whole scenes spoiled by bad writing, of phrases as brackish as so many lumps of sodium hyposulphite." Mencken goes on to say: "I often wonder if Dreiser gets anything properly describable as pleasure out of this dogged accumulation of threadbare, undistinguished, uninspiring nouns, adjectives, verbs, adverbs, pronouns, participles and conjunctions." There is no compelling reason to believe that Dreiser ever did.

Finding aesthetic fault with Theodore Dreiser is easy, a game the whole family can play. The very first sentence of *Jennie Gerhardt*, for example, contains an obvious tautology, where Jennie is referred to as "a young girl of eighteen" (as opposed, one wants to shoot back at the author, to an old or perhaps middle-aged girl of eighteen?). The second sentence isn't worthy of being engraved in marble either, for there one discovers Jennie's mother has "a frank, open countenance." Four or five more rather strenuous clichés turn up before this first paragraph of seven sentences is complete.

But after having noted this, after having established one's own superiority to Dreiser in the niceties of language, one has to admit that this opening paragraph does what he wants it to do, not perhaps brilliantly but very effectively: it sets his scene, it gets him into his story, it establishes two of his principal characters. For all of Dreiser's famous ineptitude as a stylist, whenever a dramatic scene or delicate passage has to be rendered, Dreiser's instincts seem to take over, his prose shifts into cruise control, and he executes the scene or passage with a sure and often impressive touch. Making fun of Dreiser's prose is, finally, snobbery, a game no one in the family should play. "I often think the criticism of Dreiser as a stylist at times betrays a resistance to the feelings he causes readers to suffer," Saul Bellow has written. "If they say he can't write, they need not express those feelings."

A writer of greater personal refinement and wider culture could not have produced novels of the same power as Theodore Dreiser's. ("Remove the vices of a novelist and his virtues vanish too," wrote V. S. Pritchett.) But then such a writer would not have taken up the subjects that Dreiser did: the struggle for existence, the stirrings of uncontrollable yet hopeless desire, the shame of being low-born, the at best pyrrhic battle for happiness. If a tradition for Dreiser is wanted, the line he belongs in is that of Balzac and Dostoevsky, all three being novelists who, in taking on the large subjects, make the question of style seem, at least while reading them, quite beside the point.

Jennie Gerhardt, published in 1911, is, I believe, Theodore Dreiser's best novel. In it our interest is not riven, as it is in *Sister Carrie,* between the onward and upward career of Carrie Meeber and the downward and outward career of George Hurstwood. Nor does it contain the *longueurs* of an otherwise powerful novel like *An American Tragedy.* It is more concentrated than the novels written around the career of Frank Cowperwood and less marred by the intrusive application of the Darwinian idea of survival of the fittest that dominates these novels. Yet, strong as *Jennie Gerhardt* is, my sense is that it is one of the least taught—which is probably the same as saying, least read—

of Dreiser's novels, which is a mistake, a sadness, and an injustice.

In his posthumously published *My Life as Author and Editor,* H. L. Mencken recounts his reaction to reading *Jennie Gerhardt* in manuscript. Dreiser had sent him his manuscript hoping to discover a friend and supporter for this, his second novel. Dreiser's first novel, *Sister Carrie,* published in 1900, had run into the then active censors in American life and he felt that it had also been sabotaged by his publisher, Frank Doubleday, of Doubleday, Page & Company, whose wife was said to have intensely disliked the novel. After having read *Jennie Gerhardt,* Mencken shot off a letter to Dreiser which, in part, reads:

> The story comes upon me with great force; it touches my own experience of life in a hundred places; it preaches (or perhaps I had better say exhibits) a philosophy of life that seems to me to be sound; altogether I get a powerful effect of reality, stark and unashamed. It is drab and gloomy, but so is the struggle for existence. It is without humor, but so are the jests of that great Comedian who shoots at our heels and makes us do our grotesque dancing. . . .

What Dreiser could not have known was that he was the American novelist for whom Mencken was waiting. Mencken had his own program for American fiction, which was to oppose the treacly romantic and hopelessly thin stuff produced by the genteel tradition. Dreiser was, as Mencken writes, "the stick with which I principally flogged the dullards of my country, at least in the field of beautiful letters." When Mencken wrote about *Jennie Gerhardt* in his magazine *The Smart Set,* in a review in the November 1911 issue carrying the title "A Novel of the First Rank," he held back neither the cannon balls nor the confetti, blasting the dominant tendencies of American fiction under the cover of praising Theodore Dreiser. "Hot from it," he says in the opening paragraph of his review of the novel,

"I am firmly convinced that *Jennie Gerhardt* is the best American novel I have ever read, with the lonesome but Himalayan exception of *Huckleberry Finn,* and so I may as well say it aloud and at once and have done with it."

Some might argue that a little fish tale called *Moby-Dick* ought to be allowed as another exception and a Henry James novel or two might be tossed in as additional exceptions. But none of these would quite have served Mencken's polemical purposes. Mencken's admiration for *Jennie Gerhardt* was redoubled because in it he found confirmation of his own philosophical views. Perhaps it was not so much a fully formed philosophy as a philosophical skepticism that both men shared. Mencken formulated his own skepticism best when he set out, in one of the essays in his *Prejudices* volumes, what he thought was unknowable:

> No one knows Who created the visible universe, and it is infinitely improbable that anything properly describable as evidence on the point will ever be discovered. No one knows what motives or intentions, if any, lie behind what we call natural laws. No one knows why man has his present form. No one knows why sin and suffering were sent into this world—that is, why the fashioning of man was badly botched.

In other words, everything was unknowable, according to Mencken, that it is essential to know if we are to have any hope of understanding our purpose in life. Mencken not only believed that these things were unknowable but also thought that anyone who claimed to know them was a quack, charlatan, con artist, or damned fool, and ought, therefore, to be throttled, at least in prose.

What pumped up Mencken's spirits so about Dreiser—and he felt similarly about the novels of Joseph Conrad—was that in Dreiser he had found the novelist who gave artistic flesh to the bare bones of his own strong ideas about the unfathomableness of the universe. In his novels Dreiser, for Mencken, exposed not "the empty event and act, but the endless mystery out of which it springs"; and, more, Dreiser's was "the irresistible creative passion of a genuine artist, standing spell-bound before the impenetrable enigma that is life, enamoured by the strange beauty that plays over its sordidness, challenged to a wondering and half-terrified sort of representation of what passes understanding."

True enough, passages in Dreiser do at first seem a perfect match with the main thrust of Mencken's ideas. Late in *Jennie Gerhardt,* for example, Lester Kane, the well-born and successful businessman who risks social ostracism and eventually financial ruin by living out of wedlock with Jennie, a woman socially much beneath him—this same Lester Kane tells Jennie, who has already herself taken a number of pretty good shots from life, that "all of us are more or less pawns. We're moved about like chess men by circumstances over which we have no control." A few moments later Lester adds: "After all, life is more or less of a farce. It's a silly show. The best we can do is to hold our personalities intact. It doesn't even appear that integrity has much to do with it." One can almost see H. L. Mencken, after reading that passage, doing a little touchdown dance in the end zone of his heart.

But of course neither Mencken nor (much less) Dreiser can be boiled down to his ideas. His ideas alone do not explain the wondrous exuberance of H. L. Mencken, of whom Walter Lippmann, in an essay of 1926, wrote that "when you can explain the heightening effect of a spirited horse, of a swift athlete, of a dancer really in control of his own body, when you can explain why watching them you feel more alive yourself, you can explain the quality of his influence." As for Dreiser, in the realm of ideas, he was a mess; and the more he delved into ideas, the messier he became. He dabbled with fascism and Communism, and was tainted with anti-Semitism. But so powerful was his natural talent that even the world's worst ideas couldn't destroy it. One of the things that make *Jennie Gerhardt* Dreiser's best novel is that it was written before he had really become engaged by ideas at all.

Theodore Dreiser himself had taken a few pretty good shots from life before he wrote *Jennie Gerhardt*. The first shot was his early life. Dreiser's father, a German immigrant, never recovered his ambition after a fire that destroyed his small business and caused his financial fall. Theodore was born five years after this disaster, in 1871, the ninth of ten children in a family that never climbed out of poverty and alternated in its emotional states among defeat, shame, religious terror, and social disgrace. His sisters went off with married men, and one among them returned home pregnant. He had brothers who lapsed into alcoholism and ne'er-do-wellism. The family moved often, once, in Vincennes, Indiana, living above a brothel. To these social disadvantages can be added Dreiser's personal unattractiveness. H. L. Mencken put it gently when of Dreiser he wrote that "the boon of beauty has been denied him." Dreiser had buck teeth and a right eye that refused to look straight ahead. He was tall and gangly, socially inept, sexually on fire, and flush with every kind of insecurity.

Through the sponsorship of a kind and generous high-school teacher, Dreiser spent a year at Indiana University. He then worked at a number of odd jobs, ending up in journalism. He was employed by newspapers in Chicago, Saint Louis, Toledo, Cleveland, Pittsburgh, and Buffalo. In 1894, a man named Arthur Henry, his city editor on *The Toledo Blade,* encouraged him to write fiction. Dreiser was then twenty-three years old. It was not till six years later, after he had married, that Dreiser published *Sister Carrie,* a book that, in its first appearance, brought him royalties totaling $68.40 and the obloquy of reviewers who thought he wrote an immoral book because he had failed to punish Carrie Meeber, his heroine, for living outside conventional morality. (It is another sign of Dreiser's power that radical changes in conventional morality—adults living together before marriage, easy access to abortion—have not made his novels seem historically dated or otherwise irrelevant.)

Dreiser had begun to work on *Jennie Gerhardt* soon after finishing but before publishing *Sister Carrie* in 1900. But the commercial and critical defeat dealt him by the publication of the earlier book sent him swirling into a nervous breakdown and a long bout of unemployment of the kind he had prophetically described George Hurstwood undergoing in *Sister Carrie.* Here his brother Paul, a successful songwriter of the day, came to his rescue, installing him in a sanatorium and helping him financially until he recovered. Dreiser took seven years before returning to the writing of *Jennie Gerhardt* and it was three more years before he saw it published.

Mencken, while acknowledging that Dreiser's fiction could be extremely uneven, felt that "his writing does not rise or fall with any regularity; he neither improves steadily nor grows worse steadily." Mencken did feel that it is in *Jennie Gerhardt* that Dreiser's view of the world begins "to take on coherence and to show a general tendency." I would myself go further to say that Dreiser reached the top of his form with the publication of this novel, because, among other reasons, he hadn't yet been freighted with too many of the ideas that would later overload though never destroy his work. He had already been intellectually astonished by reading the evolutionist Herbert Spencer's *First Principles,* which, he later remarked, "took every shred of belief away from me." But he had not yet made sedulous attempts to master the mechanistic theory of life from the chemical physiology of Jacques Loeb or the tenets of modern psychology from the Austrian psychoanalyst A. A. Brill. One begins to see the sorry influence of these studies in such later novels of Dreiser's as *An American Tragedy* and *The Bulwark,* with all their talk of "chemisms," moths hovering rather too patently around flames, and other lower forms of animal life consuming one another.

In *Jennie Gerhardt,* Dreiser was still working out his vision of life, letting facts suggest ideas instead of the other way around. Dreiser's position had not yet hardened, nor had his view of destiny been fixed. With the passing of time Dreiser may have grown intellectually more sophisticated—as Ellen Moers shows in her brilliant book *Two Dreisers* (1969)—but it is far from clear that, in Dreiser, whose genius was of the natural kind, sophistication necessarily made him better.

Dreiser had superior novelistic instincts. He knew that what was important is conveying life, and he knew, too, that while good intentions could have bad effects, the opposite was equally possible. A perfect illustration in *Jennie Gerhardt* is the cold disdain in which Jennie's illegitimate infant child Vesta is held by Jennie's father, old Gerhardt, for whom the child is an all too vivid sign of his family's disgrace and precipitate decline in the world. Dreiser writes:

> Although opposed to the presence of it [the child], and irritated by the thought of having it in the house, he felt as if he ought not to say anything. Jennie was working. Still he could not help considering it from a grand-parently standpoint, particularly since the child was a human being possessed of a soul, and subject to baptism and union with the church. He thought it over and wondered if the baby had been baptized.

After the infant is baptized, Gerhardt's view is utterly changed. "However much the daughter had sinned, the infant was not to blame. It was a helpless, puling, tender thing, demanding his sympathy and his love. Gerhardt felt his heart go out to the little child, and yet he could not yield his position all in a moment." Yet, from that moment on in fact, Gerhardt, for all his narrowness, takes a strong and righteous interest in the child. "There would always be her soul to consider. He would never again be utterly unconscious of her soul." Later the relationship between the child Vesta and her old-world grandfather will provide one of the small but winning touches in the novel.

What is most interesting about this is that Dreiser was no friend of organized religion. Very far from it. He had grown up under the stiff harness of his father's grinding and tyrannical piety. He lived his own life untouched by religion in the traditional or conventional sense. If anything, he was likely to have been contemptuous of it. He thought, as he says in the pages of *Jennie Gerhardt,* "unseeing man, narrowly drawing himself up in judgement," which clergymen in Dreiser's day were confidently wont to do, pathetic in the extreme. Yet for all this Dreiser attributes to religion—or, more specifically, old Gerhardt's fanatical attachment to his religion—one of the most good-hearted acts in the novel. As a novelist, Dreiser was smart enough not to allow his ideas or even his prejudices to get in the way of the higher—that is to say, the novelistic—truth about the human heart.

In the same way, there are no true villains in Dreiser, only people, the duller among whom act out their assigned roles. Those who choose not to act out their assigned roles, but to leave the track, often do so with tragic consequences. Not even Lester Kane's rather spiritually calloused brother Robert qualifies as villainous, for, rivalrous though he is and pleased though he is to have his brother set on the sidelines by his socially outraging arrangement with Jennie, even Robert Kane softens toward the novel's close and wishes a rapprochement with his brother. The reason there are no true villains in Dreiser's novelistic world is that none are needed. The world, with its many rigid conventions, and the cosmos, by arbitrarily conferring strong appetites on unusual people, supply a sufficient number of traps to keep everyone busy. "Hell," Lester Kane thinks, "what a tangle life was, what a mystery!" I believe that Dreiser thought this, too, and thinking it made him a better novelist.

To be impressed by the mystery that life presents, though perhaps a beginning, is not in itself sufficient to make a novelist great. For that at least partial penetration into the mystery of life—or into many of its sideshow mysteries—is required.

In Dreiser, one not only regularly finds such penetration but finds that many of his novelistic discoveries have taken decades to sink into the popular culture. In the unforgettable figure of George Hurstwood, for example, Dreiser discovered what the self-help industry now calls "the masculine mid-life crisis": the poor man who feels time running out on him, which is a prefatory sign of his running out on his wife with a younger woman. Although she represents much more than this, the character Jennie Gerhardt is a demonstration (roughly seventy years before the man, a rabbi, came around to write the best-seller about it) of bad things happening to good people. On this role of prophet not infrequently played by the writer, someone once told Dostoevsky that some of his characters were not true to life. Dostoevsky replied that this was nonsense and told this fellow, in effect, to stick around, for life would soon turn up exactly the kind of characters he had created. Life, as we ought by now to know, often contrives to imitate art.

"I want you to look facts in the face," Lester at one point says to Jennie, but one of these facts is that this is precisely what he himself cannot do. Yet looking facts in the face is something that, in any Dreiser novel as in life, most people have a difficult time doing. It is not by any means plain that Dreiser himself could always do so. He is doubtless speaking for himself when he has Lester Kane, in the midst of his almost endless wobbling over whether to marry Jennie or to leave her or to continue in his state of easy drift, think: "the sum and substance of every man's life was unrest and dissatisfaction."

But then Dreiser could touch more tender notes, too, as when he remarks, of the relationship between the child Vesta and her grandfather, "there is an inexplicable affinity between old age and childhood which is as lovely as it is pathetic." He knew, too, doubtless from personal experience, as he has Lester Kane reflect in this novel, that "people turn so quickly from weakness or the shadow of it" and that the worst social disease of all is failure. Dreiser was never deceived about the importance of money in social arrangements; and, as he puts it in this novel, "money was essential: for real distinction outside of the arts, a great deal of it was needed; and even in the arts the man with money was so much more distinguished." He wasn't too bad on the little touches, either, for late in the novel a minor character named O'Brien appears of whom Dreiser writes that he "was suave, good-natured, and well-meaning, even if he was a lawyer."

From a larger perspective, Dreiser has put more memorable characters into American fiction than perhaps any other novelist. Carrie Meeber and George Hurstwood from *Sister Carrie*, Clyde Griffiths and Sondra Finchley from *An American Tragedy*, Frank Cowperwood from *The Financier* and *The Titan*, and, perhaps his most impressive creation of all, Jennie from *Jennie Gerhardt*. In Jennie, Dreiser accomplished something that Dickens often attempted but never really did bring off: the creation of a thoroughly good yet entirely believable young woman.

In an impressive way, the character of Jennie Gerhardt stands as a refutation of the theory that is supposed to lie behind much of Theodore Dreiser's fiction. If for most of us life is a battle waged between egotism and altruism, for Jennie it never seems anything of the kind: egotism never has a chance. In Jennie, the sense of the pathetic is strong; decency is instinctive. When Lester Kane fumbles for reasons why he is so strongly drawn to Jennie, a young woman of good looks but no subtlety or intellectual penetration of any kind, the best he can come up with is that "Jennie has something—a big, emotional pull of some kind which held him." Lester never says it, nor does Dreiser come near to doing so, but what Jennie possesses is an uncorrupted goodness.

Dreiser puts Jennie through horrendous suffering in this novel, yet, somehow, she is not diminished by it. She is, on the contrary, made larger by her suffering, even though it is not always suffering that she understands, or can hope to understand. In the end, Jennie is a larger character—a larger human being—than Lester, who at the close of his life thinks he is without illusions. Jennie, in her more tentative, more inchoate, understanding of life is by far the more impressive. When traveling in Europe, noting how little lasts of even the grandest civilizations, she asks—and it is difficult not to think she is speaking for Dreiser here—if anything matters "except goodness—goodness of heart? What else was there that was real?" Sometimes Dreiser intercedes in this matter of understanding. And when the cruelest blow of all is landed upon Jennie, the loss of a child, Dreiser writes: "If only some counselor of eternal wisdom could have whispered to her that obvious and consoling truth—there are no dead." That is not a moment one thinks of as characteristically Dreiserian.

In her ungrudging puzzlement about the world, it is Jennie who comes closer than anyone in this novel, or perhaps in any of Dreiser's novels, to grasping the true mystery of life—not solving it, but grasping it. Though her mind never acquired any specialized knowledge, Dreiser tells us, and though she hadn't anything like conventional intellectual interests, Jennie did, owing to her experience, have "the feeling that the world moved in some strange, unstable way." Dreiser continues:

> It was not known clearly by any one, apparently, what it was all about. People were born and died. Some believed that the world had been made six thousand years before. Some that it was millions of years old. Some, like her father, thought that there was a personal God, some that there was no God at all. For her part she felt there must be something—a guiding intelligence which produced all the beautiful things—the flowers, the stars, the trees, the grass. Nature was so beautiful. If at times certain events were cruel, yet there was this beauty persisting. And color, tones, feeling, laughter, the joy of character, the beauty of youth—how these softened in between the harsh faces of hunger, cold, indifference, greed. She could not understand what it was all about, but still, as in her youth, it was beautiful. One could live, somehow, under any circumstances.

In the end perhaps it is not so surprising that Dreiser should have been so impressed, not to say entranced, by the mystery presented by life. This ugly, clumsy, in every way inelegant man, reared in poverty, ignorance, and superstition, lived to be one of his country's greatest writers. Was this not in itself mystery, indeed astonishment, enough? As with so many other mysteries, there is nothing much for it but to stand back in amazement and, because in this particular case the result of the mystery is a great artist, in appreciative awe.

U.S.A. *Today*

Not yet gone but long forgotten—such was John Dos Passos's position in American letters during the last decade of his life. Since his death, in 1970, things haven't changed for the better. Dos Passos's work has passed from general neglect to near-complete obscurity. There was a time when, along with F. Scott Fitzgerald and Ernest Hemingway, he was one of the big three of the American novel. For those of us who grew up on the fiction of the 1920's and 1930's, Hemingway represented poetic sensitivity combined with a code of manliness, Fitzgerald style and worldly aspiration, and Dos Passos politics and social conscience.

Until the 1940's, Dos Passos seems to have been as highly regarded as any American writer of his generation. Jean-Paul Sartre said of his fictional world that he knew of "none—not even Faulkner's or Kafka's—in which the art is greater or better hidden." F. R. Leavis wrote of his "rare seriousness." Lionel Trilling, in 1938, said that *U.S.A.*, the trilogy that is Dos Passos's magnum opus, "stands as the important American novel of the decade."

But today the small portion of literature from the past that gets remembered is that which gets taught. Dos Passos does not often get taught. Nor is there anything resembling a Dos Passos literary industry as there is a Hemingway or a Fitzgerald or a Faulkner industry, with its inevitable newsletters, its recurring collections of letters, and its bands of hot-handed academics mining ever thinner literary leavings. John Dos Passos is all but gone—poof!—down the history hole.

When I first read *U.S.A.,* in the summer of 1956, the eclipse of Dos Passos's reputation was already well under way, though as an unbookish boy of nineteen I had no notion of this. Nor had I any notion that Dos Passos, by his actions and his subsequent publications, had largely disavowed much in this book that was to be his most impressive claim to lasting fame. I read its almost thirteen hundred pages nearly straight through, over three summer days, sitting outside the concrete tennis courts of Chicago's Indian Boundary Park. Forty years later, I can still feel the cool shade of the park's large Dutch-elm trees and hear the *pock, pock, pock* of tennis balls being struck in the background as I read on and deep into John Dos Passos's book, until nothing in life outside that book interested me anywhere near as much as what was going on between its covers. *U.S.A.,* with its evocation of the tumult of American life in the first three decades of the century, blew me away. Dos Passos had the godlike aura of a novelist working on a vast stage with a huge cast of characters. As I read the cantering rhythms of his prose, my own mind galloped wildly off into fields until then unknown to me:

> And then they all woke up and for hours and hours the telephone poles went by, and towns, frame houses, brick factories with ranks and ranks of glittering windows, dumping grounds, trainyards, plowed land, pasture, and cows, and Milly got trainsick and Fainy's legs felt like they would drop off from sitting in the seat so long; some places it was snowing and some places it was sunny, and Milly kept getting sick and smelt dismally of vomit and it got dark and they all slept; and

light again, and then the towns and the frame houses and the factories all started drawing together, humping into warehouses and elevators, and the trainyards spread as far as you could see and it was Chicago.

Some books, if you come to them at just the right time, form you the way a crucial experience does. *U.S.A.* did that for me.

I had not then heard of the literary holy grail known as the Great American Novel, but that, of course, was precisely what Dos Passos seemed to me to have written: a vast, comprehensive work that attempted to reveal the soul of American life. Edmund Wilson, upbraiding Hemingway, Fitzgerald, and Thornton Wilder for merely cultivating their "own little corners," wrote, even before *U.S.A.* was completed, that Dos Passos "remains one of the few first-rate figures among our writers of his generation, and the only one of those who has made a systematic effort to study all the aspects of America and to take account of all its elements, to compose them into a picture which makes some general sense."

To a boy of nineteen, it made more than general sense: what Dos Passos wrote seemed above argument. Fate, *U.S.A.* announced, was not in one's own hands. Will, decency, aspiration—all were as nothing when they were set against the crushing force exerted by the current system of economics and social arrangements, which were the true determinants of personal destiny. I began *U.S.A.* as apolitical as a person can be and finished it a highly skeptical young man determined not to be plowed under by conformity, by empty ambition, by the false goddess of success. "You can't argue with success," my father used to say, with a shrug. But after reading Dos Passos I wished to do nothing else. At whose expense did the success come? At what cost? Success now stirred me only to dubiety, whereas I found failure rather noble. *U.S.A.*, in other words, gave me a politics and, with it, a ready-made position on nearly all the polit-

ical and social issues I would encounter over the next fifteen or
so years.

I myself became a writer—owing, at least in part, to my
encounter with *U.S.A.*—and, having had articles and reviews
published in *Harper's, The New Republic, Dissent,* and other magazines, was ready to write my first book. What better subject
than John Dos Passos, of whom no serious biography had yet
been written? I wrote to Dos Passos, in Westmoreland County,
Virginia, to ask for his cooperation. I soon received a reply, badly
typed, in which Dos Passos said that he would be pleased to help
me all he could, provided I put my "liberal ideology in moth-
balls" and promised never again to use the word "explicate." He
added that I mustn't expect a great deal from him in the way of
help, because he had work of his own that he wished to finish
while he "still had a few marbles left."

There was a jokey, generous spirit in the letter, and I eagerly planned for our meeting. I signed a book contract, I read
everything Dos Passos had published, I organized myself to
write a full-blown biography of the six-to-eight-hundred-page
sort that was then (and, alas, still is) in vogue. But less than a
year later, in 1970, John Dos Passos died, at the age of seventy-
four. With my subject no longer extant, I lost interest in writing his biography and soon thereafter returned the publisher's
advance.

What I didn't lose interest in, however, was my notion of
John Dos Passos as a model of the great novelist. Hemingway
said that the first requisite for being a writer was an unhappy
childhood, and here Dos Passos qualified handsomely. He was
born in Chicago in 1896, to older parents—his mother was
nearly forty-two and his father fifty-one at his birth—who were
unable to wed, because his father, John Randolph Dos Passos,
who was an immensely successful New York lawyer, was married to a woman who wouldn't release him from the marriage.
(After her death, his parents finally married; John, Jr., was then
fourteen.) The boy and his mother lived well, but not quite out

in the open. His father was a worldly man, a yachtsman, and a lavish spender; he knew Thomas Edison and he once introduced his son to Mark Twain.

Dos Passos spent much of his childhood in hotels, both here and abroad, looking after his mother, who suffered from Bright's disease. He enrolled in schools under the name John Madison. They were very good schools, to be sure—the Sidwell Friends School, in Washington, D.C.; Peterborough Lodge, outside London; Choate; and then Harvard—but much of his early life, as it is described in the pages of his novels *Manhattan Transfer* (1925) and *Chosen Country* (1951), and in his memoir, *The Best Times* (1966), was strained and lonely. Shy, myopic, and unathletic, speaking with a mid-Atlantic accent, he was scarcely built for popularity, and it was only at Harvard, among the coterie of students who fancied themselves aesthetes, that he began to come into his own.

Dos Passos was of that generation of writers who cultivated experience, in contrast to earlier generations, who simply had it. The First World War was his generation's crucial experience: its members were opposed to the war but wouldn't have missed it for the world. Dos Passos first saw the war as a member of the volunteer Norton-Harjes Ambulance Corps, then served with the American Red Cross in Italy. Unpatriotic gore was his lot in both jobs: among other tasks, he carted out buckets of amputated arms and legs from surgical theatres. I say "unpatriotic" because by 1917 Dos Passos was thoroughly radicalized, and claimed that revolution was the only hope for a rotten and corrupt world. Never without humor, he signed letters to friends "Sans culottely, Dos."

After his tours with Norton-Harjes and the Red Cross, Dos Passos joined the United States Army Medical Corps as a private. He put his First World War experience to literary use in two novels, *One Man's Initiation: 1917* (1920) and *Three Soldiers* (1921). *Three Soldiers* and *Manhattan Transfer* established his fame. Dos Passos was highly prolific, publishing his first essay,

"Against American Literature," in *The New Republic,* a few months after he graduated from Harvard. His writing was as much a profession as an art, and he turned out not only novels but travel books, popular histories, poetry, plays, political tracts—some thirty books in all, of the most varied quality.

Although Dos Passos was never a member of the Communist Party, at times he seemed close to being a fellow traveler. He was a familiar signatory to all the protests of the day, a member of the Sacco-Vanzetti Defense Committee, and voted for William Z. Foster, the Communist candidate for President, in the 1932 election. A symbolic moment occurred in his political odyssey when, in 1928, after he completed a tour of Soviet Russia, a Russian actress, who had come with him to the railroad station, called, "Are you for us or against us?" Dos Passos found himself unable to get his tongue around the phrase "For you" as the train pulled out of the station.

The exact nature of Dos Passos's politics has long been in dispute. The novelist Dawn Powell writes in her diaries about trying to explain to a graduate student that Dos Passos's leftism was in part legendary—"that Communist rallies were always advertising him when he wasn't even present, that he never led meetings, had a horror of organizations, etc." Powell, a tough judge of character, also comments on Dos Passos's kindness, calling him "one of the gentlest, sweetest, finest characters the world has known." Much evidence suggests that this is true. In a way that is rare among modern writers, there was something gallantly upstanding and honorable about him.

In 1937, Dos Passos, along with Lillian Hellman, Archibald MacLeish, and Ernest Hemingway, was part of a group that planned a propaganda film about the Spanish Civil War. He and Hemingway argued over the film: Hemingway wanted to emphasize the military aspect of the war, Dos Passos its sadness and suffering. A rupture came when an old friend of Dos Passos's, José Robles, was executed by the Communists on the charge that he was a Fascist spy. According to Dos Passos's biographer, Townsend Ludington, Dos Passos "believed that the Communists killed Robles for being unfriendly to their ulterior motives in the war," one of which was—as Orwell later confirmed in *Homage to Catalonia*—to discredit the so-called Trotskyists. Unwilling to hear anything disparaging about the Loyalist side, Hemingway told Dos Passos to cool his investigation into Robles's death. When Dos Passos told Hemingway that he was going to return to the United States to tell the truth about the Communists' role, Hemingway reportedly said to him, "You do that and the New York reviewers will kill you. They will demolish you forever." Dos Passos took no heed of the all too accurate warning.

The anti-Communism that Dos Passos absorbed from his experience in Spain evolved into a hostility to socialism and to the left generally. He had claimed to recognize class conflict in America, and to despise the inhuman quality of "our giant bureaucratic machines," but now America, once his great nemesis, became the world's great hope: liberty became his obsession, the name of his desire, and the theme of much of his fiction and other writing. All that encouraged individual liberty was good, all that stifled it—notably, big labor, big bureaucracy, big government—was detestable.

Dos Passos's transformed political views had a dire effect on his critical standing. He was seen as a sellout—a phrase that, it is useful to remember, got a strong workout among Stalinists, for whom any deviation from the line opened one to the charge that one had sold out the Communist Party. What Dos Passos was thought to have sold out, of course, was his passion against capitalism, his brilliant and unrelenting criticism of America, his belief in the cause of the underdog, his hope for revolution.

It was as true then as it is now that in the matter of politics writers can be more conformist than a Big Ten sorority during rush week. There's little doubt that Dos Passos's defection from literary leftism cost him his reputation. Hemingway had always gone out of his way to be insulting, once blasting him as "a one-eyed bastard" (Dos Passos lost an eye in a 1947 car accident, which also killed the first of his two wives); now he was joined even by Dos Passos's old friend Edmund Wilson. "In a time when the meaning of political slogans turns topsy-turvy every few years," Dos Passos wrote in *The Best Times,* "anyone who tries to keep a questioning mind, matching each slogan with its real-life application, each label with the thing itself, has to put up with having old friends turn into unfriends and even into enemies."

Dos Passos now found himself in a very different crowd. I was in the audience at Madison Square Garden in 1962 when Dos Passos received an award from a right-wing organization called Young Americans for Freedom; groupie-like, I had gone there to gaze upon a culture hero of mine. Strom Thurmond, Ludwig von Mises, and John Wayne were also given awards that evening; L. Brent Bozell delivered a let-'er-rip speech about the betrayal of America. Dos Passos, by then in his late sixties, was a fairly thickset man, bald, bespectacled, dignified. This old friend of Gerald and Sara Murphy, it seemed to me that evening, had known jollier company.

Kenneth Lynn points out that the later Dos Passos's conservatism was not nearly as dogmatic as the earlier radicalism of *U.S.A.* An air less of anger than of disappointment enters such novels as *Chosen Country, Midcentury,* and *Century's Ebb.* In *U.S.A.,* there is a clear line of demarcation between good and evil. "All right we are two nations," Dos Passos concludes near the close of his trilogy. In the books that follow, there is a sense of hangover, of mistakes made, of a world too complicated to be easily redeemed by revolution or other quick solutions. Yet these books, though they may have been written out of a greater maturity, attained nothing resembling the vitality of *U.S.A.*

What happened? In his trilogy, Dos Passos's energies were divided between his hatred for those he deemed the enemy and his sympathy for victims, whereas his later novels are concerned chiefly with liberal dupes and swindlers, and happy capitalists. The outlines are bolder and the shading is less: the politician has wrested control from the novelist. You wish that Dos Passos could have written in a plague-on-both-their-houses spirit, but such equipoise seems not to have been available to him.

The test case here is Senator Joseph McCarthy, and, sadly, Dos Passos fails it. In *Century's Ebb* he wrote a brief biography of McCarthy which made him a patriotic martyr: "Plain old-fashioned patriotism had sent him out to risk his life with the Marines. Plain old-fashioned patriotism had a lot to do with his taking up the anti-Communist cause." It was, of course, possible to be strongly anti-Communist and still have a cold contempt for McCarthy and his shabby operation. But Dos Passos chose to write about McCarthy as a martyr to the cause rather than as what he more likely was, another politician-hustler on to what looked like a good thing.

Marking the centenary of Dos Passos's birth, the Library of America has now reissued *U.S.A.*—the trilogy consisting of *The Forty-second Parallel* (which first appeared in 1930), *Nineteen Nineteen* (1932), and *The Big Money* (1936). After a hiatus of forty years, I have just reread it, and the ambition of Dos Passos in this trilogy seems even more impressive than I remembered. The plan of *U.S.A.* is panoramic: its aim is to show almost the whole picture of American life in the first three decades of this century, a carefully significant bit at a time. The three novels are composed of four distinct parts: "newsreels," in which headlines and newspaper stories, advertisements, and snatches of contemporary popular songs are placed in sometimes comic, often ironic juxtaposition; "camera eyes" (fifty-one of these), in which Dos Passos offers, in stream-of-consciousness prose, autobiographical recollections of a period he is writing about elsewhere in the novel; biographies (twenty-six of these) of great or emblematic figures of the time, such as Joe Hill, Henry Ford, Rudolph Valentino, J. P. Morgan, Thorstein Veblen, and Isadora Duncan, all of them done in Whitmanesque style, and many of them still brilliant, even after so many years; and, finally, narratives of the lives of twelve major characters, and half a dozen important secondary ones, whose experience ranges from setting type for the International Workers of the World through selling the peace at Versailles for Woodrow Wilson by means of public relations to a successful career in silent movies.

U.S.A., its present-day readers may not realize, was an avant-garde work, in which Dos Passos applied modernist means to naturalist ends. The result is something like a multimedia event within a single book. Dos Passos had devised, through a montagelike method, an impressive apparatus for delineating collective historical experience. The collectivity was his unit of choice. His book is about the defeat of human aspiration by means of dehumanizing political and social and economic arrangements. "When you're outa luck in this man's country, you certainly are outa luck," one character says. All but the very rich live in perpetual peril of going under: "Everything would have gone right if his father hadn't slipped on the ice on the station steps one January morning Johnny's sophomore year and broken his hip."

Joseph Conrad once called Henry James the "historian of fine consciences." Dos Passos was the historian of coarse consciences. His characters act and react, and, above all, they aspire, often in a dreamy way, to wealth and love and what they construe to be the good life—but they do not quite think. Dos Passos draws them with impressive specificity, but they remain types instead of becoming individuated characters. In fiction, characters can develop into types, but the reverse rarely works: types never quite become successful characters. Characters as exquisitely and inexhaustibly thought-filled as Henry James's may never have existed in reality, and characters as generally thoughtless as Dos Passos's in *U.S.A.* may be all around us, but, such are the mysteries of art, James's characters stick in the mind and Dos Passos's do not.

The problem, one feels, is that Dos Passos, whether he

wrote as a man of the left or of the right, was primarily interested in the opportunity the novel offered to make political points—to engage in what he once called "my own curious sort of political agit-prop." Dos Passos was using his characters as intellectual constructs; they remain all too true to type, and that is death for fiction. He had an odd coldness—an objectivity that never let him be more than a puppet master to his characters. Theodore Dreiser, a less proficient writer, was able, because he could express through his characters his own deep stirrings, yearnings, heartbreak, and hope, to create George Hurstwood, Clyde Griffiths, and other characters who have joined the cast of American literature in a way that none of Dos Passos's characters have.

I see now, as I did not forty years ago, that Dos Passos's design in *U.S.A.* was both grand and limited, with the limitation implicit in the grandeur. Use a wide-angle lens and you cannot expect to go very deep; use the closeup and you lose breadth of detail. It has been given to very few novelists—Balzac, Dickens, Tolstoy, and, at moments, Stendhal—to do both things well. Dos Passos was not among them.

John Dos Passos wrote the truth as he saw it, but his truths were almost entirely political ones—and such truths are all too mutable. He missed the main story, which, as Henry James once described it in *The Princess Casamassima,* his one political novel, is about the eternal confusions of human beings: "The figures on the chessboard were still the passions and jealousies and superstitions and stupidities of man, and thus positioned with regard to each other at any given moment could be of interest only to the grim invisible fates who played the game—who sat, through the ages, bow-backed over the table."

Although Dos Passos maintained his outward cheerfulness as he grew older, his views became darker and darker. He somehow lost the artistic energy that once brought life even to the wooden marionettes of his earlier fiction. Nor did his darkening views ever develop into the tragic vision that might have swept him into the front rank of twentieth-century novelists.

John Dos Passos taught me what politics was about; he gave me a strong conception of what a writer's life ought to be; and he has a permanent place in that small club of writers who not only preached but tried to live by a code of honor and decency. He ignited my passion when I was a boy; he changed my life. In the mysterious way of important books in one's life, his powerful trilogy was there when I needed it. In *U.S.A.* he may not have written a book for the ages, but it was a book for his age, and that is no small thing. I—and who knows how many others—shall always be grateful to him.

Sam Lipman at The NEA

———◆———

Sam—what a perfect fit that name seemed for Samuel Lipman. Nobody I know ever called him Samuel. He was Sam, and within his circle of friends, and even enemies, if you said Sam, it was like saying Johnny (Carson), or Frank (Sinatra), or Michael (Jordan), everyone knew about whom you were talking. I'm fairly certain Sam would not have approved those Johnny, Frank, and Michael references; I'm fairly certain he would not have known who Michael Jordan is, though Sam was a sports fan in his youth.

Midway in his more than four-year battle with leukemia, while talking about quack cures for cancer, I mentioned to Sam that I had somewhere read that Steve McQueen, in the last months of his battle with cancer, had gone to Mexico in search of a cure not allowed in the United States. "Who," asked Sam, after a pause, "is Steve McQueen?" Sam was then fifty-eight and had spent all his life in America; and I thought to myself, boy, Sam really knew how to live. How Sam lived was as an immitigable highbrow. Not long after I first met Sam, one evening when we were walking in Washington, I asked him if he watched many movies or much television. "I consider the movies and television," he said, without breaking stride, "dogshit."

Although I had been reading Sam's music criticism with admiration since he first set up as a music critic in *Commentary* in 1975, and although I was once on a panel with him discussing American culture at the Plaza Hotel in New York, I only became Sam's friend in 1984, when, partly through his urging (as I was later to learn), I was appointed a member of the National Council on the Arts, the advisory body of the National Endowment for the Arts. I accepted the appointment for no more serious reason than that I thought it might be a useful experience as well as a way of getting out of the neighborhood for two or three days every three months. Council meetings were held at the Old Post Office Building on Pennsylvania Avenue in Washington. Sam had been on the Council since 1982, and, in stark distinction to my rather larky view of the appointment, he treated his as if it were not merely a political responsibility but something akin to fighting in World War III.

"You know Sam Lipman?" Frank Conroy, the novelist who was then director of the Endowment's literature program, asked me. When I allowed that I knew Sam but didn't know him well, Frank, the one person I knew who worked at the NEA and who was normally an easygoing fellow, his mouth curling into a sneer, said: "The guy is really *sick*."

What Sam's sickness turned out to consist of was taking art and his job on the Council with deadly seriousness. How seriously he took it I saw on the Friday of the first meeting that I attended. Frank Hodsoll was then the chairman of the Endowment, but Sam, it became immediately clear, was easily the dominating figure in the room. What made his dominance so impressive was that he insisted on saying things that most people in the room had no wish to hear. Chief among them was that much of the art that the NEA was spending its $170 or so million on was either trivial or misguided or pernicious.

I have never seen a performance to match Sam's over the next four years in that long dreary room, the smell of cookies from the mall outside its doors wafting in, as he held a crowd of perhaps some two hundred people who generally disagreed with him at bay. Before each Council meeting, members, whose job it was to approve grants and set policy, were sent a thick three-ring notebook containing perhaps three hundred small-print pages of bureaucratic prose, mainly having to do with federal guidelines, grants, and reports on the status or situation or administrative problems of one or another art. These books, I soon discovered, could turn my eyeballs to isinglass in something under ten minutes flat. I read them chiefly to search for absurdities, sniffing to smell rats.

Sam read them as if they were not merely Talmud but Kabbalah, Zohar, and newly discovered Dead Sea Scrolls. He read them as if the salvation of his soul depended upon them. He did his homework like no one else on the Council. And this, combined with his powerful mind and the skill he developed in public argument, was what gave him his advantage. The Council was composed, I believe, of twenty-six members, and Sam, I should estimate, did roughly a third of the talking. Of significant utterance, I should say he was responsible for perhaps 80 percent. At one meeting, Kurt Adler, the conductor and artistic director of the San Francisco Opera and a fellow Council member, leaned toward me and, in a heavy Teutonic accent, whispered: "Zam Lifman I zink takes too great pride in his maztery of ze Englis langooage."

Soon after I arrived for my first Council meeting, Sam told me that he thought the NEA's literature program was one of its poorest, and that he would like me to scrutinize it with some care. He was correct about the dreariness of the literature grants. He had control over the music program, which had solid directors and maintained a high level of seriousness. The dance program also seemed strong, in good part owing to the efflorescence of ballet and modern dance in our day. But so much else—visual arts, design, theater, a sad avant-garde hotchpotch called inter-arts—seemed very poor stuff. There was a separate program for minority-group artists, and it was Sam's sense that this was sacred terrain and more than he could hope to take on. Folk arts—basket-weaving, bluegrass fiddling, quilt-making, and the rest—had in Sam's mind the same fecal status as movies and television, but he grudgingly left them alone. He was always suspicious of the program called media arts—each year he was the lone dissenter on a grant given to the "Bob & Ray" radio show—and generally registered his skepticism about the vast sums being spent to develop what he felt were glamorous projects that were likely to end up in the smoke of which pipe dreams were made.

At the NEA, Sam established himself as a man not to be fooled with. He was lawyerly, in the best sense of the term. He argued well and fairly—always on the issues. He never attacked anyone personally, and the one time I saw him lose his poise was when someone in the room attacked him on what he felt were personal grounds, at which point he quickly lashed back. He knew very well that his defense of high standards, his distaste for art whose chief merit seemed to be its popularity, his disdain for obscurantism, and his distrust of politicized art was not what people wanted to hear. Without Sam, the Council could have devoted itself to undeflected self-congratulation, each member happy to be associated with art, which, by absence of definition, was, as Irish widows used to say of the Church, "the grand thing, you know."

I once asked Sam how it felt to take on so relentlessly that entire room of NEA Council members and staff. "I don't enjoy it," he said. "In fact, when I realize everyone in the room hates what I'm saying, my *kischkes* churn. But what choice do I have?" With the exception of Helen Frankenthaler, Carlos Moseley, myself, and occasionally Jacob Neusner, scarcely anyone in the room wished himself to be identified with Sam's strong and always clearly articulated views. Yet during the four years I sat at Council meetings I noted a gradual building up of respect for Sam: for his concern, for his ability, for his authority as a former performing artist and a critic.

Sam loathed ignorance, and at the Endowment, both on the Council and among the staff, it was never in short supply, but, as he once confided to me, it was difficult for him to keep up his dislike of many of the people he encountered there. You spend weekend after weekend in a gloomy room with the same people, he said, it's inhuman to hold grudges or have unfriendly feelings toward them.

Sam was a hero at the NEA, but he was no martyr. Despite the uphill battle, he enjoyed the fight. He was, by temperament and metabolism, permanently supercharged, and he loved the action at the Endowment: the arguing, conniving, the deal making, however small the deals might be. Members stayed at the Hay-Adams during my early years on the Council. ("Nothing too good for us Communists," an old joke has it.) Many mornings I met Sam for the prodigiously overpriced breakfasts there, and we would review what was coming up during the long day ahead. One had to be insensate not to sense his excitement at the prospect of another day in the trenches.

Sam was not untouched by anxiety and suspicion, maladies common to intellectuals, and he combined these with insomnia, no doubt the product of a racing mind, whose motor, my guess is, only profound works of musical art could still. The insomnia gave him more time to work out the possibilities suggested by the anxiety. I remember sitting in one of the elegantly paneled, heavily draped rooms at the Hay-Adams, Sam devouring a bowl of Brazil nuts and cashews, asking me to identify (I couldn't) a piece of piano music that he had once played in concert, and laying out for me ways he thought Frank Hodsoll might be "outflanking" him. Sam was a powerful motive finder. He reminded me, in this aspect of his personality, of Metternich, who, when the Russian ambassador died on the eve of the Congress of Verona, is supposed to have said: "I wonder why he did that."

Sam was always more concerned to wield influence in the right direction than to garner praise. From time to time, I would pass along to Sam a compliment I had heard about his splendid music criticism, but he seemed little interested in these. He wanted his writing to result in change: scoundrels thrown out, people of quality put in, programs changed, argument leading to action. His days at the NEA allowed him to believe that here his influence was genuine, even though friends told him he was wasting his time. Although he had a decisive hand in a report on arts education and on the place of art in American civilization, the sad truth is that few people read such reports, and no one at all ever acts upon them, and so little evidence of his immense effort at the Endowment remains.

Sam had to have known this, and doubtless it chagrined him, especially in later years, when his six-year term on the Council was ended. If he needed a justification—and being Sam, he probably did—his personal defense of his time at the Endowment could have been that of the immensely compassionate cardinal who, when asked how he could possibly have worked for so uncompassionate a Pope as Pius XII, replied: "You don't know what I have prevented." Sam prevented a lot; things at the NEA would have been much worse without him.

They certainly would have been a great deal more boring. For twelve or so days every year, Sam demonstrated how a serious mind worked. He was almost never less than brilliant; it was his unrelieved brilliance that commanded attention. Program directors at the NEA must have trembled when they saw Sam's hand shoot up to ask a question. One of these directors once described Council meetings as days of extreme boredom punctuated by a few moments of genuine terror. The terror, my guess is, had principally to do with getting through Sam's interrogations. Sam's great advantage in all these matters, what gave him his impressive authority, was that he knew what he believed; nothing improves one's arguments and clarifies one's passion as knowing one's own true views.

I shall never forget a group who one day visited the Council to speak about minority interests in the arts. Two blacks were among the group, along with a Hispanic- and Japanese-American. Their case was that of pure victimhood: they argued that they had been too-long excluded from participation in the cultural life of the country; and now it was their turn to speak out, angrily and exclusively, about their claims against a country that had denied them their place. Naturally, everyone in the room was utterly cowed.

Except Sam. After raising his hand to respond, Sam began tentatively, saying that he didn't wish to argue about their views of their own past, only about their vision of the future. He alluded briefly to his own immigrant parents. Then, growing less tentative, gathering strength for the mounting of his real theme, Sam said that he always believed, and nothing could make him disbelieve, that the real dream of American civilization was one of unity, a large and diverse people united in a fundamental belief in merit and fairness and honorableness, and that anyone who gave up this dream was losing sight of something absolutely crucial about life in America. Sam's tone was less that of polemic than of pleading on behalf of good will in the name of good sense. As he finished, Sam had the respect of everyone in the room. In my six years on the Council, this was far and away its finest moment. God, I thought, I am proud that this man is my friend.

Sam's brilliance, I came to discover, did not exclude his being wrong. Like most intellectuals, he needed to display his brilliance. I recall one mortifying moment when, early in the day, Sam came up to me at my seat at the Council table to whisper that he needed my support on an item that was coming up for discussion. Whatever the item was, I spoke to the point, backing Sam's play. I believe we carried the day. That afternoon I made some comment about the relation between criticism and the creation of art. Sam raised his hand and said, much as he disliked disagreeing with his friend Joe Epstein, he couldn't help observing that in making my comment I was falling into the same trap Ezra Pound had fallen into in the 1930's. I'm not sure what the trap was, but, let's face it, it couldn't have been much less than proto-fascism.

I heard Sam play the piano only once—with his wife, Jeaneane Dowis, a piece for four hands by Schubert. But I always felt that Sam's experience as a piano prodigy had a powerful shaping influence on him. In nearly every aspect of his life he was, to take a word from music criticism, virtuosic. Since a little boy, he was used to captivating an audience. He was on what I think of as the concert performer's ego diet. The concert performer—usually a pianist or violinist—plays, people burst into applause, beg him to play more, afterward fête him: how brilliant you were tonight, more lobster, you must meet my daughter. I rather doubt if Sam ever quite got over all that.

I remember at the conclusion of one Council meeting Sam telling me that he had to return home to practice two Mozart pieces. "What a delight that must be," I said, envying him. "It isn't," he shot back, saying no more. I wondered what he meant. Perhaps he could no longer play to his own exacting standard and long practice sessions made this plain to him. At some point, Sam, as he once told me, knew that he could not have the kind of career at the piano that he had dreamed of since childhood. Of what did that dream consist? The concert pianist as hero, genius, conquistador; it was the hauteur of Liszt stopping in mid-performance to say ironically to Tsar Nicholas I that he didn't wish his playing to interrupt his highness's conversation: "Music, herself, should be silent when Nicholas speaks."

Did Sam ever find anything to replace that dream of power and glory that began in art? I don't know, but I do know that his conception of himself was in part heroic. Romantic music may have lent the background to this conception. One of Sam's heroes, I was to discover only late in our friendship, was T. E. Lawrence; he thought *Seven Pillars of Wisdom* one of the world's great books. The appeal of Lawrence for intellectuals, like that of Trotsky for an earlier generation, was obvious: the man who made moot the question of which was greater, the pen or the

sword, by wielding both to maximum effect. Lawrence, an out-
sider, inspired, obsessed, one has no difficulty seeing the attraction of such a man for Sam.

To have had a reasonably successful run as a young pianist,
to be this country's best music critic (and to have had one's performance in this capacity certified by Virgil Thomson), to have
been one of the two founders of an important cultural magazine (*The New Criterion*) none of this, I suspect, was quite enough
for Sam. "He who strives will never enjoy this life peacefully,"
Paul Klee wrote in his diary, and Sam was nothing if not a
striver.

In my musical ignorance, I sometimes thought Sam might
have made a great conductor, a job that would have allowed him
to use both his musical talent and executive ability and that
would have suited, in at least a small way, his taste for power. I
can easily imagine Sam being addressed as "Maestro" and lov-
ing it; I shouldn't have minded calling him that myself. He had,
when the spirit took him, the necessary imperiousness for the
job. I have seen Sam ask a waiter what kind of mineral water he
had, and when the man named no fewer than six kinds, Sam,
looking disappointed, said, "Never mind, I'll just have a beer."
On another occasion, in another restaurant, he had forgotten
his glasses at the office and asked that someone call and have
them brought to him at the restaurant. Very maestro-ish.

As for his taste for power, Sam was not only aware of it,
but could, in a rueful way, be highly amusing about it. Several
years ago, at a party in the Rainbow Room celebrating the
twenty-fifth anniversary of Norman Podhoretz's editorship of
Commentary, a party at which Sam and Jeaneane played in Norman's honor, I found myself at the same table as Sam. Also at
this party, along with their security men and their inevitable
walky-talkies, were Secretary of State George Schultz, Mayor
Ed Koch, UN Ambassador Jean Kirkpatrick, Senator Daniel
Patrick Moynihan, and former Secretary of State Henry
Kissinger. At our table sat, along with husbands and wives, the

conductor Gerard Schwarz, the novelist Cynthia Ozick, the English critic John Gross, and Hilton Kramer. Sam, checking the room, leaned over to me and said, "I see we're seated at the children's table."

Sam could be a very funny man. He liked to hear a joke and he adored conveying one. But his own wit, as in the children's table joke, was best when personal, issuing out of his perception of his own position or condition in life. Not long after he had begun his treatment for leukemia at Sloan-Kettering, he was asked, as I gather everyone who has any complicated blood work done in the age of AIDS must now be asked, how many sex partners he had had over the past decade. "Oh," said Sam, "I can tell you the exact number for longer than the past quarter of a century. But are you going to be disappointed!" And he held up his index finger.

Sam's natural tendency, his temperament, was critical. He spent a fair amount of time criticizing various people at the NEA, but the man he devoted much of his critical energy to was the chairman, Frank Hodsoll, whom, in fact, he rather liked. But liking Hodsoll did not stanch the flow of criticism. So I was surprised when one day Sam said to me, "You know one thing I really admire about Frank?" I couldn't, truly, imagine what this might be. "What I admire about him," Sam said, "is his bladder. I've been in meetings with Frank for ten or twelve hours, and not once did he have to go to the bathroom."

Sam didn't have the bladder to be chairman of the NEA, but that didn't stop him from fantasizing about the job. Just because he knew more than anybody else about it, he thought he was qualified for it. Not only did he never really have a chance for the chairmanship, but it would have been all wrong for him. For one thing, Sam didn't suffer fools I wouldn't even say gladly but at all, and suffering fools is, inevitably, a serious part of such a job. Frank Hodsoll may not have known much about the arts—an attorney and full-time public servant, he would sometimes treat us to lectures on the meaning of the avant-garde that, in the power of their tedium, could stop a race riot—but, as chairman, he was a courtly and kindly man. When someone on the Council finished speaking, no matter how high the quotient of idiocy in his or her talk, Frank would always say, quite as if he meant it, "Thank you, Francine." I once told Sam that he could never accomplish that part of the job—the "Thank you, Francine" could never get past his lips. He agreed it could be a problem.

Nor did Sam have the temperament for compromise. I, for one, am rather glad he didn't. Like the rest of us, however, Sam had his self-deceptions. One of these was his mistaken belief in himself as a public politician. In fact, he was quite good as a behind-the-scenes politician, and he regularly cut successful deals at the NEA on such matters as who would be given presidential medals in the arts and who wouldn't. (I used to tease him about these medals, which I thought a bad idea, asking if he was planning to get one for the Harmonicats.)

Sam was a man of great appetite. He not only took great pleasure in food, but wanted to acquire and devour all the good books, hear all the music (in, let me add, all its various performances), meet all the interesting people. (When he wrote about the new *Grove Dictionary of Music* for *Commentary,* he felt he had to own and study that estimable work in all its editions.) Somehow, such was his wondrous energy, it all seemed possible.

When Sam was struck by cancer in 1990—and, not long after, by a heart attack—it seemed all the crueller because his very being depended on a flow of the most extraordinary energy. Sam without this energy seemed not oxymoronic, or a contradiction, or anything but an impossibility. The truth was that his leukemia—and it was leukemia with all the most ghastly tortures thrown in, except bone-marrow transplant, which his weakened heart prevented—though it slowed his energy, didn't alter his restlessness.

The new instrument Sam began to play was the telephone. After our days at the NEA together, days that for me will always be defined by his presence, Sam and I stayed in touch chiefly through telephone calls. He was too impatient to write letters, or to wait for them; the fax machine seems to me invented just for Sam, whose patience had long been too sorely tried by the mails. He didn't call me as frequently as I know he called others, but when his health held up I would often get four or five long-distance calls a week, never at set or predictable times. These calls invariably began with the following staccato exchange: "Joe. Sam." "Hi, Sam." "Good time?" (He was unfailingly courteous in asking that question.) "A fine time." And we'd be off.

Sam's telephone calls usually lasted forty or fifty minutes, and they sometimes put to the test Mae West's dictum that you cannot get too much of a good thing. The calls themselves were pure Sam: filled with information, vituperation, often odd but always impressive cogitation. Typically, they might include White House gossip, a Rosina Lhévinne anecdote, a Jewish joke, an item about Matthew Arnold's theological assumptions, an often wild political prediction, and anything else that was on Sam's mind at the moment. And there was always a vast amount on Sam's mind.

When Sam sensed that I had run out of conversational gas, or when I had exhausted such information as I had that was likely to be of interest to him, there would be a pause, then *"Hokay,"* he would say, signing off, and hang up. I was generally ready for a walk around the room or a cup of tea or a nap after such a call. Sam, I assumed, had four or five more such calls to make after he had finished with me.

Because he was so forthright, Sam was one of those men whom, in order to like him, you had *really* to like him. His aggressiveness might have put you off, or what could sometimes be his genuine touchiness might as easily put him off you. I really liked him. In fact, I loved being Sam's friend—loved having so talented a man who was also my contemporary as a close friend. I felt that, in becoming his friend, I was admitted to a small but select club—that of the people Sam felt he could count on. Sam, an only son who himself had an only son, was intensely a family man, and he had a way of making you feel that you were part of his family, with some of the responsibilities pertaining thereto: no betrayals of any kind allowed, we stick together, we count on one another in the clutch. None of this was ever said; it didn't have to be. It was at times an obligation being Sam's friend but it was always an honor, and I hope I never gave him cause to think I let him down.

Since Sam's death, I have thought about the pattern in his life, searching, in Henry James's phrase, for the figure in Sam's carpet. I believe the figure is to be found in Sam's courage, which was courage of a particular kind—the courage of the underdog. I think of the courage it must have taken for that dark-eyed beautiful eight-year-old boy of *Ostjuden* ancestry to go on the concert stage lashed to that most powerfully complex of musical instruments, the piano; the courage even as a tennis player to be the scrambler that Sam was—a player, that is, not of first-class gifts, who had to fight for every bloody point; the courage to mount a career as a concert performer and the no lesser courage to understand that, despite his victories as a pianist, he had to walk away from it because he could not have the kind of career at the piano he wanted; the courage to begin, at forty, a new career as a music critic in which he confronted the musical establishment of his day; the courage to join with Hilton Kramer in beginning a new journal to take on, in effect, all of contemporary American culture in its dominant, one might say mainstream, antinomian strain; the courage to grapple, weekend after weekend, with a roomful of people in argument over the importance of art; the courage, finally, to stage his uncomplaining fight against cancer in one of its most horrendous forms.

I suppose that Sam died believing that, unlike his hero T. E. Lawrence, he never got to ride triumphantly into Aqaba. Yet Sam took each battle as it came, and he notched his own string of victories, by acting with honor and courage whenever those difficult qualities were called for. One of the few regrets I have about my friendship with Sam is that, before he died, I neglected to tell him that he had never been other than true to his own heroic conception of himself; and, in my eyes, a hero he was and shall always remain.